BORN READING

Bringing Up Bookworms in a Digital Age—
From Picture Books to eBooks
and Everything in Between

JASON BOOG

Foreword by Betsy Bird,
New York City children's librarian

A TOUCHSTONE BOOK

Published by Simon & Schuster

New York   London   Toronto   Sydney   New Delhi

TOUCHSTONE
A Division of Simon & Schuster, Inc.
1230 Avenue of the Americas
New York, NY 10020

First Touchstone trade paperback edition July 2014

For information about special discounts for bulk purchases, please contact Simon & Schuster Special Sales at 1-866-506-1949 or business@simonandschuster.com.

The Simon & Schuster Speakers Bureau can bring authors to your live event. For more information or to book an event contact the Simon & Schuster Speakers Bureau at 1-866-248-3049 or visit our website at www.simonspeakers.com.

Designed by Aline Pace
Cover photograph © blessings/Shutterstock

Manufactured in the United States of America

10 9 8 7 6 5 4 3

Library of Congress Cataloging-in-Publication Data

Boog, Jason.
    Born reading: bringing up bookworms in a digital age—from picture books to ebooks and everything in between / Jason Boog.
        pages   cm
    1. Reading—Parent participation.   2. Children—Books and reading.   I. Title.
    LB1050.B58 2014
    372.42'5—dc23   2014005567

ISBN 978-1-4767-4979-2
ISBN 978-1-4767-4981-5 (ebook)

For Olive and Caitlin

Contents

Foreword

by Betsy Bird,
New York City children's librarian

When a child is born, its parents are placed in a peculiar situation. Suddenly they find themselves raiding their own brains for personal skills that will, in some way, give their offspring a leg up in life. If a parent is into sports, perhaps he or she will think, "Well at least I'll be able to teach the kid how to toss the ball around." If a parent is an advocate for cleanliness he or she will say, "Well at least I'll be able to teach them how to make a bed." But no matter how many skills you yourself happen to have, there's a fear that somehow you will fail at imparting those skills to your child. You won't be good enough, your kids will never even learn to tie their shoelaces, and from there on in everything will be worry, chaos, and woe.

Alas, people who work on a regular basis with small children are not exempt from these fears. At the same time there's a strange sort of pressure. If, for example, you are a children's librarian and you or your spouse happens to be pregnant, this is what you will hear with depressing regularity until the child is born (and for quite a while afterward too): "I guess you won't have to worry about your kid liking books!"

Now here's the dirty little secret that nobody else will tell you: I know more authors and illustrators and teachers and librarians with non-reading kids than you would ever believe. It's true. If reading were a matter of genetics then these kids would be mutant aberrations. Instead, they're just not born readers. For whatever reason, books have passed them by.

You see, it doesn't matter how many picture books you know or whether or not you can booktalk the latest fantasy novel for the 9- to 12-year-old set with enviable ease. When it comes to your own kid you are bamboozled. You are up a tree. Suddenly all your training and knowledge feels moot. You may know the materials better than your friends, but that doesn't mean you feel any more competent. For many of us, the understanding that, as wonderful as it is to catch a football or to make a bed off of which you could bounce a quarter, first things first. You need to instill in your kids a love of books and reading. And what you really need when your own kid is born, whether you're a librarian or senator, a sewage treatment plant worker or a nurse, is a handbook that tells you everything you need to know about creating the most intelligent child possible through literature.

Enter Jason Boog.

What Boog has managed to do here is create the go-to manual that every parent should be required to read upon exiting the hospital with a newborn in tow. It should be as standard a baby shower giveaway as *Goodnight Moon* and *The Very Hungry Caterpillar*. In short, if you read only one book before having a child (or even if you've recently had the kiddo) read this one.

Why? Because Boog's no expert. I mean that as a compliment. He wants you to be able to read a book to your kid with ease and skill, and to do that he's not going to come at you like he's some know-it-all while you barely know anything. He is perfectly aware that while you're good at other things in your life, maybe the simple act of reading something like Nina Laden's *Peek-a-Who?* to your infant can be potentially terrifying. Relax. He's been there. And he's going to get you through this so that your kiddo not only knows books but loves them as well.

Part of the appeal here lies in the fact that the man knows his material. There's not a book recommendation mentioned in this title that feels out of place. Then there's the fact that when it came to getting his facts down, Boog contacted experts in every possible field. As a result you'll read statements from child development specialists to educators to authors as diverse as Jon Scieszka and Stan Lee. Then he took all the research and made it fun and understandable for you, the parent. This isn't simply the work of a single man but the combined intelligence and experience of hundreds of people working in the field with the sole purpose of getting your child into books and reading.

This is particularly useful when the discussion of shiny rectangles comes up. I am referring, of course, to screen time (the amount of time your child spends on digital devices). Now forgive me, reader, for I shall now lay before you my own app-related sins. I admit it, I may have succumbed to temptation and allowed my own offspring a taste of the addictive lures of my iPad in exchange for 20 minutes to cook dinner or a scream-free car ride that lasted for more than several hours. Keeping your child screen-free for the first two years is certainly a challenge. But Boog isn't here to judge us. He doesn't sneer at electronic babysitters or condemn screen-addled children to a bookless life. Instead, he is gentle with his guidance. He shows you where you have strayed and then leads you back onto the path. Most importantly, he offers guidelines on where to find the best possible apps for our children. The great English poet and novelist Walter de la Mare once said that "*only the rarest kind of best* in anything can be *good* enough for the young." That goes for apps as well as books.

Born Reading cleverly uses Boog's relationship with his own daughter as a springboard for a variety of different discussions. And as I read about Jason's relationship with Olive, I was able to draw parallels between my own child and myself. This involved understanding events like how big a step it was when my two-and-a-half-year-old starting making her stuffed animals talk to one another so that they could become active participants in her own made-up stories. Other times it was a little sillier. For example, while Olive had a tendency to latch onto pseudo-children's books that weren't really written for a kid market (*All My Friends are Dead, Dick and Jane with Vampires*, etc.) my own kiddo would certainly do the same with books like the existential but oddly entrancing *Bob & Co.*

As I read this book, I found myself consistently jotting down recommendations not just for apps and books but also presents for other members of my family and their children. Then I started applying Jason's reading techniques to my own kid. Some of his tips I'd already incorporated into our regular readings. Other ideas had never occurred to me but felt so natural when I used them that it was like I'd been doing them all along. Mind you, a person can go overboard at times. My husband and I have a tendency to pause a little too often and ask my daughter questions while reading a book to her. Fortunately, she knows how to tell us when our perpetual questioning is distracting from her enjoyment of the story. Quoth she: "I can't know everything!"

Maybe not, but you can. Everything there is to know about making your kid a born reader, that is. Because let's face facts: there's nothing else like this in the marketplace today. When was the last time someone handed you an interactive reading pamphlet? Do your co-workers swap tips on the best ways to bring *Chicka Chicka Boom Boom* to life? If you're looking to give your child a leg up and establish a deep and abiding relationship with books that can't be replicated by any other form of media out there, this is the handbook you've been waiting for.

✐

Betsy Bird is currently New York Public Library's Youth Materials Collections Specialist. She has served on the Newbery award selection committee, written for *The Horn Book*, reviewed for *Kirkus* and *The New York Times*, and has also written the picture book *Giant Dance Party*, illustrated by Brandon Dorman. In 2014, Candlewick will publish *Wild Things: Acts of Mischief in Children's Literature*, which she co-wrote with Jules Danielson and Peter Sieruta.

You can follow Betsy on Twitter @FuseEight.

Introduction

The Born Reading Playbook, or How to Use This Book

Reading a book to a kid is harder than it looks.

Every day for more than five years, I wrote about books and publishing news at the popular GalleyCat website. Thousands of readers visit the site on a daily basis, looking for book recommendations and guidance through the literary world. I've always been a reader, and while working this beat, I got to know the business side of publishing inside and out.

So when I had my daughter, Olive, in 2010, I wanted her to love books as much as I do. But when it came time to choose the actual books I was going to read to her, I was completely clueless. Even though I spent my entire working day immersed in the world of literature, I had no idea what books to read or what to do while holding a book in front of this mute newborn.

Very few parents have the necessary skills to turn a book into an exciting and enriching experience for a toddler (let alone an infant). I certainly didn't. I'm not an educational expert, a librarian, or a children's book writer. I'm a journalist and a dad, and I happen to have a passion for books and reading. It's a passion that I want to relay to my daughter, so that reading will bring her as much pleasure in her life as it has brought me. So I took the skills I do possess—curiosity, a love of the written word, and a dogged determination to get the story—and I embarked on a quest to find the best books and the best ways to read with my baby.

Born Reading is a personal, quirky book. I'll tell you a lot of stories about my daughter and our lives together—what we read, what reading techniques my family tried, and what worked for us. But at every step along the way, I did the research and asked the professionals for their insights. This book is built upon the experience and deep knowledge of the librarians, authors, publishers, technology experts, psychologists, and others who live and breathe children's literature. I was hardly a parenting expert when I started writing this book, but I learned from some of the most inspiring leaders in the field about how to be a better parent. You can learn along with me.

Is There a "Right" Way to Read to Your Child?

So as I started my research, I began in a different way than most people. I started reading about, well, reading. It turns out that all reading is not created equal.

Perspectives on Psychological Science published a study in 2013 that validated the hours I spent chasing my daughter with picture books, and forever changed the way I thought about reading to a child. In a research paper with the evocative title "How to Make a

Young Child Smarter," researchers tabulated data from eight scientific studies of childhood development.

They reached an eye-popping conclusion: the right kind of reading—interactive reading—can raise your child's IQ by more than six points.

Let me repeat that, because I don't want that crucial piece of information to get lost. Interactive reading with your child can raise his or her IQ by more than *six* points. Even more surprisingly, they found that "the earlier the interactive reading takes place, the larger the benefits." They ranked interactive reading on par with vitamins and a healthy diet.

But here's the key: Just having books around the house is not enough. Parents need to provide an *interactive* reading experience to reap the intellectual rewards inside of books.

Hospitals should be handing out interactive reading pamphlets along with diapers as new parents head home. We spend thousands of dollars on school, tutors, test prep, and supplies, but this powerful reading method is an absolutely free gift that every parent can give a child after an hour of practice. But nobody is teaching parents these simple skills! That's what *Born Reading* is all about. It teaches parents specific ways to implement these interactive reading techniques into your own life with your child.

By the end of this introduction, you will have a powerful toolkit for turning your family reading sessions into a rich interactive experience. Even better, you and your kids will have more fun reading together. You won't need smartphones, tablet computers, baby videos, or expensive courses to learn how to use these techniques. But if you have access to digital devices, this book will also share tips for how to use them to enhance your child's reading experiences.

When your child refuses to go to sleep or pitches a book

across the room, you will wish there was a handbook to guide you through the endurance test of parenthood. This book is the missing owner's manual to understand the reading, writing, and storytelling parts of your child's brain.

Now I know how hard it is to find time to read a parenting handbook during these busy days and nights. If you only read one section of this book, I hope it is this introduction. Don't worry, I won't be offended. These first few pages introduce strategies for the rest of your child's life, a simple set of interactive reading activities that anyone can perform.

What is interactive reading? No parent can ignore this amazing mental boost for his or her child. To find out more, I caught up with John Protzko, one of the New York University researchers behind "How to Make a Young Child Smarter." Protzko summed up the most important aspect uncovered by the study: "Interactive reading is not just about a parent and child sitting down and reading a book, but is instead about creating a dialogue with the child and the book. Asking them wh- questions (such as, why do you think the rabbit took so many breaks?), following their interests, and not letting them provide one-word answers but really having them elaborate their thoughts."

Protzko traced the development of interactive reading strategies back to Dr. Grover Whitehurst, a child development expert who would go on to serve as director of the Institute of Education Sciences at the Department of Education. Whitehurst developed a program called "dialogic reading" 25 years ago, a groundbreaking way to help prepare lower-income kids for school.

Back in 1988, most experts agreed that reading with children would make them smarter, but little research existed to back it up with cold hard evidence.

Whitehurst launched a landmark study monitoring how interactive reading helped children aged 21–35 months. Half the parents in his sample group read books to their children in the standard, normal manner—a one-way recitation from parent to child. It's the way most of us grew up hearing stories from our parents: parents talk, kids listen.

But the other half of the parents received a priceless education in the art of "dialogic reading," a set of best practices for parents to both read and discuss a book with their child. In short, the second set of parents learned the type of interactive reading techniques we'll be discussing in this book.

After four weeks, both groups were given three tests of verbal abilities: the Illinois Test of Psycholinguistic Abilities wherein the tester offers the child an object and asks him or her to tell the tester about it; the Expressive One-Word Picture Vocabulary Test wherein the tester asks a child to name objects based on pictures; and the Peabody Picture Vocabulary Test wherein the tester names an object and asks the child to point to a picture of the object.

The results changed the art and science of reading with children forever. Whitehurst found that those kids given the full interactive reading experience—the ones whose parents just learned a few new tricks and techniques for reading with their toddlers— were *eight and a half months ahead* of the other children on the Psycholinguistic test, and they were *six months ahead* on the Vocabulary tests after four weeks of interactive reading. Even better, the interactive readers continued to hold a six-month advantage over the control group almost a year after the study.

Whitehurst did not develop a fancy education program for parents or a complicated mental workout for the kids. His study noted that it only took an hour to teach the parents how to read interactively with their children.

Whitehurst's results still boggle my mind—the idea that these kids whose parents had read to them interactively were *six to eight months* ahead of other kids, even those who were also lucky enough to have books in the home, is amazing. It turns out that it's not only important *that* you read to your kids, but it's also important *how* you read to your kids—and the techniques for proper interactive reading are within every parent's grasp. This revelation has the potential to change lives.

But what really got to me is that these techniques have never really made it out of academia. Studies have proven the power of interactive reading over and over again, and ordinary parents deserve to learn these techniques. We've had this earthshaking revelation for more than a quarter century, but nobody told me about it when Olive was born! That's what *Born Reading* is intended to do—teach parents the surprisingly simple techniques that can improve the way your child learns and foster a lifelong love of the written word.

So how can parents learn this interactive reading method? After interviewing a long list of child-development experts and combing through 25 years of research, I distilled these interactive reading techniques into a set of skills parents can use while reading with children.

I call this collection of reading strategies the Born Reading Playbook. I identify them all at the end of this introduction, but I will give practical explanations and illustrations of each skill throughout the book. I will show you how to share the gift of interactive reading with your child from birth all the way to kindergarten.

Years before the child in your life learns to read or write, interactive reading can give them a powerful boost. We should be training parents, grandparents, brothers, sisters, babysitters, nannies, and all our caregivers in interactive reading techniques, just like we take practical courses in CPR, nutrition, or childbirth to keep our babies healthy.

What about Digital Devices?

Born Reading will teach you a new way to read and interact with your child. But this book also acknowledges that reading and learning—even for small children—is happening more and more on screens and online. Whatever your feelings about that, it's a truth to be embraced, not shunned. So in this book, alongside reading recommendations and interactive reading techniques, I'll also offer suggestions for great learning apps, vetted by educators, librarians, and other parents (including me). Interactive reading is more important than ever in this digital age, and the techniques can be applied to all media, not just books.

Interactive reading will give you ways to talk to your children about books, apps, TV shows, or even video games, sparking conversations that will continue for your child's entire lifetime. They will help you raise a media-savvy child capable of analyzing complex stories on college entrance exams, but they will also show your child how to choose the best books, movies, and games in a world cluttered with useless media.

Teaching children a love of reading is ever more important in this digital age, when so many different devices are battling for our time and attention. I spoke with Harvard children's literature professor Maria Tatar, one of the most eloquent defenders of reading with children. She urged parents to remember the first time they read a book and entered the "comfort zone" of the imagination.

She explained: "It was someplace where we were liberated from authority and we navigate ourselves. You experience it. You witness it. You are exploring a new world. It opens up possibilities that go hand and hand with cognitive gains. It opens up curiosity, makes you want to know more about the world and how it operates. There are cognitive gains—you are processing language and learning how to use print media. Once you have access to that, you can do anything. It is wonderfully liberating to be at ease in the world of words." In a world that can seem positively overwhelming, being comfortable with the written word will give your child a sense of power and control. What an amazing gift to offer.

Even if you hate reading books or the idea of discussing kids' books drives you nuts, you still need to do it. And you should teach all the caregivers in your child's life how to do it too. But here's the good news: the Born Reading Playbook isn't intimidating or scary for caregivers. In fact, most parents find that it makes them enjoy reading time with their child even more than before. Reading will seem less like a dull chore and more like a fun experience—something parents, caregivers, and kids will all appreciate.

The best way to prepare yourself is to simply cut out the pages of the Born Reading Playbook and put them up on your refrigerator. Gradually these techniques will sink into your brain and become part of the way that you read to a child.

If this long list of reading skills seems daunting, don't despair. Throughout this book, I will provide plenty of book recommendations and examples to illustrate how the methods work.

Don't stress out and try to cram all of the Born Reading Playbook techniques into a single reading session. You do not need to use all 15 techniques at once any more than you would use a vacuum cleaner, hammer, and a tire jack to hang a picture in your living room. Use the techniques that feel most natural for a particular book or reading session.

So many people want to give you advice about raising your baby. Some parents play classical music in utero, others buy educational videos for infants. Some guidebooks will tell you to be stricter, others will tell you to relax. I won't tell you what to do. I will show you my journey as a father learning how to read with his daughter, and I will teach you everything I learned along the way.

I've been reading to my baby for her entire lifetime, and I think it is the quickest and most useful way to become a better parent. By sharing our story, I hope you will find ways to make reading a part of your child's life.

Together, we can figure out how to raise a generation of born readers.

The Born Reading Playbook

1. **Read together.** Researchers call this co-play, sharing a book, app, eBook, audiobook, or any kind of literary experience. Don't let your kid spend too much time alone with a device. Make sure you play games and read together every single day.

Conversation starters: *Could we read that book together? Can you show me how to cook something on this app?*

2. **Ask lots and lots of questions.** Questions are the foundation of interactive reading, and you can ask them even before your child can answer with words. Be sure to ask questions before, during, and after the reading experience.

Conversation starters: *Where did the rabbit go? What color is the flower?*

3. **Share details about the book.** Point out your favorite illustrations, name the colors, animals, people, and feelings on the page. At first your child will not be able to join you, but he or she will pick up your interactive habit as they grow.

Conversation starters: *That car is red—do you see anything red? Do you want to count the animals?*

4. **Dramatize the story.** You can mime sweeping when you see a broom or pretend to eat the character's food. This will help your child match the concepts to the words, a pillar of the interactive reading experience.

Conversation starters: *Then the caterpillar ate one _____. Then he saw somebody—who is it?*

5. **Help your child identify with the characters.** Start by talking about simple emotions. These skills will scale as your kid gets older, when you can ask more complex questions.

Conversation starters: *The bunny is sleepy—could you rub his head? Have you ever felt mad like that baby?*

6. **Compliment your child as you read.** Reward your child for simple responses, cuddle them after a reading session, and praise him or her for choosing good books or apps.

Conversation starters: *I'm so glad you picked this book. Great job counting on the iPad!*

7. **Discuss personal opinions about a book.** If your kid loved a book, find out *why.* If your child wiggled away while using a storybook app, find out why. Both questions will help you build a stronger reading relationship.

Conversation starters: *Did that book make you happy? Why do you want to read that book again?*

8. **Follow the things your child loves.** If your child loved a book with panda bears, ask the librarian for more panda books. Read the books your child loves, use apps, videos, and online research to help him or her learn more.

Conversation starters: *Do you want to read more about panda bears? Should we ask the librarian about this?*

9. **Stop and talk about what happened.** Too often adults speed through these books or apps to get to the end, but these pauses are crucial for your child's comprehension.

Conversation starters: *Should we stop and look at this mountain? Should we take a break and talk about what happened?*

10. **Guess what happens next.** These questions will reinforce a sense of narrative and enhance reading comprehension. Kids' books are perfect for these questions, following easy patterns

with fun exceptions. These questions can spark long conversations that continue into adulthood. I still play this game while watching movies.

Conversation starters: *Who do you think will win the race? What do you think is in the box?*

11. Continue the conversation. Don't stop talking about a book or digital reading app after you've ended the reading experience. Reference the book in real life and keep asking questions.

Conversation starters: *Should we look at pictures of porcupines now? Do you remember what an accordion is?*

12. Guide your child beyond what they already know. Researchers call this "scaffolding," and it can be as simple as reading to your child because he or she does not know how to read. As often as possible, guide book reading into new material.

Conversation starters: *Do you know why his car did not work? Should I tell you how he cooked the soup?*

13. Show your child the world outside your neighborhood. As a kid growing up in rural Michigan, this was crucial. Before I saw France or New York City or Guatemala or the Pacific Ocean, books showed me these places. Make sure you choose books that explore diverse places, cultures, and stories, and follow your child's interests when he or she loves a setting.

Conversation starters: *Do you want to know about Antarctica? Should I show you where France is?*

14. Compare the story to personal experiences. Help associate the book with the experiences that obsess your child. This is how human beings understand the world; applying something in a book or app to real life is a crucial skill.

Conversation starters: *Did you see that kind of animal at the zoo? Did you get mad when we left the park too?*

15. Encourage your child to recount the story. I loved making Olive tell me her favorite stories over breakfast, the perfect way to reinforce a reading experience and teach storytelling.

Conversation starters: *Can you read that book to your teddy bear? What happened after the elephant dropped his ice cream cone?*

These 15 skills have been integrated into every chapter of this book, showing you how to apply the fundamentals of interactive reading during every stage of your child's life. You will see Born Reading sections in every chapter, using age-specific examples to guide you through each technique and to help you master these important skills. The Born Reading Playbook works for digital and print reading, and we'll be moving into the issue of digital reading right away in the next chapter—exploring some of the toughest decisions you will make as a parent.

Chapter 1

Before Your Baby Is Born

When the doctors finally let me hold my daughter Olive in the delivery room, she was wailing at the top of her lungs. All throughout my wife's pregnancy, I would lie beside her and sing "Tiny Bubbles" to our baby before she went to sleep. It was the champagne anthem that ended *The Lawrence Welk Show*—my late grandmother's favorite song and the first tune my wife and I played at our wedding reception.

At some point, I changed the lyrics:

Tiny Olive, in my arms
Makes me happy,
Makes me want to go home.

So I sang that song in the delivery room, holding my swaddled caterpillar for the first time. Olive looked at me with her deep hazel eyes, staring like she had known me for a long, long time.

Experts affirm that it wasn't just my imagination: babies can hear sounds in utero, and newborns can emerge from the womb responding to sounds they heard before birth. Something as simple as reading to your child in utero can have a profound effect on his or her future. Education and child development expert Gordon Wells explained how important this in-utero reading time is for children: "There seems to be quite a lot of evidence that the fetus responds to the audio as well as the physical environment. And that the sound of mother reading [or, in my case, a father singing] is preparing the child to continue that experience after they are born."

Beyond all the developmental and educational benefits of interactive reading with your child, the most important advantage is that the time you spend together is helping you create a stronger bond. That bond can start immediately at birth—or, if you're a goof like me, even earlier.

In this chapter, we'll talk about some of the things you can do to influence your child's love of reading from the beginning of his or her life—or in some cases, decisions you can make even before birth to help put him or her on a path toward readership. These are fun, empowering decisions for any parent. But I discovered that you also have to think about how you will limit certain experiences in your child's life. If you take the time to read to your child in utero, you might as well tackle some of these tough conversations early as well.

One of the first decisions you're going to have to make as a parent—ideally, it's something you should start thinking about before your child is even born—is how early, and how often, he or she will be exposed to digital media and devices.

Introducing Digital Devices: How Much Is Too Much?

Early in my adventures as a new parent, I uncovered one of the most controversial videos I ever shared with my online readers at GalleyCat. I watched it over and over on YouTube, fascinated at first, but I felt uneasy the more I watched it.

A cute baby in a sundress plays with an iPad. She squeals with pure joy, realizing that she can actually control something in the world. She shuttles icons, flips the iPad, and spins pictures in a thrilling series of motions. This adorable baby instantly grasps motions that take some adults weeks to learn: the double-fingered swipe to make an image bigger, the single click to open a new application, or even the casual flip that changes the orientation.

The video cuts to the same baby on a deck someplace sunny and warm, where she struggles with a hefty print edition of *Vogue* magazine. She tries all the same swipes and button pushes on the static magazine cover, but nothing changes. The pictures stay the same and the text never rotates as she tilts the pages.

The video undoubtedly demonstrates the power and innovation of Apple engineers, and the baby's parent posted a short manifesto about the future of reading at the end of the video: "For my one-year-old daughter, a magazine is an iPad that does not work. It will remain so her whole life. Steve Jobs had coded a part of her OS."

Those parents intended the video as a tribute to the late Steve Jobs, a man who did indeed change the world. The millions of iPads he sold to parents don't matter in the long run; his profound triumph lay in the video. Jobs managed to change the way the children of those iPad owners interact with the world. Our children will never know a world without a tablet computer, smartphone, or laptop. And that means the decisions about how, and when, to expose them to these devices begin immediately.

Jobs rewired an entire generation of adults to spend ever-increasing amounts of time in front of screens. In my own life, thanks to work, smartphones, and digital books, I spend hundreds of hours in front of screens every year. And of course, while this transition happened during most of our lives, our children will live their entire lives in a world both enhanced and dominated by digital devices. As a new dad, I realized very quickly that despite all my noble ideas about reading print books, Olive will likely spend her whole life seamlessly toggling between digital and print worlds—indeed, she may not even perceive the difference as starkly as I do. After all, she has been exposed to digital technology since the very first moments of her life.

Within moments of Olive's birth, I was taking pictures of her cradled in her mother's arms. Minutes later, I was calling my parents on my cell phone and emailing them photographs. With smartphones, tablets, and digital cameras, we have documented every developmental milestone or important moment of her life.

When I rocked Olive for hours during her colicky first few months, I would read digital books on my Kindle. While hanging out with her on sleepy mornings before work, I would make silly videos for my family about this little creature in my life—dressing her in funny hats or signs.

All this device usage happened before Olive was coordinated enough to reach out and grab my phone. Once her fingers worked, Olive seemed to instinctively understand how touchscreen devices worked. By the time she figured out how to grab things with her bitty fingers, the smartphone was the very first thing she wanted.

From that moment onward, all parents begin an epic tug-of-war that will last until that baby grows up and goes to college. It will happen with any device: an iPod, iPad, smartphone, or even a TV remote.

When a device plays a big role in your life, your children will want to use it too. Look in most kids' toy boxes and you will find toy phones, dead cell phones, or even toy computers that play insipid songs and imitate the real thing that adults use all day long.

How much time should children spend with these devices? Parents have debated this question for years. Throughout this book you will get recommendations from experts about using devices, but no one has the hard and fast facts. Kindles, iPads, iPhones, and other digital devices are simply too new—researchers are only beginning to measure their effects on the infant brain. We know that too much TV can be bad developmentally, but these are different kinds of devices.

The truth is that child development experts and pediatricians still do not have enough research to tell us definitively how much is too much when it comes to screen time. Parents operate with little or no guidance from doctors about using the mobile devices that have quickly swallowed huge chunks of our lives. While we wait for the official research about the effects of touchscreens on growing brains, we will still have to make these decisions for our families in the meantime.

These devices will be a part of your child's life, there is no way to avoid it. Many of the crucial decisions you will make about your children's reading and media usage should be made (or at least considered) before they're even born. In the absence of data,

I think we should be more cautious. We laugh about our grand-parents' bad parenting decisions now: dry cleaning bags on kids' heads, cigarettes in the house, letting kids watch six straight hours of television. Someday our descendants will roll their eyes at our own parenting decisions. What mistakes are we making that we don't even realize yet? We hardly understand the effects of apps on growing brains. But it's an area of robust research, and experts are starting to gather information to share with those of us who want to make up our own minds.

Professional Guidelines about Device Usage: What Do the Experts Say?

In 2011, the American Academy of Pediatrics (AAP) released a strict set of guidelines, urging parents to not let children younger than two years old consume any sort of media, from television to smartphones to iPads. The recommendations aimed at extending "unplugged play," a cognitive stepping stone every bit as valuable as learning how to walk or speak.

The AAP dispatch explained: "Pediatricians should explain to parents the importance of unstructured, unplugged play in allowing a child's mind to grow, problem-solve, think innovatively, and develop reasoning skills. Unstructured play occurs both independently and cooperatively with a parent or caregiver. The importance of parents sitting down to play with their children cannot be overstated."

At the very least, parents should set strict media limits, to make sure the child devotes enough time to "unplugged play." The AAP even recommends that children older than two years spend less than two hours a day in front of a screen. If you compare that to the staggering amount of time adults like me spend working in front of screens, these guidelines seem nearly impossible to enforce. That's why you should think about these philosophical questions months before your baby ever touches an iPad.

A team of AAP doctors summarized a year's worth of research into the dangers of excessive screen time for children in a frightening paragraph: "Time spent watching television is associated with a number of negative health behaviors and outcomes among children, including overweight, irregular sleep, insufficient consumption of fruits and vegetables, and disordered eating. Excessive television viewing has detrimental effects on prosocial behaviors, such as spending time with parents and siblings, doing homework, or engaging in creative play, and is linked with getting lower grades, getting into trouble, and feeling sadness and boredom."

Yikes. If smartphones and tablets are not used in the proper context, we are basically giving kids televisions they can carry anywhere they want. While researchers don't have enough data to make many conclusions, parents should not underestimate the dangers posed by too much screen time—no matter what device they use.

University of Washington professor of pediatrics Dimitri Christakis explained in an online interview: "The newborn brain triples in size in the first two years of life, and it does this in direct response to external stimulation." Every time I get sick of reading the same book over and over or just want to watch television instead of offering a bedtime story, I think about my baby's growing brain. Especially during those first few years, reading to your baby really does make a difference. Christakis concluded: "When a television is on, or a screen is on, the child is engaged in watching that program, and the parent is talking to their child 80 percent less of the time. That talking time is really critical for a child's language development, because hearing the words and hearing their parents talking to them is helping them understand the language and grow their communication skills. Making use of those times when you're busy doing something else is really valuable time for your child."

Even though the research is only beginning, any parent can clearly see the powerful sway these devices hold over a child. So what's a parent to do? While experts don't agree 100 percent on what exactly the best practices are for device use for and around children, a few guidelines do emerge.

Think carefully about how early (and how often) to introduce devices.

Some groups believe we should keep devices out of our kids' hands until after elementary school. The Alliance for Childhood published a huge report called "Fool's Gold," calling for an "immediate moratorium on the further introduction of computers in early childhood and elementary education, except for special cases of students with disabilities. Such a time-out is necessary to create the climate for the above recommendations to take place."

The Waldorf Education approach to early education actively discourages the use of devices with young kids. The educational philosophy developed from the work of Austrian philosopher and teacher Rudolf Steiner. Steiner founded a revolutionary school in the 1920s, developing a curriculum years before television or computers. His philosophies spread to 900 Waldorf schools in 83 different countries.

The school has a strict policy about devices inside the classroom, and many teachers discourage computer use in the home as well. The movement's official page makes the policy clear: "Waldorf teachers feel the appropriate age for computer use in the classroom and by students is in high school. We feel it is more important for students to have the opportunity to interact with one another and with teachers in exploring the world of ideas, participating in the creative process, and developing their knowledge, skills, abilities, and inner qualities. Waldorf students have a love of learning, an ongoing curiosity, and interest in life. As older students, they quickly master computer technology, and graduates have successful careers in the computer industry."

In an online interview, Washington pediatrician Don Shifrin noted that "two-thirds of kids ages 4 to 7 have already used an iPhone or an iPod Touch," a staggering statistic if you consider how relatively new these devices are.

Even the people building digital experiences for children struggle with the question of how much time to spend on a device. App designer Christoph Niemann shared his own family device usage guidelines for his children: "I don't want [my son] to have something like that in his room, where he can drag it out in the middle of the night and play for two hours. The first thing is basically that they can only do it with their brothers, together. I don't want this to be a solitary thing. The second thing is limiting time, extremely." Whatever you and your family decide, the general rule, say experts, is to monitor your kids' time on and access to electronic devices. Unfettered access is generally not recommended.

End each day with a book, not a device.

In practice, most parents will allow their children some sort of monitored or restricted device usage. But there is one important principle that nearly every expert agrees upon. Keep the device outside of the bedroom. Shifrin advises parents: "Media in children's and even teenagers' bedrooms is a detriment to their health, their family health, their ability to connect with the family, their ability to get information unfiltered into their brains and also the ability to go to sleep."

As parents, we can make a commitment to end our child's day with a print book, rather than a cartoon or digital book in the bedroom. Keeping devices and eBooks out of the bedroom will build better sleep habits and put your child on a healthier course as they grow up. You can model the behavior with your own device usage, by setting (and keeping!) your own digital boundaries inside the house. No devices at the dinner table, anyone?

Be mindful of what other toys are in the house.

This is also a great time to think about commercialism in your child's life. Harvard Medical School psychiatry instructor Susan Linn has spent years fighting corporations sneaking into your child's toy box and has written a number of books about commercialism. She leads the Campaign for a Commercial-Free Childhood, a nonprofit group waging a very active war against marketers and corporations who target children through digital devices, television shows, and toys. "Parents can be conscious of the commercial onslaught even before their babies are born. Set limits in early childhood. If your baby is inundated with Elmo or the Disney princesses, if the baby's room is decorated with media characters, if the baby's toys *are* media characters, those media characters are going to become incredibly important to your child and it's going to be harder to set limits later," she said. "It's easy to limit commercialism in the life of a baby and a toddler, because they're not asking for it."

As you've probably already realized, you don't need to buy a single media-branded item for your kids ... because your family and friends will likely do it for you. But this is an invaluable conversation to have before your child arrives, setting family rules about the oncoming deluge of toys that encourage kids to watch more TV, buy more breakfast cereal, or spend more money on other branded toys. Remember, you are ultimately in charge of what toys come into your house (and which ones stay there).

The Three C's of Responsible Device Usage: Making Devices More Interactive

Before Olive could talk, she recognized the words iPad and iPhone. Her eyes lit up like a trained monkey when we used those magic names. Once she could talk, one of her first words was iPhone. Who could blame her? This device has been stuck in her face at every major moment in her life, from birthday parties to first steps to video chats with her grandparents back in Michigan.

Nevertheless, our first impulse as parents was to limit her time on the device.

While raising her children during the early 2000s, journalist Lisa Guernsey struggled to strike a similar balance with device usage. With two young kids running around the house, she discovered how DVDs could bring a little bit of domestic peace to these creatures with boundless energy. She interviewed a host of experts, writing an entire book called *Into the Minds of Babes: How Screen Time Affects Children from Birth to Age Five.*

I caught up with Guernsey for some advice in my own life, and she urged parents to think less about time spent on a device and more time worrying about the three C's, her strategies for thinking about screen time: "content," "context," and your "individual child." She explained (emphasis mine): "One is the *content*, knowing whether the material that the children are seeing on the screen makes sense to them or not. But then there's the *context*, which is whether there are moments for conversations about what they are experiencing on the screen. . . . The third C is your individual *child* and recognizing how every child is so different. They will come to that screen media experience in a different way because of that child's own experiences that they've already started building up and their own disposition and their own interests."

Interactive reading can be a powerful kind of early stimulation. By using Guernsey's three C's and the Born Reading Playbook, you can make sure digital reading is more constructive as well. By choosing the right eBooks, apps, and media, you can make sure your child receives the kind of stimulation the growing brain needs.

I applied the three C's during an adventure I took with Olive when she was two and a half years old. At this point in her life, Olive spent about 15 minutes a day using an iPad, and she was learning to use a storytelling app that involved playing with digital treasure boxes and castles.

Following Guernsey's advice, I knew that the *content* made sense to my toddler. Olive clearly understood what was happening. She repeated the words "treasure" and "castle" often and spent one morning decorating cardboard castles with her mom. Olive pronounced the word "treasure" with a tiny lisp, the word brimming with joy like the word "surprise" or "present."

That morning, I took the combination of app games and real life games a step further, inventing a simple castles and treasure game at the park. We played treasure hunters for an hour at play structure "castles," digging through the sand, wood chips, and dirt to uncover imaginary treasure boxes.

By playing in the park, I extended the *context* of the app into the real world, giving Olive a chance to use the words she had learned by playing with the device in a physical (if imaginary) game. We added tigers and snakes that guarded the treasures, and I would wrestle play monsters while she grabbed the treasure.

As the game continued, I recognized my *individual child*'s passion for our digital devices. At this point, we still had to battle her if she happened to grab one of our smartphones. Olive would whine and use all her delay tactics before reluctantly returning the device.

So I decided to let Olive have some extra smartphone time in the park, teaching her how to take photographs of our imaginary castles with my iPhone. She got her wish to use our devices and I got my wish for a more interactive experience with her, based on the imaginary world that we'd first encountered in the app.

What Makes a Good App?
The Key Is Parental Interaction

In this book, I generally advocate following the AAP's guidelines for digital devices: no screen time before age two. Once your child turns two years old, these digital boundaries need to be reconsidered. Children need digital literacy to be a part of contemporary culture, and there is a vast pool of resources they can explore with digital tech. But parents need to negotiate this world carefully.

When you make the decision to let your children use a device, your life becomes complicated in another way. You must decide how long they can use the device and what is the best way to pry it from their hands when they have reached that allotted time. I am convinced that most kids would use these devices until they keel over from exhaustion.

We kept Olive's time under control with a sophisticated parenting tool: the kitchen timer. "Five minutes," I would say, plunking her down at the same chair in the same corner of the kitchen table every time. She grew so accustomed to using that corner of the table that she refused to sit in "the iPad chair" when she was eating.

After a few days of timer training, she would surrender the device without a big fight when the timer beeped. She would use a variety of delay tactics to extend her time by a minute or two, but generally, she would give it up without too much whining—no small feat for a two-year-old.

Tablets require more participation than television, creating the convenient illusion that the device is healthier for your child. App developer Andy Russell explained the classic dilemma that parents face: "A lot of parents see these things as digital pacifiers and they think, 'Oh, it's the iPad, it's good for my kids,' much the same way that they look at PBS TV shows and say, 'Oh, it's better for my kids than *Power Rangers*, so I'm just going to pop my kid down in front of PBS and it's going to be good for them.' And that is less bad than just popping them in front of *Power Rangers* or *NYPD Blue* or something like that, of course. But it's not necessarily good for them. Kids don't just learn by soaking up information."

While the iPad instinctively feels like a solitary device, parents should make it a communal experience. Remember all the talk of "interactive reading" in the introduction? We'll come back to that again soon, but the key takeaway applies to digital media as well as print books—the learning is in your *interaction* with your child, not in the content itself. The temptation is to leave and do something else during these moments when your child is in a state of deep focus on the device, but these are actually the moments to engage, not walk away. If it's a learning app, you can guide your child through these simple games, helping him or her spot letters, numbers, and shapes. As you read this book and take interactive reading to heart, you need to change all your ideas about media. These scary facts and figures about screen time need to be balanced by a healthy attitude about media consumption.

For instance, we all grew up thinking that *Sesame Street* was "good for you," that the creators had developed some intelligence-increasing recipe, like the media equivalent of eating your vegetables. Russell turned those ideas upside down. He explained why the classic show *Sesame Street* was good for kids: "The best thing about *Sesame Street* isn't that it's got this incredible curriculum that no one else does. The best thing about *Sesame Street* is that it's appealing to both kids and parents. The kids love the Muppets and the parents love the satire. That there are all sorts of funny little puns between Grover singing 'Letter B' instead of 'Let It Be,' to them doing spoofs of *Mad Men* to Will.i.am coming on and performing music videos. There's always something in every *Sesame Street* episode that's going to make the parents smile. And that's why parents love sitting down with their kids and watching it. And that, to a certain extent, is why kids love watching *Sesame Street* because it is something they can do with their mom or dad."

So instead of obsessing about how much time your kids spend in front of screens, you should focus more on the quality of your interaction while they are using these devices. This chapter covered many of the negatives parents should consider about device usage, but upcoming chapters will explore the entire range of digital reading available to twenty-first-century parents. These chapters will help you build a digital library for your child, no matter what kind of devices you have at home. These powerful tools will reinforce your print library and help your child grow as a born reader.

Questions to Ask about Devices before the Baby Is Born: A Checklist

1. What kind of devices will you use around your child?
2. Will you let your child use devices before the age of two?
3. If you will let your child use devices, how much time will he or she spend on them?
4. If you do allow devices, what apps, videos, or cartoons can your child watch?
5. What will you do when you need downtime?

Beyond Devices: Reading Matters More than the Format

In this chapter, I've talked a lot about the earliest decisions families will have to make about digital devices—when they will be introduced, how much time you should allow your children access to digital devices, how you can use them to actually enhance your child's early learning. But the most important thing to remember, no matter what your device strategy, is this: tablets and smartphones will never replace good old-fashioned reading time with your children.

Lisa Guernsey explains: "I know it sounds kind of obvious, but when you look back on some crazes around technology and media, we become so focused on the device or the baby video moment or whatever that parents can kind of feel like they aren't necessary. I really hope we don't fall into that same trap again with apps."

Just like walking or talking, kids need lots of practice reading books. You are laying the foundation for literacy, but also a host of other important skills: a lifetime of attentiveness, patience, and good study habits.

Before your baby is born, you need to decide to make reading a part of your family routine.

Babies and toddlers depend on routine: they want the same person to tuck them in to bed every night, they need the same toys in the bathtub, and they will freak out if you suddenly remove a well-loved chair from the living room. You will not always feel like reading a book every day, but you should put books into your routine. Olive spends my workday at day care, so these reading moments are precious. I love to read a book in the morning and a book at night.

This all depends on a collection of good children's books. Despite writing about the publishing industry for my full-time job as a blogger, I had absolutely no idea what books to buy my baby. Our friends did all the work for us at my wife's baby shower, giving us a bookshelf filled with lovely books—including many of the classics mentioned later in this book. Olive still reads many of those gifts. If you are expecting, you should ask guests to bring a copy of the book they loved most as a child to your baby shower—it's a great way to explore the crowded world of kids' books.

In addition, every chapter of this book will conclude with a list of ten books I recommend. Olive and I have tested every single book mentioned in these pages, and I'll describe the book and include some ideas for how to read them as well.

But don't just depend on my recommendations. Ask family, friends, and co-workers for their favorite books. Grilling parents on book ideas became a habit for me at play dates or in the park. These suggestions will make your personal collection and visits to the library much more exciting. By the time you finish this book, you should have a hundred books to consider for your children's library.

We will also explore the crowded and confusing world of digital books for children. From two years old and onward, I will include another list of ten recommended eBooks for children—helping parents stock their Kindles, iPads, smartphones, Nooks, and other devices with the best stories for kids. I'll even show you how to create your own digital books for kids.

As you will see while reading this book, digital books will give children some amazing reading experiences we could previously only read about in science fiction novels. They will take smartphones and tablets for granted, a printed book will be equally exotic or dull to them as a digital page, and they will have no associations with books, no reason to value one or the other.

But we can make sure they are born reading, building them a powerful foundation before they ever have to choose.

Questions to Ask about Print Books before the Baby Is Born: A Checklist

1. What books do you want in your library?
2. Did you ask your friends for books and book suggestions?
3. When will you schedule reading time during the day?
4. Who will read the bedtime story?
5. If you don't allow devices, what will you do when you need downtime?

Encouraging Diversity

Once your baby is born, you won't have time to take a shower, much less worry about the diversity of your kid's library. However, I think all parents should take a hard look at their child's personal libraries, making sure each child can have the most diverse reading list possible. There are some excellent organizations out there that are committed to bringing resources, both digital and print, to all early readers.

First Book is a literacy nonprofit that pledges to bring more diverse books to thousands of classrooms around the country. CEO Kyle Zimmer says, "We've heard time and again from the educators we work with that one of the biggest challenges to helping kids become strong readers is the desperate lack of books that are culturally relevant to these kids' lives. One of the best ways to turn children into readers is to give them stories with heroes and experiences they can relate to."

And that exposure goes both ways—educators say it's important to expose *all* children, regardless of their background, to a broad variety of characters, some whose experiences and cultures are familiar to them, and some whose are not.

I have worked to fill this book with recommendations that show a variety of perspectives on race, class, ethnicity, and gender. If you are looking for more diverse reading, I recommend you start at the Goodreads social network for readers. You can find hundreds and hundreds of recommended books in the "Diversity Book Lists" section of that site—each book is suggested by one of the millions of avid readers on the site. You can compile a long list of books to find at your local library.

It takes conscious effort to build a diverse bookshelf. But at the end of the day, our kids deserve to read books about cultures from around the world.

Interlude: How Sign Language Can Change Your Baby's Life

The first word that Olive learned in sign language was "more." Months before she turned one year old, she would make the sign by tapping the fingertips of both hands together when she wanted *more* food, *more* books, *more* toys, or *more* attention from her parents.

Teaching your baby sign language is an amazing way to ease the frustration of those months before your child learns how to speak. Using a collection of simple American Sign Language (ASL) signs, you can vastly improve your baby's communication during the first year of life. We started saying basic words and making signs within the first few months of our daughter's life.

To find out more about baby sign language, I spoke with Lissa Zeviar. Her parents are both deaf, and she works as a professional sign-language interpreter. She also created Babygebaren, a company offering classes, tools, and research assistance for teaching your baby sign language. "Most of the people that I work with see the pure, two-way communication that you can have at an age when babies really do want to communicate," she told me. "You can just tell by a baby's body language they want to share so much."

She urges parents to start baby signing as early as they feel comfortable. There will be an indefinite period where your baby will not respond or appear to recognize signs, so it requires a bit of patience. All children are different, but Zeviar set six months as the developmental moment when "babies are more likely to possess the ability to remember signs and the motor skills to produce them."

The primary benefit of baby sign language is that you will be able to understand what your child wants during those early months before your child can speak. You can avoid frustrating tantrums and defuse anger with a little bit of communication. But your child will also learn about both language and reading.

By the time Olive was a year and a half old, she could identify all the signs in her favorite baby sign-language book. She could read the book years before she was actually literate—a powerful tool to bridge the gap between reading with a parent and reading by oneself.

"Once that sign becomes letters 'B-O-O-K' they've already made the link that a symbol can also represent something," explained Zeviar, illustrating how baby sign language can augment a lifetime of reading.

"My kids could go through flashcards of signs and they could actually read the signs, because they could see what the sign means. They couldn't read at all, but they could read the picture," she said. "That's what you need for reading. By the time they do start to read and write, they've already practiced that in a much younger and natural way. To encourage reading, it's done naturally."

Literacy is much, much more than simply reading letters on the page. By showing your child how to read sign language both in sign-language books and with you, you show them how to decode language. These are the primary building blocks for a lifetime of reading and storytelling, tremendous gifts to give your child even at this young age.

As you teach your child this basic vocabulary, Zeviar urges parents to seek words that their child wants to learn. Instead of only teaching words that parents need (like "hungry," "wait," or "stop"), make sure to teach your child the words for things that fascinate them. How can you follow a child's interest if they can't even speak? It is easier than you think.

What does your baby stare at all day? Those are the words that they want to know. "The sign for 'light' can really start the process early. Light is often one of the first signs that a baby makes. Anytime they see a light, they are mesmerized," explained Zeviar.

"If you want a child to sign back, follow their interest," she said. If you teach your baby the word for that mysterious brightness on every ceiling, you will help them solve a concrete language problem months before they can speak.

As your child grows older, you may be tempted to stop using sign language, but you may also decide it is worth keeping in your life. Sign language could help your child communicate with sign-language users in your school district. Zeviar explains that instead of separating deaf children, schools now mix them together with all kinds of students. "Schools these days are being much more mainstreamed," she said. "Deaf people are not being stuffed away in deaf schools anymore. [Hearing children] will encounter deaf children."

But sign language is used by a variety of students, and kids with sign language can interact with them as well. "There is a quite large group of children who grow up very intelligent but for one reason or another can't speak or use language. But they can use sign language," she concluded. With the gift of sign language, your child can make friends in this new diverse environment.

Below, I've collected a few books and apps that you can use to teach sign language, but you can find many, many more resources online for other languages.

Print Sign-Language Resources

Baby Fingers series by Lora Heller
Simple, easy-to-understand photographs of toddlers making important signs—a good basic introduction.

Baby Signing Time book series
Inspired by the PBS show *Signing Time*, this board book series covers signs for everything from food to friends to going to sleep.

Little Beauty by Anthony Browne
A book about a gorilla and a cat becoming friends in captivity. Sign language plays a key role in the plot, prompting conversations about signing.

Digital Sign-Language Resources

Signing Time
http://www.signingtime.com/resources/
This PBS show has a free set of guides, coloring pages, and other resources for parents and children learning how to sign.

"The Art of Sign Language, for Babies, Boobs and Bobs"
A TEDx talk by Lissa Zeviar, outlining why sign language matters for babies and sharing her personal story.

Scholastic Storybook Treasures: Goodnight Moon . . . And More Great Bedtime Stories
A sign language DVD that adapts some classic stories in American Sign Language, teaching your kids with their favorite books.

Baby Einstein: My First Signs
A DVD for babies introducing key signs. Actress Marlee Matlin leads the show with puppets.

Chapter 2

First Year of Life

The very first book we read with Olive was *Goodnight Moon* by Margaret Wise Brown. Olive was one week old, bewildered as a space alien who accidentally crash-landed on our planet. She could barely even rock her body, much less wiggle away if I was reading. So I filled her spare five-minute stretches of happiness with that little storybook. Laying on our bed, I sat Olive on my stomach with her back balanced against my knees. I could hold the book in between us, a cozy set up that only works for the first month or so of your baby's life.

You can buy many editions of *Goodnight Moon*, from gorgeous large hardbacks to miniature editions that fit in one hand. We ended up with a "board book" edition of the classic kids' book, the pages printed on sturdy cardboard that can survive baby chewing, ripping, and spills. The 5 x 6-inch dimensions were perfect for reading to an infant.

The book tells the story of a baby rabbit going to sleep, saying goodnight to a collection of toys, animals, clothes, and celestial bodies. Every page captures the bunny's room from a different angle, a masterpiece of composition. One page shows the whole room, grandma rabbit knitting in the corner, while another page focuses on the sleepy bunny wiggling into his bed, trying to avoid sleeping. Another page zooms in on a painting in the bedroom, showing a scene from *Goldilocks and the Three Bears*.

The zoomed-in scenes appear as gentle black-and-white illustrations, while the wide shots are in color—the perfect contrast for Olive's brand-new eyes. I read the drowsy rhymes out loud over and over, repeating goodnight to all these objects she'd never seen. I pointed to everything inside the pictures: the tussling kittens, the slow moonrise, and the bitty mouse spotlighted by a pool of mysterious light.

On good days, Olive could make it through the whole book before she needed to be fed or walked or bounced. During these brief readings, her big eyes locked on the book. She'll never be able to tell me how much she absorbed during those first weeks of reading, but she accepted the motions of reading almost immediately. Reading became a regular part of this new world.

Harvard professor Maria Tatar started reading to her kids as soon as they could sit up by themselves. She reminds parents not to worry about comprehension during these early months. The experience is the most important part. She explains: "Sometimes it's not just for the baby, you are teaching them about the object, the artifact. How to turn pages, it's more of a kinetic than a cognitive activity at that point."

Storytelling Lessons: *Goodnight Moon*

1. Point out all of the animals and objects in the carefully painted scenes.
2. Make the sounds for each animal in these scenes.
3. Customize the story, identifying parents or grandparents in the scenes.
4. Repeat the names of objects on every page to reinforce the vocabulary.
5. Choose the right size of the book for your baby: large paper pages or smaller board book edition.

Reading during the First Six Months: Practice for You and for Baby

Will *Goodnight Moon* work for you and your baby? You won't know until you try. Librarian Betsy Bird of the New York Public Library has some selection advice for these first picks: "Be sure you get the right kind of board book. There are some out there with *way* too many words or with soft contrast pictures that bore babies to blazes. Find out what the best board books are and latch on to those. And when they're good at reaching out and grabbing things, encourage them to help you turn the pages in a book."

Olive's first three months were relentless. She had colic, a mysterious ailment that tortures unlucky babies during the first weeks of their lives. We had little slivers of happy baby time, half-hour intervals scattered over the course of her day. I filled as many of those hours with books as possible.

That was the beginning of a much longer and complicated voodoo to get her to sleep. I would swaddle her after reading her goodnight book, sit on a yoga ball in front of our stereo, and bounce for half an hour or an hour until she would relax. Olive always wailed for the first few minutes, and then ever so slowly, she settled. I could balance her tiny body along the crook of one arm, her eggshell head in my palm.

As we bounced, the radio played songs by Bob Dylan, Wilco, and a Hawaiian cover of our favorite "Tiny Bubbles" that I still have memorized to this day. When I stopped bouncing too soon, Olive would scream and the whole ritual would begin again. On the days when she wouldn't stop screaming, I could play her a homemade white noise track. After discovering that people managed to charge $10-15 online for recordings of vacuum cleaners, I made my own recording of a blow dryer, looping the sound over and over for an hour-long track on my laptop. The "Blowdryer!" track on my iPod still sends shivers down my spine when I see it on my computer.

We kept reading, forming daily rituals around the handful of books she could enjoy. At night, we would sit in our rocking chair, the pocket stuffed with a couple handy books, repeating the reading ritual and rocking. These early reading experiences shaped her first bedtime routine, something that would pay off months later when her colicky period ended.

These routines are very important to babies. They want the same person to sing the same song and tuck them in at night. You will be tired after a long day of work, and you will not always feel like it, but you should incorporate books into this routine. It is the best time of the day for reading, especially if your child spends most of the day at day care or with someone else.

When is the right time to read to my baby? I kept asking friends, doctors, and publishers, but the best answer I got was simple: "Whenever you want." The American Academy of Pediatrics (AAP) advises parents to start reading at six months, but I tell all new parents to start reading during those first weeks. It is thankless work at first, but you will never forget those early reading experiences.

Born Reading Playbook: Read together.
Researchers call this co-play. Make sure you play games and read together every single day.

Ideas for parents: *You will spend most of these first few months staring at a mute baby. Why not pass these quiet days with books?*

According to development experts at the Mayo Clinic, babies begin to focus on faces, shapes, and colors within the first few weeks. These newborns react to parents' voices from birth onward, and reading is the perfect way to encourage your child's earliest language development. By six months, babies can follow a book and imitate a reader's sounds, even though they seem immobile.

Reading is a habit more than anything. Betsy Bird explains: "Essentially a kid can be read to pretty much from the get-go. . . . In the earliest weeks babies can't actually see anything very well, so their ability to understand a book is going to be pretty limited. Even then there are things you can do. You can get awesome titles like Tana Hoban's *Black & White*, an accordion book that you spread out in their crib. The sharp contrast is fascinating to babies. Once their sight is better you read to them while they're lying in their crib. Then after that, when you can prop them up on your lap, you read to them there. So basically you read to them as early as you can and by the time they're able to latch on to things, books are going to be amongst their favorite toys."

Using the American Academy of Pediatrics' developmental charts, I plotted reading milestones in your child's development as he or she grows during these early months.

How to Read during the First Six Months

1. Your baby always enjoys human interaction; books are the perfect introduction.
2. By three months, hands and eyes coordinate. Start touching books!
3. Between four and seven months, your baby can sit up to read.
4. Memory increases dramatically over these months—they will remember books.
5. Babies learn cause and effect by playing with objects— including books.

Early Reading: Planting the Seeds for Later

Even though it doesn't seem like much is getting through to your child during those first several months, you may be surprised at what he or she retains. Olive was born in the middle of a vampire craze in the publishing industry, so I had a copy of *Dick and Jane and Vampires* lying around the house. Intended for older readers, the book was a sly mash-up of the classic Dick and Jane storybook series and a campy vampire straight out of a black and white movie.

The book poked fun at 1950s nostalgia, much like the television show *Mad Men* gives us a glimpse of white suburban parents during an economic boom. At one point, Dick and Jane's mother hands out dry cleaning bags, letting the kids wear the plastic over their heads as they run around the backyard. The vampire begins as a hip gag, but ends up warming your heart as he performs weak somersaults and gamely wears baby clothes for the kids.

During the first six months of Olive's life, I spent a lot of time hanging out while she sat in her bouncy chair. Invariably, I would run out of amusements, so I introduced Olive to the book. It made me laugh, and I wanted her to think it was funny too. So I reenacted the book endlessly, turning the pages for her and exaggerating every joke.

I would read the book and shout "*vampire!*" every time the purple-caped villain would show up, hiding in the bushes, under the bed, or dangling upside down in the closet. She sat in her blue bouncy chair, mute and rubbery, but her eyes were so bright.

After a few days, Olive would smile every time I yelled "*vampire!*" Every time I shouted the magic word, she would giggle and grin this shy grin that I interpreted as, "I don't quite know what you are talking about, but I think you're hilarious so I'm gonna laugh like I get it."

One year later, I pulled the book out of a box and reread the book to my toddler. Suddenly Olive started repeating all the old gags I taught her the year before. All my "*vampire!*" training came back to haunt me, because suddenly Olive wouldn't read anything else.

The 130-page book became tedious to read over and over, and as her vampire phase peaked, she wouldn't touch anything else. I tried to bury the book under other books, leave it behind downstairs, or lure her to one of her old favorite books. It never worked. She would shrug her shoulders going, "Huh? Huh? Huh?" until I acknowledged she was looking for the vampire book. Then she would yell "wham pie ur!" toddling around the house until we could find the book.

During those first few months of acting out the story, I was learning how to read my daughter's reactions—a crucial skill for interactive reading sessions.

This simple playbook technique works for both books and digital media, straight from child development expert Lisa Guernsey. "You also have to watch your kids' faces. Read them at the same time you are reading the text," she explains. "There are nonverbal cues that kids can give us about what they are really interested in."

Make sure these rituals are cozy experiences. Children's author and book designer Sara Gillingham urges parents to turn these cuddly moments into an interactive experience: "One thing I love about reading to small children is that the best position is holding them in your lap. The fact that a snuggle often goes hand-in-hand with a book is a powerful association."

She also explains how this will actually lead to more intimate reading. As you hold them, it is easy to guide these slow-moving creatures through the book-reading experience. She concludes: "To keep babies interested in a book, I'd encourage them to touch, turn and play with them, to show them that books are colorful, tactile objects with moving parts [and] pages, not just things they need to sit and look at passively."

Betsy Bird also urges parents to find more interactive books: "Get some nice tactile books with touchable insides. That can be a big hit at a certain age."

Born Reading Playbook: Dramatize the story.

You can mime sweeping when you see a broom or pretend to eat the character's food. This will help your child match the concepts to the words, a pillar of interactive reading experience.

Ideas for parents: *Can you help your child touch the illustrations? What actions or sound effects make your baby pay attention?*

So what's the point of reading to a mute and passive baby?

Publisher Roger Priddy thinks it helps a lot: "Babies don't do much for a while, and then you can see they start to engage with things around them. Six months to a year is a great period, it's when they start to recognize things around them—they aren't necessarily following a story, but they pick up on images."

I would read *The Very Hungry Caterpillar* by Eric Carle while I watched Olive during those early, quiet days. I would lift her finger to touch the pages so she could feel the dents in the page and count the different-colored food devoured by the title character. About the same time, Olive tried to gnaw on all her books while we read. Without discouraging the act of reading, I'd try to dissuade her.

Once she ripped an entire magazine out of my hands and started munching. I remembered in a flash how paper tasted and how I used to put books and magazines in my mouth. Magazines had the crunchiest, the most satisfying glossy taste. As I wrestled for my reading material, I wondered how old that memory is.

It may feel like you are reading to thin air those first few months, as the only thing to read to are her eyes. But at six months everything changes: baby wants to eat pages or crawl away or wiggle, and those moments when she is calm and reading are glorious.

Despite the lack of participation during these early months, Sara Gillingham advises parents to introduce books as early as they introduce toys into a baby's life. She had this advice for reading to very young children: "I'd choose books that feature visuals or words that are familiar to your child. I'd play with your voice, volume, and pacing as you read, because I find the energy we put into reading to children is contagious. And finally, I'd put age-appropriate books out at playtime alongside blocks and stuffed toys as soon as a baby begins to show interest in toys. A child doesn't need to be able to read, or be read to, to enjoy the tactile qualities of a book from a very young age, and to begin to think of a book as a friend."

Storytelling Lessons

1. Start reading to your baby at least once a day in the first months of life.
2. Don't worry about keeping the books safe. Roger Priddy explains: "When a book is beat up, it's had a good life."
3. Read a book with words and sounds, even though the baby can't understand them.
4. Don't stop reading until your baby wants to stop.
5. Watch your baby's reactions to the book and respond to these cues.

Reading from Six Months Onward: Recognizing and Responding

By six months old, you have an entirely new kind of reader. Your child can respond to a book and interact with the pages. Instead of a mute passenger in your lap, your baby can make sounds and wiggle to share his or her opinion about a book. He or she will probably start to grab books out of your hand and even nibble on the pages. Board books are your friends during these months, and your favorite books will likely emerge with gnawed-upon edges. It's all part of your child's exploration process.

Every year in your baby's reading life will begin and end with a totally different creature. In the course of those first 12 months (the fastest 12 months of my life), Olive traveled from a mute, immobile worm to a wiggling, busy baby cruising along furniture.

After six months, I walked around the neighborhood with Olive strapped in a baby carrier facing outward. Even though she couldn't answer me, I started naming every object we saw and talking about our books in an endless monologue.

Olive could only babble during this period, but I knew she was absorbing books, words, and life. Even though she couldn't explain what was going on inside that little head, you could see the training wheels turning.

Using the AAP's developmental charts, I plotted five reading milestones in your baby's development as they near one year old.

How to Read with a 6- to 12-Month-Old Baby

1. Your child will be able to look for a familiar object on a book page.
2. Your baby will touch, chew, stare at, and otherwise examine books.
3. Your baby can search for hidden objects, opening flaps in a book.
4. Your baby can sit up without assistance, the perfect time to stick a baby-sized book in his or her hands.
5. Your baby will be testing the size, shape, and texture of the world around him or her, perfect time for tactile books with fabric or scratchy or shiny surfaces to explore.

The exciting thing about reading with babies from about 6 to 12 months old is that they start to "wake up" to the world. Even if they aren't responding directly to your stories at first, they're starting to connect the words, stories, and images. And by the time your baby nears one year old, he or she may surprise you with glimmers of recognition or understanding about those stories you've been reading all this time.

That was certainly the case in our family. Our friends gave us a copy of *Lost and Found*, a lovely book about a boy who befriends a lost penguin. The boy spends the entire book helping the penguin get home, only to realize that the penguin just wanted to be his friend. One technique you can employ in books like these to really engage your child is to substitute your child's name for the child in the story. It makes for a customized reading experience, and for this book Olive particularly loved it.

We kept reading until one seemingly routine evening when Olive was around six months old. I was reading her *Lost and Found* for what felt like the fiftieth time. The book climaxes after the boy paddles through Antarctica looking for his friend the penguin, realizing that they should stay together. Among the icebergs and gorgeous dark blue painted ocean, we see the penguin as a shadow in the distance—the lonesome bird floating on an umbrella to reunite with his friend.

I can still recite my particular rendition of the story from memory. "Somebody was coming closer and closer and closer. Who was it? Who was it?" I always paused for effect, savoring the big climax came when the tubby penguin embraced his friend on the next page. "*The penguin! It was the penguin!* And he gave Olive a big hug."

On that momentous night, I swear to god, Olive frowned when the penguin went missing and she cheered when the penguin appeared on that shimmering white ice shelf. I will defend that moment until my dying day, it was the first time my baby *believed* in a story. It wasn't just my voice or some pretty picture, she giggled and babbled with joy, she actually grasped the story and understood that the penguin had been lost and found. I scooped her up in my arms and held her, in love with this new creature.

It is so exciting to start to see emotions and responses to a story playing out with your little one. These first reactions were the beginning of an ongoing reading conversation in our family. Maria Tatar explains that this developmental milestone is key to children at 6–12 months, as your child "wakes up" to the world. In her family, they set aside time every night to read, continuing the practice all the way through high school. She urged parents to go beyond passive reading and pose questions about the characters, settings, and emotions in the book.

As your baby nears one, the first words will emerge. This is your chance to begin talking about books. Tatar thinks this ongoing conversation had a profound impact on her relationship with her children: "They share a lot more with me because of that experience, talking while reading. The story helped them process things that were going on during the day. It gave them the words to talk about feelings, responses, and emotions. I don't think anyone will be able to quantify that that experience created a relationship that made it easier to talk about a lot of things that were taboo when I was a child."

I encourage you to break reading rules regularly. According to the packaging, books like *Lost and Found* should be read to older children. I've been reading longer storybooks to Olive for most of her life and I haven't seen a single side effect. Pick a few storybooks that you enjoy and give it a try.

We need to change our whole attitude about reading. There is absolutely no substitute for reading to your baby, no television or app can do that for you, especially not during the first year of life.

Buying this book is a good first step, but you need to commit to years and years of reading together to make it work. Your baby is worth it.

Storytelling Lessons: *Lost and Found*

1. Substitute your baby's name for the main character.
2. Use a stuffed animal as a prop for the penguin.
3. Painstakingly explain every drawing.

4. Act out the character's emotions dramatically.
5. Add movement to the drawings: brush your hands on the page for ocean waves and trace the momentum of a boat.

To help you with your reading journey, the following chapters of the book will end with some books that I loved to read with my daughter. Enjoy my book recommendations, but the most important books are the books that your child loves to read.

Researcher John Protzko summed it up: "One of the main aspects of interactive reading is to follow the child's interests. In this way, the best question is not whether I have any books I would recommend but what books the children doing the reading would recommend."

Caregivers and children must make these decisions together. You can make the final decisions with the child in your life at bookstores, libraries, or digital app stores.

Born Reading Playbook: Share details about the book.

Point out your favorite illustrations, name the colors, animals, people, and feelings on the page. At first your child will not be able to join you, but they will pick up your interactive habit as they grow.

Ideas for parents: *Can you mime objects in the pictures? What images draw your child's attention?*

Books for the First Year

Goodnight Moon by Margaret Wise Brown
The book tells the story of a baby rabbit going to sleep, saying goodnight to a collection of toys, animals, winter clothes, and celestial bodies. Every page captures the bunny's room from a different angle, a masterpiece of composition. I recommend adding your baby's name to the book, showing your child how "little rabbit _____ is going to sleep."

F Is for Farm by Roger Priddy
This oversized board book features high-resolution photographs of farm dwellers against an empty white background. Each page carries a brief verse that will be burned into a young parent's mind forever: "Yellow digger, have you seen one bigger?" or "The duck says 'quack' as he looks for a snack."

Ten Tiny Tickles by Karen Katz
Perhaps one of the cuddliest books on the market, filled with Katz's signature baby illustrations with big expressive faces and rosy cheeks. The board book counts tickles on baby bellies, giving you an early way to interact with your baby while reading— well before they can talk.

The Going to Bed Book by Sandra Boynton
This modern-day classic shows a crew of lovable animals getting ready for bed. These cuddly creatures will make your baby feel cozy, and the simple, catchy lines will lull them into bedtime.

Good Night, Gorilla by Peggy Rathmann
With barely any words, this impeccably paced book shows a gorilla helping the entire zoo escape before bedtime. The animals end up following the zookeeper home, where sleepy hijinks ensue. Olive loved to point out the pacifier, bottle, and doll in the armadillo's pen, a quiet allusion to your baby's own life.

Mommy, Carry Me Please! by Jane Cabrera
This cozy book shows a menagerie of animals hugging their parents, perfect for giving your baby a hug while reading. The different animals hold on to different parts of their mommies, a good way to introduce head, neck, tail, and other words your baby will master in a few months.

Lost and Found by Oliver Jeffers
The story of a boy who befriends a lost penguin. High-contrast, simple, and elegant illustrations on giant pages make this an ideal book to read with a young baby. Even though they don't understand narrative, these vivid pictures will hold their attention.

Ten, Nine, Eight by Molly Bang
In this sleepy book for toddlers, a girl gets ready for bed, saying goodnight to stuffed animals, putting on her yellow sleeping dress, and curling up with a cozy white bear to sleep. The book is lovingly painted by Molly Bang.

Baa Baa Black Sheep by Tomie dePaola
This book reframes classic Mother Goose stories with striking illustrations that will catch the attention of any baby.

Who Said Moo? by Harriet Ziefert and Simms Taback
  (illustrator)
The colorful and dramatic rooster in this book searches the farm to answer the burning question: "Who said moo?" The equally colorful farm animals respond, teaching your baby the primary animal sounds—an easy and early way to encourage interactive reading.

Device Decisions during the First Year of Life: Most Experts Suggest Less (or None) Is Better

In 2013, the Campaign for a Commercial-Free Childhood filed a complaint with the Federal Trade Commission alleging that two companies "falsely market their popular tablet and smart-phone apps for babies as educational."

With legal assistance from the Institute for Public Representation at Georgetown University, they hoped to strike back at what they called the "genius baby industry." They described their battle against apps aimed at babies under two years old: "We're shining a much needed spotlight on two important issues—that there's no evidence that babies learn anything meaningful from screens, be it television, DVDs, smart phones, or tablets, and that media companies claiming that their products are educational for babies are violating consumer protection laws."

If you want to let your baby use devices before two years old, there are thousands of apps you can try. Some of them are even marketed as educational. But remember, I discussed in chapter one that the American Academy of Pediatrics recommends that you should wait until your child is two years old to bring digital devices into his or her life.

"Our mission is to limit commercial access to kids, and one of the primary ways that marketers target children is through screens," Campaign for a Commercial-Free Childhood president Susan Linn told me. "There is a lot of indication that screen time is increasing for children in this country and that it's linked to some potentially unhealthy and concerning outcomes. There is also evidence that screen time is habit forming, and so that's one of the reasons that our focus has been on babies. There's some evidence that some screen time is beneficial for older kids, but there isn't that evidence for babies."

We mostly obeyed the AAP recommendation during Olive's first two years of life. We occasionally let her play with the smartphone, iPad, iPod, or laptop computer. She understood how all these fancy machines worked, flipping through her baby pictures on the iPhone or turning the screensaver portrait on the iPad or laughing at the lion cub screensaver on my laptop. However, we never let her sit and watch a screen for longer than a minute.

As you will see, any decision to limit screen time will make parenting harder. You lose free time and relaxation that you could have while the baby watches something for a few minutes. But remember: your child will have his or her entire childhood to use these devices. What's the rush?

In our house, we made the choice to hold off on tablets and televisions until my daughter turned two. And don't worry about kids "falling behind" on digital literacy—Olive caught up instantaneously with these devices once we introduced them.

Sara Gillingham also kept devices out of those early years. As a designer, she appreciated the range of "interactive and creative apps" available for kids, but she decided to wait. "As a mother, I've chosen to delay the use of digital books/apps with my kids as long as possible. I like the fact that paper books are something we need to do together. And I also find it easier to explain and enhance the content when I'm directly engaged in it with them."

No matter what your childcare situation is, a baby under two years old requires constant supervision—so why not fill that time with human interaction?

Finally, every parent knows how to use digital devices as the Pacifier of Last Resort. When your child gets out of control on a plane or in a checkout line, or in another situation you cannot escape, you can always give him an iPhone on which to browse through pictures of himself and your family. Babies can stare at pictures of other babies for hours, and parents fill their smartphones with baby pictures.

Storytelling Lessons: Device Usage before Two Years Old

1. Treat devices with screens as the treat of last resort.
2. Don't allow unsupervised time with devices.
3. Keep device use under a maximum of ten minutes a day.
4. When the device is turned off, be firm about keeping it off.
5. No using devices in the bedroom.

Betsy Bird agrees: "Plenty of research is being done on kids these days, and in spite of the proliferation of videos like *Baby Einstein* and the like there is significant evidence to suggest that allowing your baby to watch and play with screens for extended periods of time can hurt rather than help their development. Their head isn't going to explode if you occasionally seat them on your lap while you finish a spreadsheet on the computer, but plopping them down in front of the television for even a half an hour every day is a definite no-no."

In chapter 4, I will explore a variety of ways to introduce digital media into your child's life. Many of the experts in that chapter see digital media as a more productive tool, if used in moderation. During these earliest years however, you should be more cautious.

Olive's generation will play a crucial role in the future of books. I grew up in a world where books were the only option. Home computing didn't arrive until I had started school. I had a deep affection for books and paper, but I could adapt to the computerized world as it arrived. We are the last generation that can pass along both a lifelong affection for both print and digital tools to our children.

Betsy Bird adds one last bit of advice for parents: "Try avoiding, what my brother-in-law likes to refer to as 'shiny glowing rectangles,' until the age of two. At that point they've hit a stage in their development where they can handle the vast amounts of information hitting them. And if you've managed to inculcate them with a love of books from the get-go, they may be more than happy to play in their playpens with a couple board books strewn about them. Those beat electronics any day of the week."

Your children will be fascinated with all the digital devices you use every day, but nothing in popular culture will help our children learn the value of printed books. We must show them that we care about print books from the very earliest moments of their lives.

Interlude: Raising Library Babies

I first visited the library as a three-year-old kid. We had cards at three different libraries: the Lyons Village Library, the Portland Public Library, and the Ionia Public Library. My mom let us check out five books a week, and I devoured shelves of books over long lazy summers.

I've spent countless days in libraries as an adult. My happiest days as a journalist came as I chased stories in the stacks, exploring crumbling newspaper archives, microfiche records, and forgotten books.

Even though the Internet can help kids churn out a million soulless term papers, there is so much left to discover in the world of printed books. Digital devices should not replace libraries in your child's life, but they should augment your child's reading, writing, and research.

"I can see the amazing difference when kids are coming to the library right from age zero and then transitioning into day care or preschool," librarian Paige Bentley-Flannery told me. She's worked as the children's and community librarian at Deschutes Public Library in Deschutes County, Oregon, for years, sharing her knowledge with other librarians through the Association for Library Service to Children.

"They are already library users. It's not new for them," Bentley-Flannery continued. "It's part of their routine, making the library part of your day."

Libraries are stuck in a curious situation in the twenty-first century. With dwindling budgets they can barely afford to give kids library access to these revolutionary new digital tools.

A recent Pew Internet Life study looked at what people want from their libraries, and it found that 98 percent of parents thought that libraries were still important and wanted digital help at the library. Even beyond that, librarians can model more productive useful activities. However, without the budget and training to keep libraries functional in the digital age, whole communities could be abandoned.

Librarian Cen Campbell thinks that librarians should help guide communities through the digital transition. "The image that we have of children interacting with devices in mainstream media is usually a picture of one child and one device," she told me. "These devices are used as babysitters. And that's kind of the default setting right now. That is my challenge. To train other librarians to help their communities see that these devices should not be predominately babysitters."

Campbell founded Little eLit, a site that reviews apps and eBooks for children aged two to five years old. She also serves on the Children and Technology Committee in the Association for Library Service to Children, the part of the American Library Association focused on born readers.

Take *Born Reading* to the library with you. Find as many of my recommended books on the shelves as you can—it is the most affordable and fun way to introduce your child to the library. You will also give them the beautiful experience of researching something at the library.

You can even play library at home. When Olive was a toddler, a friend gave us an old-fashioned library kit as a present. It contained a simple stamp and library card pockets to put inside your favorite books. Olive adored this collection of obsolete library tools, and played library for hours with her personal bookshelf.

We would pull books off the shelf, give them to her so she could stamp the card, and pretend to scan her homemade library card. It was an easy and interactive way to revisit her favorite books. I could ask her to read a book to her doll or ask her to tell me about her favorite book.

Library reading programs are essential; you should find out all the offerings at your local library and attend them. Your library needs your support, and these librarians are interactive reading masters—both you and your child will learn something.

We discovered the Pacific Palisades branch of the Los Angeles Public Library when Olive was about nine months old. It was walking distance from our house, and I could take her there a couple times a week.

Our library has three baskets filled with board books. Babies and toddlers crawl through these stacks of reading material every day and discover books. Many of the books that I discussed here were discovered in those same baskets. The library also includes blocks and toys for kids to play with, adding a little bit extra to these baby book stacks.

But Olive figured out very quickly what the library was for. As soon as she could walk she would proudly carry her chosen book all the way to the checkout desk. I will never forget watching this pint-sized human waddle the entire length of the library carrying a book about puppies that was half as big as her. I knew from that moment on that I had a born reader.

Beyond all these cute experiences, our local library introduced Olive to her community. Olive also had crafts, story times, puppet shows, summer reading programs, and lots of other activities. Even though she could spend her entire life only looking things up online, I hope I have shown her the value of meeting other people at the library and exploring community resources together.

When Olive was one year old, I signed her up for her first summer reading program. She got a sheet to mark how many books she read and got small prizes for reading books. These programs reward your kids for reading, but they also help them see how other kids in the community are reading.

Each child participating in the summer reading program colored a small square on which his or her name was written, and the librarians stapled them to the wall. Olive could see spread before her all of the children who loved to read just as much she did— her very first community.

Book Recommendations for Library Babies

Curious George Visits the Library by H. A. Rey, Margret Rey, and Martha Weston (illustrator)
The mischievous monkey wreaks havoc at his local library, but introduces young kids (two years old and up) to the mechanics of the library.

Library Lion by Michelle Knudsen and Kevin Hawkes (illustrator)
This best-selling picture book shows how a lion discovers his purpose at his local library, helping out among the stacks. Kids of all ages will respond to these beautiful drawings and slightly surreal story.

Library Mouse by Daniel Kirk

An award-winning book about a mouse named Sam who lives in the library. He starts writing his own books, and gets discovered at the library. Gorgeous illustrations will help your kid explore the library. Recommended for kids aged three and up.

The Inside Outside Book of Libraries by Julie Cummins
 and Roxie Munro (illustrator)

This nonfiction book will help your child see a variety of libraries, from the Library of Congress to a prison library to an aircraft carrier collection. Written by a New York Public Library coordinator of children's services, this book will inspire kids four years and older.

Bats at the Library by Brian Lies

Some bats sneak into the library and learn about some great books inside. A great way for parents to introduce four-year-old kids and older to the library.

Digital Resources

Start with a Book

http://www.startwithabook.org/

A free website that lets your child pick from a long list of themes, including dinosaurs, bugs, superheroes, art, or the ocean. The site will give you free recommendations of great books for kids you can find at your local library around that theme.

International Children's Digital Library
http://en.childrenslibrary.org/
A vast collection of free digital books for kids. It features more than 4,600 books in over 60 languages. Explore this safe and inspiring collection with your child to show him or her how libraries work online as well.

Library of Congress—Virtual Tour by the Library of Congress
This free iPhone, iPad, or iPod Touch app helps kids tour the vast Library of Congress holdings, sharing both images and resources at our nation's most powerful library.

Chapter 3

Reading with a One-Year-Old

The spookiest thing about one-year-olds is that they understand everything you say, even if they can't speak more than a few words. Most of your life is spent trying to decipher their gibberish, but they will comprehend way more than you expect.

When Olive was one, magic words like "food," "nap," "milk," or "library" would generate a range of emotions before she could even speak. She would say "buh buh buh" for everything, testing different syllables and intonations—decoding how to be understood. She couldn't speak yet, but she used a combination of sign language and babble to communicate. As she got older, she would get visibly upset if we couldn't understand her messages.

Around this time, Olive and I spent an afternoon flipping through gossip magazines on the coffee table. She fixated on a photograph of Johnny Depp wearing stylish glasses on the cover of a magazine.

"Who is that?" I asked, just to see what would happen.

"Dada!" she cried, pointing at Depp and making the American Sign Language sign for "glasses." "Dada! Dada!"

I love telling that story because my brilliant child compared me to one of the most handsome actors of our time. But it also illustrates how crucial interactivity is during this period in your child's life. You need to ask questions constantly when your child is one year old, about everything from magazines to books to street signs.

Even though these toddlers have an extremely limited spoken vocabulary, you should strive to expand the boundaries in conversation and with books. When reading a book, point out the colors, the names of animals, and ask for answers. Even if your baby only says "buh buh buh," he or she is communicating something. The more you encourage this and respond, the less frustrated your toddler will feel.

Born Reading Playbook:
Ask lots and lots of questions.

Questions are the foundation of interactive reading, and you should practice even before your child can answer with words. Use sign language for "yes" or "no" and acknowledge any sort of response from your baby.

Conversation starters: *Can you make a sound like the kitty? How does the duck go?*

Your Toddler's Brain: Primed to Learn

To find out more about a child's brain during this period, I spoke with Dr. Stuart Shanker, the director of the Milton and Ethel Harris Research Initiative in Toronto. His center studies the "processes that promote the development of a healthy mind in young children."

He shared some recent discoveries from the world of neuroscience, explaining why digital devices pose risks during these years. "We think of the first 48 months as being especially important," he explained. During this period, babies enter a crucial stage of "brain plasticity." "The newborn brain is relatively underdeveloped and there is an explosion of brain growth at birth (as much as 700 new synapses form every single second)." In these first several months of a child's life, the brain is like a plant in the spring that's been fed Miracle-Gro—it is growing wildly, abundantly in every direction. In fact, says Shanker, "there is an *over-profusion* of synaptic growth, so that, at eight months, these connections start to be 'pruned' or 'sculpted.' Those connections that have been most useful will be preserved."

So from eight months onward, your child's brain will start to pick which of these neural connections will be fed, and which will be left to wither from disuse. And these momentous changes are all guided by speech. The verbal stimulation your child receives during this critical time will directly determine the connections made in the brain. All of these changes happen during the first two years.

But it's not just talking to your baby that can help feed and develop these healthy connections in the brain. During the first

48 months, your efforts to soothe your baby are also vital. Shanker explains that "down-regulating" a baby (soothing them, through reading, quiet time, or other activities) also plays a role in brain plasticity. Reading, in particular, serves a particularly effective role in this down-regulating process—Shanker explains that "the sound of your voice, vocal rhythms, being held, just having one-on-one time," all help a baby's brain start to make the connections that are necessary for speech and further development.

There is no better way to have one-on-one time than with a book. Using the American Academy of Pediatrics' developmental charts, I plotted five reading suggestions for a one-year-old kid.

How to Read to a One-Year-Old

1. Imitation is the primary mode of learning, encourage it.
2. Make animal sounds together, while reading books as well as when you're not.
3. Complete simple fill-in-the-blank questions: "The dog is yellow," "The boy feels sad," etc. This works best with repeated books.
4. Set routines about how many books and stories you read at bedtime. Don't use devices at bedtime.
5. Encourage your baby to choose books at the library and at home.

Making Connections:
Using Books as a Tool to Discuss Real Life

After a year of immobility, your one-year-old becomes an interactive reader during this amazing year. Sometimes this interaction can be a bit frustrating for parents: for the first time, a baby can recognize a favorite book . . . or toddle away when he or she doesn't want to read something. Your child can shred books . . . or make you read the same book over and over again for hours. It's both adorable and maddening. Don't let these behaviors discourage you. Make the one-year-old noise and fuss part of your reading.

But the other thing that's exciting about reading to children at this age is seeing kids recognize elements from the real world inside of books. One favorite title for toddlers (and their parents) is Mo Willems's modern classic, *Knuffle Bunny*. Whether or not the Brooklyn setting is familiar to your child, the emotions Willems captures on the page will resonate with kids (and parents).

The pages mix photographs of Brooklyn neighborhoods with illustrations of a cute toddler named Trixie who loses her favorite bunny. The book brilliantly evokes the world of one-year-olds. They are perfectly aware of everything around them, but they can't explain the problem to the adults around them.

After Trixie leaves her prized stuffed animal at the laundromat, her parents spend the rest of the book looking for the missing bunny. Since Trixie can't talk, her frustration grows into an epic temper tantrum. They finally discover the lost bunny in an emotional reunion.

The pages lend themselves perfectly to an interactive reading; the build-up to the baby's breakdown will be all too familiar for parents and kids. As you read, make the same sound effects that your kid makes.

I caught up with Mo Willems while writing this book, getting the great writer's advice for reading his books. He had two simple and useful sentences: "Yell and act a little crazy. This is also my advice for visiting the DMV."

That advice seems glib at first, but once you read this book with a one-year-old you'll understand exactly what he means. Olive visibly responded as Trixie's frustration mounted in the book, and I think there is something cathartic for a toddler to see this baby freaking out over the lost bunny and recovering once the stuffed animal is found.

The more dramatically we would read the story, the better Olive would also react. We were teaching her the very early outlines of storytelling and she loved our theatrical reenactments of the baby's mighty wail.

As we shared this book with Olive, we missed our Brooklyn friends as well (we live in Los Angeles, but Olive was born in New York City). When I visited Brooklyn with Olive one year later, she stared in dumbstruck awe at the rows of washing machines inside a local laundromat. We stood for 15 minutes one winter's night as this California girl watched someone's Brooklyn laundry go through an entire cycle.

She made us wait there until her mom could catch up and then she showed my wife too. "*Look!*" she exclaimed, pointing at the hypnotic soap and water swirling behind the industrial washing machine's glass window. Every time we read *Knuffle Bunny* after that, she associated a new set of powerful memories attached to her birthplace.

What's exciting for parents to see at this age is that the ongoing monologue you've hopefully been having with your child since birth—the narration of everyday life, including your explanation of what's going on in the books you read—starts to become a little more two-sided. As your kid starts to slowly understand and recognize things from the books you read in the world around her, it's an opportunity to keep the conversation (and the learning) going.

While you navigate this communication gap with your baby, it is the perfect time to use the interactive reading techniques outlined in the Born Reading Playbook at the beginning of the book. It might seem odd at first, but you can test many of these skills, even if your baby can't respond yet. By the time he or she actually starts talking, your child will be used to reading experiences where you are asking questions and interacting. These early interactions lay the groundwork for stronger reading and communication skills.

Lisa Guernsey urges parents to make the effort to hold one-sided conversations with their kids during this time, no matter how difficult it seems and even if you're not sure what your child is picking up on. "Before the age of two, the conversations that adults have with children on their own are so valuable." Besides being an author, Guernsey is also the director of the Early Education Initiative at the New America Foundation, exploring how these early interactions between parents and children can have a profound impact on academic performance later in life.

"Sometimes we as parents struggle a bit," she said. "We don't always elicit clear expressions from our kids because they are still at young ages trying to figure out how to express themselves and what they want to say. And so keeping things simple and being open to hearing what they have to say, even if it is bits and phrases and not full thoughts, is really important."

One-year-olds also begin to communicate, making this the ideal time for them to respond to a parent's spirited reading. Researcher Grover Whitehurst reminds parents: "Don't wait until the child can be expected to actually talk about the pictures in the book. Start very early and develop the habit of book sharing between parent and kid at the very outset."

Dr. Stuart Shanker outlines the delicate neurological balance inside your toddler's brain during this year. "The story about early development here is one of balancing two opposing systems, the sympathetic nervous system and the parasympathetic nervous system. The better these are balanced the better the child's physical, psychological, cognitive, social, emotional development. The human voice is one of the most effective and important tools we have for dealing with this system in our baby."

According to Shanker, the sympathetic nervous system readies your body for activity, and the parasympathetic nervous system works to relax your body after activity. Stress or overstimulation can keep the sympathetic system activated, hindering a child's ability to learn. When the two systems are working in concert, children are calm and primed for learning. Your voice and interaction will help teach your baby how to balance these complex systems.

You cannot underestimate the power of a parent's reading during this period. Your voice, your explanations, help your child make sense of the confusing world around him or her.

The Baby Goes Beep was one of our favorite books during this year. Olive discovered this book in a library basket and fell in love with the bare-bones plot: a baby with a single curl on his head acts out the average one-year-old's day. Each page shows the baby doing something new: he bangs a pot, splashes in the bath, and cuddles with his parents. A cute pet cat shadows the baby, and I would always point out the cat and "meow" for Olive's benefit.

After a few reading sessions, I think Olive understood everything in that book. On one page, the baby "flip flip flips" the pages of a baby board book. In the book, the baby discovers a picture of a juicy fruit, foreshadowing lunchtime with his family on the next page. Without fail, the picture always inspired Olive to make her sign for "food" as well. Like Pavlov's dog experiment, this book showcases a baby's most basic instincts.

Six months later, Olive was eating supper. She couldn't talk yet, but loved to make fragmentary stories with a mix of sign language, syllable imitation, and a few stock words. She banged her spoon like the kid in her library book, so I quoted it: "Baby goes boom!"

Suddenly Olive launched into storytelling mode, reproducing the gestures of the baby in the book. She spit food, splashed in the bath, and mimed kissing goodnight like the baby. Playing along with the game, I reenacted the "flip flip flip" part of the story. "Meow meow" she responded, remembering how a cat perched over the baby's shoulder.

After months of reading that book, Olive was telling me the story. It was a strange and beautiful moment. This book had taught her how to describe what she did during the day. Even though she couldn't talk yet, she could tell stories.

Born Reading Playbook:
Share details about the book.

Even though your one-year-old can't be too chatty, you can share all the details as you read. Point out colors, shapes, numbers, and letters and help them decode the book. As your baby gets older you can share more complex details like emotions or action verbs. Eventually your child will learn to perform this interactive activity him- or herself.

Conversation starters: *What is that baby doing? How does the cat go?*

The Dangers of Screen Time: It's Still Best to Limit It

It is always going to be tempting to give a digital device to your toddler when you need some personal time, but as we've discussed earlier, most health and educational professionals urge parents to follow the American Academy of Pediatrics' suggestion to avoid screen time and devices during the first two years of your baby's life.

Neuroscience has uncovered some remarkable insights into your baby's brain development, and all parents should weigh these findings as they make device decisions. Above all, parents should understand the crucial role that reading print books plays in neurological development.

Reading books and talking to your child is the only way to help him or her through this momentous period in neurological development. Dr. Stuart Shanker explains: "Basically, what is critical in the first 48 months of life is the development of the social engagement system. This is absolutely essential for how the child responds to stress throughout life. Nothing can take the place of the nuanced interactions with a caregiver in the development of these systems. Plus, we don't know the effect of electronic media on developing brains, but have reason to be concerned."

The most important thing you can learn from this research is that we need to read and talk with our children as much as possible during these critical first two years. *You* will stimulate neural pathway functions and help your child have the best grasp of language possible when they finally start speaking.

Beyond neurology, reading print books will help your child learn how to interact with a book and develop a lifetime relationship with print.

Maria Tatar actually worried that the new forms of digital reading could reduce the tactile experience that kids have with books. "There is something about the serene effect of a book," she explains. "I mourn the fact that there are less bookstores so parents can go in and touch the books."

If you struggle with the tablet or smartphone time, Lisa Guernsey has some advice about ways to buy time without shoving a device in your child's hand. "At very young ages, if it is a short amount of time, sure you can pull the pots or pans out of the cupboard or have them engage with some other hands-on toy. Sometimes that works and is more helpful than an iPad app because it's easier to get them to transition. You don't have to be yanking the iPad away from them when they are done."

If you do use devices with your baby during this year, minimize that time as much as possible. Here are five alternatives to using devices (including television) if you need some extra time.

How to Avoid Using Devices

1. You can put your child on the kitchen floor with you to play with pots while you cook.
2. You can give your child a pile of magazines to play with and even destroy if they so choose.
3. You can give your child a stack of board books. This won't last forever, but Olive enjoyed holding the books over her head and staring at the pictures.
4. You can put your baby in a carrier, moving around the house as you do work.
5. You can put your baby in the high chair with clay, dough, or another engrossing substance.

Ultimately you will find that limiting screen time will be a bigger adventure when your child gets older. TOON Books founder Françoise Mouly suggests that parents try having occasional unplugged weekends for the whole family. "There are times when you want to spend an entire weekend where you can tell stories, draw stories, and read books but not go online. It's a space that you can experience with your kids. Makes them realize that it is a really rich space for pleasurable activity."

You can still use devices without giving your child screen time. I encourage all parents to share music with kids during this year. While driving in the car, Olive loved to play nursery rhyme songs. She particularly loved *Sesame Street: Kids' Favorite Songs* album: "ABC Song," "Baa Baa Black Sheep," and "Twinkle, Twinkle Little Star" in a nursery rhyme medley. We listened to these songs on countless car trips. By the time Olive neared three years old, she could sing these songs all by herself. Sometimes she would sing them as lullabies to her dolls, soothing them with the musical stories she learned as a baby.

Reading before Your Toddler Can Talk: Get Your Child Involved

When Olive was one year old, she adored *Baby Touch and Feel: Animals*. It is part of DK Publishing's series for babies, and it and similar books about other topics appealing to toddlers—like cars, trucks, wild animals, or pets—are all rendered with vivid, close-up photographs.

Whenever we checked the book out at the library, Olive always insisted on reading it as we walked home in her stroller. She would bury her face in her favorite pages, kissing the high-resolution photographs of cute animals. Reading is a very tangible experience for these babies, and she cooed with joy as we rolled home.

Watching Olive cuddle her book, I could see why print will never die out—as long as we give these babies powerful, happy, and early associations with these beautiful books. You should reinforce the motions of reading during this year. Stick a book in your kid's hands while riding in the stroller, let her hand the library card to the librarian, or carry a book to the bookstore clerk.

One-year-old readers will spend a lot of time with animal

books. Two favorites in our house were *Mister Brown Can Moo! Can You?* by Dr. Seuss and *Ask Mr. Bear* by Marjorie Flack, books that have taught animal sounds to generations of kids.

Ask Mr. Bear follows a blond and gullible kid named Danny who consults with various farm animals about the best birthday present for his mom. The animals follow him in a strange parade, repeating their bleats, honks, and moos every couple pages. At the end, they send the kid (perhaps unwisely) to visit the bear by himself. I won't spoil the ending, but the bear doesn't kill our young hero.

The Dr. Seuss book takes a lively approach to common sounds, showing a mustachioed man who likes to imitate the world around him. The book has a natural call-and-response action built in, getting parents and kids to make the sounds together. Even before Olive could speak, she could make those animal sounds, a crucial step between speaking and identifying things in the real world.

One-year-olds are in a constant state of imitation. They will laugh, stretch, jabber, and cruise along furniture in a never-ending quest to do what you do. The best kids' books replicate this experience, from yoga stretches to pot banging to dancing. Whenever a book shows a specific movement, you should model it for your toddler.

Storytelling Lessons: *Ask Mr. Bear* and *Mr. Brown Can Moo! Can You?*

1. Make all the animal sounds, no matter how painstaking and repetitive.
2. Encourage your child to repeat the sounds as you read.

3. Quiz your child about the sounds when you are out and about.

4. Find the animals in other books.

5. Draw the animals and quiz your child on the sounds they make.

Olive and I were both captivated by a book called *Willy the Dreamer* when she was one. Artist and author Anthony Browne uses famous artwork as a plot device. The book focuses on a monkey who falls asleep and dreams his way through famous twentieth-century paintings by Salvador Dalí, James Whistler, and Frida Kahlo.

Olive could stare at these intricate and witty paintings longer than most books. With a little help, she could spot bananas, cats, monkeys, and cats with bananas hidden inside the oversized pages. All the dreamy symbolism seems a little, well, Freudian, and the great psychoanalyst himself makes an appearance in a jungle scene. There are entire master's theses to be written about the symbolism and play in these paintings.

I asked Anthony Browne if he had any advice for parents reading his books to their kids. He focused on the power of illustrations: "I think one of the most important things to do when sharing a book with a child is to talk to them, not just read the words. Talk about the pictures, the characters—what do you think they are feeling or thinking about? What do you think will happen next? Does this remind you of anything or anyone they know? Try to encourage the child to identify with characters in the book, to empathize."

On a particular page of *Willy the Dreamer* (inspired by Dalí), a burning banana floats in the sky. This surreal joke made me laugh and I kept pointing it out to Olive. It never failed to make her grin.

Even when we weren't reading the book, Olive could remember that joke. "Did you see the burning banana?" I would ask her and laugh. "Bah bah" she would answer, making the sign-language sign for banana. Then she would scrunch her nose, squinting and giggling, like the hilarity had overwhelmed her.

Even though one-year-olds can't use words, they love to participate in stories while you read. "Reading a book with a young child can be a lot like taking a walk with them: you'll need to make many stops along the way," children's author Sara Gillingham told me. "I think it is ideal to welcome and encourage those stops as opportunities to be interactive. Ask questions, or have your child point to objects they might know. As they grow, ask them to identify colors and shapes and visuals. Then, once your child knows a book, encourage them to fill in the blanks as you read."

Born Reading Playbook: Discuss personal opinions about a book.

If your kid loved a book, find out *why*. If he or she wiggled away while using a storybook app, find out why.

Conversation starters: *Did you like the burning banana? Does that silly picture make you laugh?*

Reading with a Bad Mood: Play Like a Child

At one point during this crazy year, Olive had a particularly bad day. She skipped her afternoon nap and broke down crying at every juncture of the evening ritual. When I told her it was time to go to sleep, she scrunched her forehead and prepared to let out a mighty wail. My wife and I scooped her up to read the old favorite, *In a People House*, but she wiggled away before we could finish.

All she wanted, it turned out, was her favorite doll. She held it as we kept reading, and when we turned the page to see a doll inside the book, she shoved her own doll against the page—she wanted to stick it inside the book. She had a simple vocabulary at this point, and her participation got louder. She shouted words she knew and cried "*more, more!*" as we turned the pages for her second trip through the book. For a few minutes, we channeled her bad mood into a spirited reading. Instead of getting frustrated during difficult moments, use books to explore what is going on inside the head of your toddler.

In the 1980s, LeVar Burton helped found the groundbreaking TV show *Reading Rainbow*. I watched the show throughout my childhood and contacted him as I wrote this book. He gave me some fantastic advice that applies to reading books with kids of any age, but I think it is especially important to remember as your child turns one. "Remember how to play like a child when you sit with the child to play," he told me. "Don't sit with the child and expect the child to play like an adult. When you sit down and play with the child, remember how to play as a child—let your imagination guide you."

That advice seems so simple in theory. But when you actually sit with your child and really *read* a book, you will understand what Burton means. You might need to read a few books with your kids before you "remember how to play like a child." When you finally reach that state, you will know exactly what he is talking about.

Endowing your baby with books will help him or her understand emotions and learn patience at a very young age. If you follow a few simple techniques at this early age, you can lay a powerful emotional foundation for your child.

At 16 months, Olive and I went to the library and I grabbed a copy of *Please, Baby, Please*, solely based on the fact that it had been written by the great movie director Spike Lee. While Olive munched on carrots for supper, I offhandedly picked up the book and started reading.

It was the first time we'd ever brought out a book while eating, but it was a major hit. Olive giggled at Kadir Nelson's vivid illustrations of a baby ignoring her parents' repeated pleas to stop shoveling sand into her mouth, scribbling on the walls, or splashing in the tub. As the parents struggle to control their toddler, they chant "Please, Baby, Please!" repeating a famous phrase from Lee's *She's Gotta Have It*.

Olive stopped eating after the first time through the book, but I told her to eat some carrots before I would read more. She dutifully shoveled cooked carrots into her mouth fist by fist. Olive howled with anger when we finally pried the book out of her hands for her bath.

More than a year later, this book became a way to talk about temper tantrums. We revisited *Please, Baby, Please* when Olive was a toddler, and she was fascinated by an illustration of the main character throwing a tantrum because she doesn't want to leave the park. In the painting, the kid's screaming hypnotized her. "What makes you mad?" I asked, and Olive talked about freaking out when we took the iPad away, took a bath, or went to bed early.

We could talk about these emotions through a favorite book, helping Olive explain these crazy new feelings. Everything happens in present tense to a toddler, but books gave Olive some of the earliest memories she could access.

Storytelling Lessons: *Please, Baby, Please*

1. Point out familiar locations in the book, like parks, bedrooms, bathtubs, or cribs.
2. Identify the mother, father, and objects in the books. Ask your child to point them out, help them point if they can't.
3. Discuss the emotions on each page: "She is so happy to be in the bath!" or "She is so mad that she has to leave the park!"
4. Exaggerate the role of the parent in the book. Channel your own parental frustrations when you yell, "Please, baby, please!"
5. Try reading the book while your child is performing the same actions as the main character: eating, bathing, or going to sleep.

Dramatizing Books: Another Tool for Interactive Reading

We discovered the *In My* . . . series by Sara Gillingham when Olive was one year old. All the books in this crafty series contain a finger puppet animal in the middle of the book—a fish, a monkey, an owl, or a dolphin—making it easy for the parent to create an interactive reading experience.

These puppets fascinated Olive; she could spend hours exploring, pushing, or chewing on the fish puppet in our edition of *In My Pond*. I even have a fond memory of her battling another toddler for control of *In My Nest*, Gillingham's book about a cute little owl.

I asked Gillingham for some advice about reading these types of uniquely interactive books with young children. "For some kids, the simple act of wiggling a soft, friendly, finger puppet creature in the middle of their book is mind-blowing," she laughs. "For others, they need the finger puppet to perform lots of actions." Gillingham explains that any kind of book that has an interactive element can be improved by using that element to actually animate the words on the page—bunnies can nibble, dolphins can jump, owls can hoot. "Other more sophisticated readers may be engaged with more of a story, so it can be fun to get them to animate the action even further, by playing out (using words and puppeteering) what else might happen in a baby animal's home . . . you can ask your young reader about the animals, and encourage them to bring their own stories to the visuals and puppets," she concludes, touching on a bedrock principle of the Born Reading Playbook.

Simple dramatization can make any book a better learning experience for your one-year-old. There are scores of children's books that actively encourage simple play-acting and imitation, but there were a few books that worked best in our family.

While crawling through the baby board books at our local library, Olive discovered *Eat!* by Roberta Grobel Intrater. The book is part of Intrater's Baby Faces series of board books, indestructible pages with close-up photographs of babies. Each book revolves around a single baby theme: smiling, hiding, sleeping, or eating.

Eat! features photos of babies covered in spaghetti or mashing bananas in their hair. "It's not easy being neat when you're learning how to eat," the book explains with simple captions. Olive thought it was hilarious to see other babies making a mess, and that refrain is still burned into my head after reading that book hundreds of times. This series creates a powerful sense of identification for a one-year-old.

Between 12 and 15 months, these types of photography-based books are very comforting, giving babies familiar and friendly faces to study. They help bridge the gap between learning simple vocabulary and understanding more complex sentences. And repeated readings build the cornerstones of your child's growing vocabulary.

No No Yes Yes is the perfect book for a parent learning how to dramatize a book for a one-year-old. Leslie Patricelli's board book features bright and compelling pictures of a bald toddler causing all sorts of trouble. As the baby pulls the dog's tail or throws toys in the toilet, the book says "No no." When the same baby scribbles art on paper or pets the dog, the book says "Yes yes."

With that simple setup, the parent has no choice but to make the sounds of the dog or the splashes in the bath. Olive's grandmother compared the book to a baby version of *The Anarchist Cookbook*, but I think it gave Olive a chance to explore the world a bit. At a moment when Olive's comprehension far exceeded her spoken vocabulary, this book never failed to entertain her as we dramatized the mischievous toddler's adventures.

We had taught Olive the signs for "yes" and "no," so she could actually read the book with some simple prompting. Should the baby write on the wall?" I would ask, occasionally getting a "No" from my little baby. To this day, Olive can spot Leslie Patricelli's distinctive art on a crowded bookshelf at the bookstore. Her books cover a number of excellent themes for the littlest readers, ranging from *Baby Happy, Baby Sad* to *Big Little* to *Potty*.

You can reinforce these new vocabulary words even when you aren't reading. Olive adored *Silly Lilly and the Four Seasons* by Agnès Rosenstiehl, a French kids' book about a little girl playing during all four seasons. Olive particularly loved the section where Lilly samples an entire basket of apples, giggling whenever I made the sound effect of biting into an apple.

As we walked through our neighborhood on various errands, I would quiz Olive about the book. She couldn't talk, but she would mime eating apples whenever we "discussed" the book on these walks. *Silly Lilly* existed outside of the pages of the book— Olive was using her imagination for the very first time.

When your one-year-old graduates from these simple books, I recommend the *No, David!* series by David Shannon. These books feature dynamic painted illustrations, showing a kid named David causing all sorts of trouble. Just like *No No Yes Yes* or *Eat!* create a sense of identification, your child will connect with this kid as he tracks dirt through the house or splashes in the bath.

"No, David!" his parents repeat throughout the book. We never see more than his parents' legs, but their voices drift over his head—an experience all toddlers can relate to. The book climaxes with David sobbing after he breaks a vase, but his mother comforts him with a giant bear hug.

The complete series includes a book about going to school and another about Christmas. The illustrations are the best part, every scene filled with little details you can't help but point out when reading with your kid. For example, David doesn't just track mud through the house, his hair is sprouting mushrooms. When he opens his mouth during dinner, we glimpse a sea of vegetables inside of his mouth. For months, we pointed out these pictures until Olive could start saying the words herself.

Storytelling Lessons: *No, David!*

1. Make dramatic sound effects for all of David's accidents and encourage your child to make the sounds.
2. Act out the motions: running, chewing, and most importantly, hugging.
3. Let your child stare at the vivid illustrations. Point out colors, objects, and funny details.
4. Teach your child how to help turn the giant pages of this book.
5. Bring up the book when eating, taking a bath, or running around. Compare your child to David.

Learning Your One-Year-Old's Interests: Build on What They (and You) Already Love

What illustrated books did you love as a kid? Try to track down a copy of your favorites and share them. It is part of your literary inheritance, a way to pass along your unique taste and memories to your child.

As I revisited some of my favorite books, the nostalgia almost swamped me. Some pictures seemed amazingly vivid, like my lost memory of that picture had hardly decayed over the last 30 years. I remembered giggling while reading *The Monster at the End of This Book* as a kid, a classic *Sesame Street* best seller that debuted during my childhood. On every page, the lovable Grover begs the reader not to turn the page and get closer to the monster at the end of the book. Obviously, you keep turning the pages, and you're greeted with pop art explosions and mounting rubble as you continue. Grover forces you to break through ropes, wood, and bricks before turning the page. Best of all, Grover's speech grows more and more elaborate as he gets closer to the end of the book, his words projected in bombastic fonts.

The great comic book creator Stan Lee knows a lot about what kids enjoy and what they're looking for in the story. He co-founded some of the most beloved comic book characters of all time, including Spider-Man, the X-Men, the Incredible Hulk, and the Fantastic Four. Lee recently founded his own kids' book imprint called Stan Lee's Kids Universe, launching a number of titles aimed at children within the Born Reading demographic. I asked Lee if he had any advice for parents trying to instill a love of reading at a very early age. "Read, read, and read some more with your children," he urged. "Encourage your children to pick up a book on a daily basis. Act out some scenes from their favorite books. Use different voices for the characters. Show your children that you are having as much fun as they are."

His advice is so crucial, especially when your baby can't yet speak. Don't sit there and wonder what they are thinking. If you're enjoying the book, they'll enjoy it too.

As a child, my wife loved Oscar the Grouch's *Go Away and*

Stop Bothering Me! The *Sesame Street* book reframed the antisocial muppet in various settings, trying to hide from or escape the reader. His escape scenes and the vintage fonts grow more elaborate as the story progresses. We still have my wife's copy of the book. Olive loves to point out the page where her mom (as a toddler) had scribbled on the pages with a green marker, filling the margins with her own emphasis. Olive didn't quite understand these books as a one-year-old, but the kinetic illustrations and giant fonts make any baby pay attention.

In 1996, Janell P. Klesius published a paper called "Interactive Storybook Reading for At-Risk Learners," showing parents, teachers, and caregivers how to adapt these techniques for struggling students. The researcher stressed the importance of dramatization, both as a way to keep kids interested in the reading experience and as a way to *show* a child what an unfamiliar word means. Remember this as you act out the story for your very young child—you are literally helping him or her to decode new words through these noisy reading experiences.

Storytelling Lessons: *The Monster at the End of This Book* and *Go Away and Stop Bothering Me!*

1. Dramatize the story by imitating the voices of these famous muppets.
2. Use your hands and sound effects to punctuate the bombastic crashes and bangs.
3. Let your child turn the page, or at least help him or her turn the pages to make the excitement of the reading more vivid.

4. Turn the book into a prop, moving it up and down with
   the story's physical action.
5. Quiz your child later about the book, even if they can't respond. "Remember when we were reading about Grover?
   What did he say?"

By revisiting the books you loved as a kid, you will start to
understand the colors, characters, themes, and books that inspire
your toddler as well. As your child begins to interact with books,
you can start following his or her interests—a lifelong project
and one of the most important skills you can take away from this
book.

These educational habits can begin years before your child
ever enters school. Even at one year old, your child can send you
plenty of signals about what he or she is interested in and what
kind of books he or she enjoys. I'm not saying your child should
be performing science experiments or playing piano concertos at
this age. Just watch your child over the course of a few days: what
activities make him or her happiest? Is he really into monkeys?
Does she perk up every time a bicycle appears on the page? I can
guarantee that there is a kids' book that focuses on just about any
topic your child is interested in. Explore your library or do a little
online research to find those books.

Child development expert Gordon Wells spent most of his
professional career helping school teachers learn how to let kids'
interests guide the school experience, rather than relying on pre-
planned curriculum. One of his greatest joys is watching the way
kids get enthused about learning when it's their passions and interests that are leading the way. "They are so excited about what
they can do—about what they *could do* if they could only break

through the shackles that are imposed on them," he told me. "Parents have the same opportunity. Respond to children, don't tell them what they should think."

If I had to pick Olive's biggest interest at 12 months old, I would have to pick sand. We lived close to the beach, and she spent hours sifting beach sand with shovels. At our neighborhood park, she would hunker down with any toddler playing in the sand, sharing trucks, buckets, and shovels for hours. At the library, we found a board book called *Sandbox* by Rosemary Wells. The book is a baby board book version from Wells's beloved Baby Max and Ruby series, a collection of books about the mundane adventures of some lovingly drawn rabbits.

The book shows baby rabbits playing in the sandbox, the board book pages textured with grains of sand or bits of birdseed. The main character goes "Pat pat, dig dig" in a bucket of sand, mimicking the primal motions of a toddler in a sandbox. This scene fascinated Olive at this age, and she made us read it over and over. The tactile book was perfect for her little fingers, and the sandy texture enthralled her. We would reenact the book whenever we visited the park, and the words became some of her first: *blueberry, pie, sand,* and *dig.*

Born Reading Playbook:
Follow the things your child loves.

If your child repeatedly reads a book about panda bears, ask the librarian for more panda books.

Conversation starters: *Do you love the sandbox? What sound does the bus make?*

During this busy year, Olive also had a major bus phase. Every time we saw a bus parked on the street, she made us stop so she could scrutinize every inch of these enormous machines. By the end of the year, I started taking her on bus trips to the Santa Monica public library on a big blue city bus. We read Karen Katz's *The Babies on the Bus* to let her follow one of her earliest interests. The book features adorable bobble-headed babies driving a bus around town. Suspending the reader's disbelief, these toddlers do not crash or stall the bus.

The book can be read or sang to the classic "Wheels on the Bus" tune. Olive sat rapt as we took turns singing the classic song. After many repeated readings, Olive shyly joined in: singing "la la" with the babies, telling noisy riders "shhhhh," and crying "wah wah wah" along with a sad toddler. She made us sing the song over and over. Suddenly reading wasn't just about good pictures or parent performance. It was a sing-along.

Storytelling Lessons: *The Babies on the Bus*

1. If you can sing when reading a book, you should sing!
2. Ask silly rhetorical questions, even if they can't answer: Can a baby really drive a bus? Why is the baby saying "Wah wah wah"?
3. Give names to the babies on the bus using your child's toddler friends and family.
4. Dramatically emphasize the sound effects on each page.
5. Keep singing the song, even when you aren't reading the book. Encourage your kid to sing along with the sound effects.

I'll never forget when we introduced Olive to *Little Fur Family* by Margaret Wise Brown. The book had double the word count of *Goodnight Moon*—some pages were almost filled with text. I laughed at the book, the front cover with a baby bear's fuzzy tummy poking out.

The story moves at the woozy pace of a toddler exploring the world. The little bear wakes up, eats breakfast, and explores the forest outside of his house. He meets his grandpa, a bug, and fish before heading home for supper. The little fur animal skirts the edges of the dangerous adult world, but never gets threatened.

At one point, he discovers the tiniest fur animal of all, a miniature version of himself scurrying into a cozy hole. Brown constantly evokes smaller worlds within worlds, zooming in on pictures hanging on the wall in *Goodnight Moon* or cuddling her bunny under a tree in a rabbit warren in *The Runaway Bunny*.

After rereading this book 50 times to Olive, I felt like I had tumbled into her world, the little microcosms that babies encounter every day, sharp eyes exploring lost threads and paper scraps in a rug or scrutinizing wallpaper patterns. Brown lived in their imaginary worlds somehow, smoothing the edges by calling a bear a little fur animal or having the cub perch on the edge of a speeding river with no fear of drowning.

Her rhymes sank into my head over the next few months, and the unexpected rhythms and narrative seemed as natural as any novel. At the end of the book, the bear's parents sit beside his bed singing a lullaby. Their mouths are open, full-hearted singing, in the book's final illustration. The baby bear curls in his blanket, holding their hands. I can't read that passage anymore without holding her tiny fist. Both of us have agreed on this before we could even talk about it. I hold her hand and we read.

"This is a song. This is a song," the book ends as the bear family sings. I've never found a logical storytelling reason for that repetition of the obvious, but after months and months of singing those lines with my invented melody, I can tell you with certainty: it is the most beautiful way to end a book.

Book Recommendations for One-Year-Olds

Baby Faces series by Roberta Grobel Intrater
These marvelous books feature stunning photographs of babies performing common baby tasks: smiling, eating, playing peek-a-boo, or kissing. These books instantly encourage participation and identification. No matter what book in the series

you choose, your child will be able to read these vibrant photographs.

Brown Bear, Brown Bear, What Do You See?
  by Bill Martin and Eric Carle
This classic kids' book features simple, repeated text. The book poses the question "What Do You See?" to a variety of animals, ending with a classroom full of children looking back at your child. Olive loved to name the kids in these gorgeous illustrations.

Baby Happy, Baby Sad by Leslie Patricelli
Patricelli's simple line drawings and bold colors will capture any baby's attention. Her board books star a baby in a diaper learning about the world. In this edition, the baby experiences happy events (new ice cream cone) and sad events (spilled ice cream cone). *Happy* and *sad* are key early words, and this book gives your child the perfect introduction.

Ten Little Fingers and Ten Little Toes by Mem Fox and
  Helen Oxenbury
This simple little book shows cute babies around the world being bathed, tucked into bed, and getting kissed by their parents. The illustrations are comforting and charming.

Whose Knees Are These? by Jabari Asim and LeUyen Pham
Another book focused on simple body language, its gorgeous paintings show a toddler marching, climbing, and cuddling, his knees featured in every picture. The sing-song text makes for an easy board book reading experience, and encourages your little one to move all over the room.

Bears in the Night by Stan Berenstain and Jan Berenstain
This early story by the Berenstains lacks all the life lessons, dialogue, and formulaic structure that dominates the later books in the series. This dreamy book shows a group of little bears sneaking out of bed for a wilderness adventure.

Watch Me Dance by Andrea Davis Pinkney
    and Brian Pinkney
This book features a dance-happy little girl teaching her baby brother how to dance. Her brother is stuck in the playpen, but she teaches him simple moves: jumping, arm waving, and more. These uncomplicated pictures model the mirroring that all one-year-olds undertake, imitating our every move.

Hug by Jez Alborough
This beautiful book contains only a handful of words, showing the adventures of a sad little monkey looking for his mother in the jungle. He enlists the help of tigers, giraffes, and snakes until he finally gives his mother a hug. This is the perfect book to cuddle with your baby and read.

In My Pond by Sara Gillingham and Lorena Siminovich
    (illustrator)
This sturdy board book has a fish finger-puppet embedded in the middle. As you turn the pages, the baby fish floats through different parts of the pond. The illustrations are high contrast and simple, and your baby will try to touch, kiss, and eat the cloth fish as you read the book. This is part of a whole series of finger-puppet books, and your baby will love them all.

Please, Baby, Please by Spike Lee, Tonya Lewis Lee, and
  Kadir Nelson (illustrator)
This kinetic book follows a toddler around an unnamed city as
she plays in the sand, throws food, and splashes in the bath.
While your baby won't get all the references yet, the vivid illus-
trations will keep his or her attention.

Interlude: How to Inspire Reluctant Readers

What happens when your kid doesn't like to read? That's the
toughest question facing any parent reading this book.

There are a variety of reasons why kids might not want to
read: maybe they like video games better, maybe they don't like
to sit still long enough for a book, maybe no one has ever read to
them in an effective way, or maybe they think books are boring.

Nevertheless, parents need to make their kids comfortable
with reading, even if they don't share your love for reading. These
skills are absolutely vital for school tests and the work world, and
parents need to at least help their children be comfortable with
books. I asked librarians, teachers, and development experts for
suggestions on helping to deal with reluctant readers.

Society of Children's Book Writers and Illustrators president
Stephen Mooser offers the most basic advice: "Unless the reluctant
reader suffers from dyslexia or other reading disorders, the key is
to find books that interest the child."

He says that snobbery has no place on a toddler's bookshelf.
"It does not matter what they read. Reading is like anything else,
it requires practice. Once they are proficient they will pick up

things that interest them. Whether a magazine about airplanes, a book about strange creatures at the bottom of the sea, or a fan magazine about their favorite movie or TV show . . . it all comes down to first getting them reading well enough so that it is not a chore, then getting them access to things that interest them."

And it's no surprise, but making sure your child has ready access to books all over your house is essential. "The more books there are around, the more likely a child is to pick one up; it's that simple," Sara Gillingham explains. "A reluctant reader may not have found the book that sparks his or her imagination yet—and that might be all it takes—so it's great to be persistent, and continue to offer your child lots of options."

And while book options should be vast, don't be hesitant to curtail other, less desirable choices. Gillingham continues: "With my own children, I've made a habit of offering books instead of electronic devices as entertainment on road trips or during long waits. When entertainment options are limited, and there is a designated reading time built into the daily routine, there is a greater chance a child will pick up a book."

If you have a very young child who doesn't like to read, try puppets. Librarian Paige Bentley-Flannery uses puppets and stuffed animals to get babies involved in her library story time at Deschutes Public Library in Oregon. She uses Penelope, a huge pink dog that doesn't talk. "But it has huge hands, a great nose, eyes, and ears so I could focus on those areas," she says.

Honestly, you don't even need a stuffed animal to charm a reluctant reader. Once I pretended my coffee mug could talk, and from then on Olive continued to have daily conversations with a dilapidated mug we dubbed "Coffee Man." To coax Olive into reading, I could pretend that Coffee Man needed help reading a book.

As your kid gets older, puppets may not do the trick anymore. With older readers, I recommend trying Jon Scieszka's *The Stinky Cheese Man and Other Fairly Stupid Tales*. It is a collection of cock-eyed fairytales that reworks the stories that jaded children have heard too many times. If your kid thinks books are boring, this might be a way to reframe the argument.

Scieszka has some advice for parents reading to kids as well. "I would be careful about abusing the idea of 'interactive reading' with kids," he said, urging parents not to stress out about the reading experience. "Just the fact that you are reading to kids or with them is wonderfully, emotionally, perfectly interactive. Have fun reading with your kids. Laugh at what you think is funny. Point out illustration details that crack you up. Let kids have their own opinion about their reading."

Scieszka also echoes the advice to pay attention to what your kid is reacting to in a story, and then do everything you can to ham it up. In his book, for example, he says, "Different kids respond to all different parts of the book. Your daughter may love the Ugly Duckling growing up to be a Really Ugly Duck. Your son may howl at the word 'funky' describing the Stinky Cheese Man's smell. You may chuckle to see the title page is nothing but huge type that says: 'TITLE PAGE.'"

Ginjer Clarke is a best-selling children's author who has made a career writing fun and informative science books for kids. She suggests that parents try to use the squeamish, gross, and otherwise compelling parts of science to get these kids reading. "I sometimes think reluctant readers are just kids who haven't found the thing that they love to read the most yet," she says. "It's true that many younger boy readers end up gravitating toward non-fiction, as well as comic books and graphic novels. Perhaps they just prefer information in smaller, more digestible bits rather than a longer narrative form. So I give that to them, and I provide a frank discussion of real-world topics (poop, vomit, prey/predator relationships, etc.) that they seem to find irresistible."

She concludes with a bit of advice for parents: "I suspect that these books are not always the favorite of parents to real aloud together with their children, but my advice for parents of kids who haven't found books that they love yet is to keep trying and to look for books that tie in with their other interests." She urges parents of reluctant readers to increase, rather than decrease, trips to the library or bookstore. The more chances your child takes on different kinds of books, the better the odds are of discovering what he or she loves.

Others agree that it's vitally important to let your child read not just *what*, but *how* he or she wants to read. Once your child is old enough to use devices effectively, let him or her read digital books if that's what he or she prefers. If you find that games or other interactive features distract your child, try mixing it up with less interactive digital books. Give your child as many different format options as possible, because each format is another potential way to excite him or her about books.

"Find traditional storytelling reference points in other media," Catherine Connors advises. Connors is the editor in chief of Disney Interactive, overseeing the popular parenting site *Babble*. "Once you've got their interest piqued in the stories themselves, whether it be a movie or TV show or a bedside story at night, that becomes a portal. You get them hooked." Her husband used that technique with her son, downloading a copy of *Jack and the Beanstalk* and reading it to his child on the iPhone. Suddenly, her son became obsessed with any storybook that mentioned Jack's story.

"He became so familiar with the story, he wanted to see it wherever it was," she said. "If you get a kid hooked on the story itself, regardless of whatever medium it's being presented in, then that becomes a gateway drug for the story in other forms."

First-grade teacher Karen Lirenman explained how devices can actually help shy students or open up a world of opportunity for kids with learning disabilities. "I have a student who is super, super quiet. I give her an iPad, if she goes to a private space where nobody can hear her, she has no problem recording her thinking privately. In a regular classroom without that technology, we would never have gotten her voice. You don't know what they are holding back on until you give them a tool that allows them to express themselves."

Kids can use a storytelling app like My Story, Toontastic, or Draw and Tell to record their voices while telling a story. When students struggle with writing, Lirenman tries these apps instead. "They don't have the skills to show they're learning in written words, but they actually know it," she explained. "They are being held back by not having the writing skills at the level that they are thinking. You lose all that data and information about the child when you close down those options. The iPad opens up the world to that many more options for them to show and share their learning."

Book Recommendations for Reluctant Readers

In My Jungle by Sara Gillingham and Lorena Siminovich
  (illustrator)
Part of Gillingham's great series of books for babies and toddlers, it includes a monkey puppet inside the book, bringing the reading experience alive.

The Stinky Cheese Man and Other Fairly Stupid Tales
    by Jon Scieszka and Lane Smith (illustrator)
Recommended for kids four years old and up, this book takes a sly spin on old fairy tales. If your kid is bored with reading, this book might wake him or her up.

Fantastic Mr. Fox by Roald Dahl and Quentin Blake
    (illustrator)
A classic book by the author of *Charlie and the Chocolate Factory* that recounts one fox's battle with farmers. You can also sweeten the pot with a movie adaptation of the book once your kid finishes it. Recommended for kids six years old and up.

Squish by Jennifer L. Holm and Matthew Holm
This graphic novel series for kids follows the silly adventures of a comic book–reading amoeba. Recommended for kids seven years old and up.

The Adventures of Captain Underpants by Dav Pilkey
Recommended for kids in second through fifth grade, this book shows the adventures of two fourth graders who create a comic book about an unusual superhero.

Best Books for Kids Who (Think They) Hate to Read by Laura
    Backes
A guide for adults struggling to find books for their kids, it contains 125 powerful recommendations that will work for a variety of reluctant readers.

Chapter 4

Reading During the Terrible Twos

Children will follow the media habits of the adults around them. I spend most of my working day staring at a computer and talking on my smartphone. For a long time, Olive told people that I worked at "pushing buttons," the only obvious activity I performed as a writer working from home.

Even before she turned two years old, Olive would mimic my cell phone cradle with various phone-shaped objects. I designed a pretend computer out of a cardboard box and an abandoned computer mouse, and Olive would dutifully plug in the mouse and press imaginary buttons on the box just like daddy.

Once Olive turned two, we began to let her use digital devices for five-minute stretches. Every morning I opened up my portable writing desk and Olive followed me with the battered iPod we kept in her room. As I started work in the morning, she would sit on the couch doing imaginary work with the device.

We loaded that iPod with all sorts of audiobooks, bedtime

music, and sing-a-long albums. I made a point of putting my favorite music on there as well. At one point, I was on a major classical music kick and added hundreds of Brahms MP3s to the device. We would listen to his dazzling compositions while Olive played beside me.

One day, Olive stopped in the middle of playing and asked me, "What Brahms look like?" Digital devices are perfect for moments like that, giving me a chance to share my music and have an interesting conversation with my daughter at the same time. We surfed Google as she sat on my lap, flipping through countless paintings of the great composer online: young Brahms in a dapper suit and the old Brahms scowling behind a thick beard. I spent so many hours playing my favorite music for Olive through these devices, and it was amazing to be able to answer her questions while listening to one of his great concertos.

Digital Reading During the Terrible Twos: It's OK to Allow Some Screen Time

During this overwhelming year, your baby morphs into a little person—capable of sharing books, telling stories, and exploring the world with you. But these terrible twos will bring temper tantrums, willful disobedience, and endless whining. If used correctly, smartphones, tablets, eBooks, and apps can be powerful tools during this time in your child's life.

The transition from two years old to three years old is astounding. I get misty-eyed watching a video from Olive's second birthday party. She looks so small, barely peeking over the picnic table and almost bursting into tears when we sing "Happy Birthday."

Six months later, Olive would wander around the house and randomly burst into "Happy Birthday" or the ABC song—testing out her lungs and the rush of new words and ideas. In this short period of time, she grew from an unsteady walker to a little imp who could bolt out of the room if she did not want to read a book. The mysterious year also amplified her frustrations; reading the wrong book or saying the wrong thing during a reading session would send her into a mysterious rage. Even worse, she hated to part with digital devices (like most kids). Our transition from the iPad to another activity could send her into crazy tantrums if we didn't handle the tradeoff carefully.

Using the American Academy of Pediatrics' developmental charts, I plotted five digital storytelling milestones in your child's development as they reach this wonderful and confounding age.

How to Use a Digital Device with a Two-Year-Old

1. Your child can scribble with a finger or a stylus on a touchscreen.
2. A toddler can identify familiar objects when asked, either by an interactive app or by a parent.
3. Kids begin to understand colors and shapes, key components of many interactive apps for toddlers.
4. Your child can repeat some words introduced in apps.
5. Your child begins pretend play, able to have fun with imaginary characters on a device.

In previous chapters, I shared advice for how to limit time on these devices. As your child gets older, it becomes more important to worry about the quality of the time your child spends with devices. I asked Lisa Guernsey to explain how parents can apply her three C's theory of "content," "context," and "your child" to the brand new world of apps and tablets.

For *content*, Guernsey urges parents to be aware of usage, especially with apps that drill children on numbers, phonics, or the alphabet: "You want to figure out whether the content is actually being retained by children or whether they are simply flipping through things because they like seeing new pictures on the screen." We've probably all seen kids flip through photos in an iPhone faster than anyone could possibly see or retain that information. Visual stimulation for its own sake isn't necessarily helpful at this age (or any age). Instead, be sure you're taking the time to see, understand, and explain any digital images alongside your child.

As for the *context* of an app, she tells parents to think about "what they can do outside of their screen media experience that helps to elevate or spring from that little screen experience." Use digital content as a starting point for further learning and discussion. Often, Guernsey says, "there is a way to translate [that content] to their physical world that can enable some deeper learning or make some deeper connections for them."

One app that meets both of those criteria is Petting Zoo, a storybook app designed by Christoph Niemann. The artist had published work in the *New Yorker* and *New York Times*, but wanted to explore the interactive storybook space. Frustrated while playing a complicated soccer video game with his kids, Niemann was inspired to create something entirely new.

He created an interactive picture book with a yellow background and simple line-drawing animals that wiggle on the screen. Each page features a different animal, ranging from porcupines to giraffes to lions, each outfitted with a compelling response to your child's touch on the digital page.

The app gave Olive plenty of ways to plunk the screen and see silly responses on the page. She especially focused on a dachshund that twisted into a pretzel, a cat that swatted at a butterfly, and a mole that tossed mud at a spider.

The Petting Zoo designer made sure to include something beyond that basic function, answering Guernsey's call for a useful context outside of the app. As kids play with his dreamy figures, the ultimate point is to encourage them to create. He explains: "The whole idea of the drawings is not to make them look so overly complicated, that a kid could actually look at the deer or the rabbit and say, 'I'm going to draw my own, I'm going to draw a camel and make a knot in its legs.' That would be the ultimate achievement. That would be great, if parents were involved to say, 'Let's draw something for ourselves.'"

Over and over, the experts told me: parents need to be involved. That's crucial, said Andy Russell, a toymaker turned app designer. After finishing his Master's degree in Learning, Design, and Technology at Stanford, he co-founded a company called Toontastic, developing story-oriented apps for kids.

We will explore his apps in later chapters, but Russell introduced me to one of the core principles of the Born Reading Playbook: co-play. No matter what kind of media your child is using—book, audiobook, iPad—make sure you have plenty of co-play time with your child. This can be as simple as holding your child on your lap and oohing and aahing as he or she discovers things inside a picture book. It can be as complicated as taking a trip with a digital device–obsessed toddler to the zoo or the park to photograph the world with your smartphone to build a digital scrapbook later.

The idea behind co-play is sharing the experience and learning how to tell stories together. Russell explains: "Learning is an iterative process. It is something that you do by trying things over and over and over again. By trying it the first time, you learn what's working and what's not. And then you adapt your behaviors and your ideas, and you try them out again and again. And eventually, you land on the thing that actually works, that's actually right. That's how you learn."

Sara Gillingham kept devices out of her young kids' lives in her family, but she urged parents to use iPads, computers, and smartphones together: "I'd set clear limits on where and when digital devices are used, and I'd use the device together with your child, so that you can stay in touch with how they're understanding and enjoying whatever they're reading."

Apps, eBooks, and other digital programs promise that they can create an interactive experience, but they still can't come close to the print reading experience with a parent. Child development expert Gordon Wells offers some words of caution for parents bringing apps into children's lives: "There's something missing when a child's experience of storying is impersonal in the sense that they do it alone, listening to the voice of an unknown person. I don't think it can take the place of sharing a story with somebody else who can read well and who is willing to interact about the story."

Nobody knows the world of story apps better than an app creator. Christoph Niemann told me: "Having small kids, this whole OD-ing part is something I'm very concerned with. I really think Petting Zoo is not a game. I really see it more as a picture book where you can go back and forth, I hope it is addictive from an artistic point of view, when the kid likes the book and wants to keep looking at the same book."

Niemann also offers some timing guidelines for parents as well: "I would be flattered if a kid wants to spend 15 or 20 minutes with it. After 20 or 25 minutes we would rather say, 'Let's look at this thing tomorrow again.' I think they should spend as much time with a book as they possibly want, but especially with smaller kids, I would say 20 minutes would be enough."

Storytelling Lessons: Petting Zoo

1. Sit with your toddler for the first few sessions.
2. Name all the animals for your child.
3. Share your kid's delight when the animals move on the screen.
4. Make the animal sounds for your child as he or she moves through the app.
5. Encourage your child to draw after using the app.

One time, Olive and I were playing a highly rated app for learning the alphabet. It was a fairly useful app, but then I noticed the banner ads at the bottom of the screen pitching adult products ranging from Netflix videos to cars.

Why were those ads running inside an app designed to teach a kid about the alphabet? They can't serve any purpose beyond getting clicks for an ad network someplace. I discourage the use of these free apps that run ads at the bottom. Still, for families of limited means or teachers working on a tight budget, these free apps are some of the only resources available. If these are your only options, parents and caregivers should monitor ads. I hope that developers can sort out some of these problems in the future.

The worst part about free kiddie apps is how some companies try to make extra money through deceptive clicks. A coloring book app I found offered free coloring pages mixed in with paid pages. Every time I let Olive use the app she would end up visiting some ad-supported webpage or yelling while the iPad asked her for my password to buy something new. These are infuriating moments as a parent, a kind of practice we would never tolerate in children's television or print books.

Even *The Monster at the End of This Book* app has ads for the next book in the series, an advertisement that literally dangles from a rope at the top of the page reminding the kid they can buy something else. Olive would never let the book close without clicking on that advertisement. The app world is an unregulated jungle and kids need help.

I would advise parents to avoid downloading the most popular apps for the sake of downloading a popular app. The app marketplace is a complete mess right now, filled with hundreds of thousands of digital products sorted by a lousy search mechanism. Worst of all, words like "educational" get bandied about without any oversight or guidance in these marketplaces.

Download recommended apps instead. Beyond the app suggestions in this book, ask friends, family, and other kids for advice. If you are looking for webpages, Google algorithms can pinpoint your request in seconds. But app store searching can take hours, and the biggest factor driving sales is popularity. Don't let popularity determine your app consumption.

But even digital content without ads or tricks to fool kids into buying other things can be distracting. Watch for elements in an app that might lead your child astray of your learning goals. Fred Rogers Center director of education and research Michael Robb notes that some apps distract children with "seductive details," content that can distract a young learner from the point of a learning experience. Parents should watch for these moments that can spoil the learning possibilities on a digital device. He explains: "Seductive detail is a feature that might be very effective, but potentially distracting from whatever the main point of the story is. This is a term that comes from the textbook literature, for people who have done research on textbooks."

He warns parents to watch for seductive details in both apps and books. Robb used the example of a Benjamin Franklin history lesson. Textbook creators discovered that kids could read a whole history lesson about Franklin's influence on our country, but at the end of the day, all they remembered was the "seductive detail" that he once flew a kite with a key attached to it during a storm. That fun, vivid element distracts kids from Franklin's more meaningful accomplishments.

Robb concludes: "If you have a specific educational goal or outcome that you are trying to reach, then you want to make sure kids are tracking toward that outcome. If they are getting sidetracked by pushing a button or making something jiggle there, then you're diminishing your chances that a kid might get what you've wanted them to get."

If an app has a distracting feature like the ability to tickle a character, produce a silly noise, or an entertaining error message, Olive could spend ten minutes pressing the same button. I've watched her mindlessly flip through an app, getting the same error messages over and over—as if the error messages themselves were a game.

Beyond these relatively abstract problems, you should test all your apps before letting your child play them alone. So many things can go wrong on a technical level: they can accidentally send an email, delete an important document, or land on the dreaded frozen screen.

That is the worst, the moment you have a two-year-old and a malfunctioning device. Olive had no patience for slow-loading content or apps that crashed while she was having fun.

Toddler frustration is a wild thing and there is absolutely no way to explain technical difficulties to your little human being. Olive's whole mood for the morning could change if an app froze and she had time to dwell on the frustration. It's best to move on and not spend time making it worse while you try to fix it.

Storytelling Lessons: Digital Troubleshooting

1. Test apps before playing them with your child.
2. Close all open apps on your device before playing with your child.
3. Reboot your device before playing.
4. Make sure your child cannot purchase items while playing.
5. Monitor the advertising inside the app.

When using apps, we can apply Born Reading Playbook principles to these digital tools. Michael Robb has some advice for parents to make the app experience more interactive. He suggests that parents treat the device experience in the same cozy way you would treat reading a book. Playing with an app, he says, "is a time to get close; if it is a young child, maybe put that child in your lap. Take the opportunity to point out the things you see on the screen. Ask questions about what they see. What's going on here? Try to go beyond just questions that only elicit a yes or a no."

Lisa Guernsey reminds us of a simple but powerful tool that works for both print books and digital books: Don't forget to pause the experience frequently, giving your child time to process. She explains: "We have such an opportunity with digital media and young children, because we can literally hit the pause button. You can do this with print books, and that's why they are still valuable and need to be a part of children's lives in as many ways as possible. We can always not turn the next page and stop on that one page. But we can also do that when we are playing games with apps or reading eBooks. I think it would be smart for more developers of games to put into the functionality a way to just pause the action for a moment so there can be some reflection on what's going on."

Born Reading Playbook:
Stop and talk about what happened.

Too often adults speed through these books or apps to get to the end, but these pauses are crucial for your child's comprehension.

Conversation starters: *Should we stop and look at this mountain?*
Should we take a break and talk about what happened?

Olive became obsessed with the game called Toca Kitchen, a game where you prepare a variety of food for a boy, girl, sloth, or cow that visits the app diner. The game includes a blender, skillet, pot, and knife, tools that no toddler could use. Olive loved dropping and dragging ingredients, feeding the characters to see their reactions.

While this wasn't exactly reading, it became part of our integrated experience.

We had read books about cooking since Olive was one year old, starting with Rosemary Wells's *Sandbox*, a delightful introduction to the world of Max and Ruby, her two most famous rabbit children. The book shows baby Max making blueberry pies in the sandbox, the pages filled with textured birdseed and sand for little hands. When she grew older, Olive loved *Bunny Cakes*, a longer book by Wells with more dialogue and baking ingredients for making cakes.

Cooking was a part of her daily life as well. I would bake bread with Olive or her mom would make pancakes. Olive had a stool she could stand on, intently measuring and stirring the ingredients (sneaking handfuls of dough at the same time).

So it was easy to create questions about cooking while Olive played the app, helping her combine the fun activity with our reading about kitchens and our real-life play. Olive had already mastered the basic vocabulary and we could extend the conversation into real life. From books to bath-time soup making to playground cake baking to the Toca Kitchen app itself, play-baking extended well beyond the confines of the iPad.

Storytelling Lessons: Toca Kitchen

1. Tell your child what's happening to the food in the kitchen.
2. Create stories for the characters as your child prepares food.
3. Show your toddler what these characters eat in real life.
4. Help your child read the reactions of the characters to the food.
5. Extend the learning by letting your toddler help in the kitchen.

During one of our library visits, I held my two-year-old daughter squirming above the kids' shelf, plucking books and flashing covers with my free hand. I pulled a copy of *The Tale of Tom Kitten* by Beatrix Potter and Olive went "Oooooh" as she grabbed a miniature hardcover edition of the beloved kids' book.

Despite the charming nineteenth-century narration, the book moves at the disjointed pace of a baby's experience. Moving through life like a restless toddler, these kittens accidentally cause all sorts of trouble: losing clothes, tumbling into bushes, and chasing ducks.

I never felt any purist urge to read the story to Olive exactly as Potter wrote it. I provided abridged versions for my baby, letting her savor the pictures.

These classic books have entered the public domain, so you can sample free eBook versions of all the books online. I recommend starting with *The Tale of Tom Kitten* or *The Tale of Peter Rabbit*, excellent introductions to Potter's world. With an iPad or a computer, you can actually show the illustrations to your baby, seeing what animals catch his or her eye.

After a few reads, Olive kept making me turn back to the section where the naughty kittens meet a duck family. Olive loved reading while the ducks tried to wear the kitten clothes, everybody looking rumpled and silly. In Potter's world, these characters reoccur and are connected in other adventures. Olive and I moved to the duck book next.

With tablet computers and digital libraries, you can sample the whole series and quickly find connected books. With a simple editing program like iBookstore's Author, Photoshop, or even Microsoft Word, you can build an online collection of your child's favorite Potter books, bringing the nineteenth-century classics into your child's life.

If you visit the Born Reading website, you can download a free picture book I created, combining all of Olive's favorite Potter books in glorious color.

Born Reading Playbook:
Follow the things your child loves.

If your child loves the Beatrix Potter digital book, ask the librarian for more books in the series. Read the books your child loves and use apps, videos, and online research to help him or her learn more.

Conversation starters: *Do you want to read more about Tom Kitten? Should we find these characters?*

Digital Recommendations for Two-Year-Olds

The Monster at the End of This Book by
  Sesame Workshop Apps
This was one of the earliest kids' book apps and it stands the test of time. It takes a beloved Grover story and makes it interactive. Be sure to cheer your child on occasionally while playing.

Available in the Apple App Store; works with iPhone, iPod Touch, and iPad.

Requires iOS 5.0 or later.

Available in Amazon Appstore for Kindle Fire and Android Devices

Fiete by Wolfgang Schmitz and Ahoiii
This book app chronicles the adventures of a sailor crossing a fairy-tale seascape. Instead of nonstop action that defines the video game genre, it tells a quiet story of fixing hats, putting wheels on cars, and playing a good old-fashioned record. Most two-year-olds can master the simple navigation, perhaps prompting some sailor adventures around the house.

Available in the Apple App Store; works with iPhone (3GS, 4, 4S, and 5), iPod Touch (third, fourth, and fifth generation), and iPad. Requires iOS 4.3 or later.

Interactive Alphabet by Pi'ikea St.
This app introduces toddlers to uppercase and lowercase letters, giving kids a chance to play with an olive-eating ogre, a Jack-in-the-box, and an old-fashioned quill pen that really works on the screen. Includes a letter-tracing function for older kids.

Available in the Apple App Store; works with iPhone, iPod Touch, and iPad. Requires iOS 5.0 or later.

One Fish Two Fish Red Fish Blue Fish by Dr. Seuss
and Oceanhouse Media

This is a great way to introduce kids to Dr. Seuss's master story-telling. If your kid loves the print edition, try this eBook version with a professional reading and interactive words that literally pop off the page.

> *Available in the Apple App Store; works with iPhone, iPod Touch, and iPad.*
> *Needs iOS 5.0 or later.*
> *Available in Google Play for Android devices.*
> *Available in Amazon Appstore for Android devices.*

What Color is Bear's Underwear? by Todd H. Doodler
and CJ Educations

When your kid starts talking about potty training, you should try this gentle storybook introduction to post-diaper life. A sweet teddy bear sings a catchy song about undies and your child can explore the storybook three ways, with interactive, traditional, and video options.

> *Available in the Apple App Store, but only works with iPad. Requires iOS*
> *4.3 or later.*

Pango Book series by Julien Akita and Studio Pango SAS

This lovable storybook app series features the adventures of a cute raccoon. The book app offers simple gestures and games to make the books interactive. The gentle app will transfix your child without overwhelming him or her.

> *Available in the Apple App Store; works with iPhone (3GS, 4, 4S, and 5),*
> *iPod Touch (third, fourth, and fifth generation), and iPad. Needs iOS 4.3*
> *or later.*
> *Available in Google Play for Android devices.*
> *Available in Amazon Appstore for Android devices.*

StoryKit by International Children's Digital Library
A clever app that requires significant parental involvement. Your child can create a simple digital book by photographing the world and drawing or writing extra pages. Olive and I took the app around our neighborhood, giving her a chance to use the iPhone for a more useful purpose and learn about photography.

Available in the Apple App Store; works with iPhone, iPod Touch, and iPad.
Requires iOS 3.0 or later.

Endless Alphabet by Originator Inc.
This is my favorite letter-oriented app—a crew of mischievous monsters teaches your kids letters, phonics, and a huge set of 25-cent words.

Available in the Apple App Store; works with iPhone, iPod Touch, and iPad.
Requires iOS 5.0 or later.

ArtKive by The Kive Company
If you have a kid who loves drawing, painting, or scribbling, you can use this app to preserve digital copies of his or her masterpieces. It will help your child be proud of his or her work and see how useful the device can be.

Available in the Apple App Store; works with iPhone (3GS, 4, 4S, and 5),
iPod Touch (third, fourth, and fifth generation), and iPad.
Available in Google Play for Android devices.
Requires iOS 6.0 or later.

Wheels on the Bus by Duck Duck Moose
An animated version of the classic song that most kids learn during this time in their lives. The app shares the lyrics in five different languages and adds interactive features to make the song more engaging—a good way to make device time more active.

Available in the Apple App Store; works with iPhone, iPod Touch, and iPad. Requires iOS 5.0 or later.

Available in Google Play for Android devices.

Reading Print Books during the Terrible Twos: Follow Their Lead

Don't forget books during this lovely period in your child's life. Kids are unpredictable and mysterious at two years old, but they learn at a mind-boggling pace. A particular book might be too challenging for them to follow one month, but then become their favorite book the next month. Keep trying new offerings (but don't be surprised if they start to fixate on specific books or characters at this age).

Ignore recommended reading ages on books, and instead read what your kid wants to read—which can mean reading above or even below the recommended reading level. During this year, Olive devoured everything from baby board books, to age-appropriate picture books, to learning-to-read books intended for second graders. We read whatever she wanted and she loved every minute of it.

While it helps if you have been reading to your kid since they were a baby, the terrible twos present all sorts of reading challenges. Most significantly, your toddler is now mobile, able to escape any reading experience and chase other distractions.

Using the Association of American Pediatrics' developmental milestones chart, I found five important reading achievements your child will reach as he or she turns two years old.

How to Read a Book with a Two-Year-Old

1. If you ask him or her to find a familiar object in a book, your toddler can touch the page to identify the object.
2. If you ask questions about a book, your toddler can answer with a vocabulary of 50 to 100 words.
3. Your toddler can repeat words you highlight in a book.
4. Your child can start to pretend with books and toys.
5. Your kid can scribble with crayons, pens, or markers, taking first steps toward writing and art.

You can't plan reading time during this busy year. Once, I took Olive to the library and then brought a load of new books to an outdoor mall so we could have some quality print book reading time during lunch.

Olive had other plans, spending the entire meal staring at a big-screen television behind our table. The flashy digital billboard advertised a kids' movie with a cute saber-toothed tiger that licked the screen. "Kitty!" Olive yelled, over and over and over at the commercial in an endless loop. Instead of reading a book, she was staring like a zombie at a food court advertisement.

Despite (or maybe because of) all this excitement, Olive skipped her nap that afternoon—even more frustration in a day that was not going how I planned. As I reluctantly let her get out of her crib after the botched nap, I ended up reading Dr. Seuss's *The Cat in the Hat* and *The Cat in the Hat Comes Back* in a rare literary double feature. We sat in a cozy chair and read two books in a row while she zoned out in my arms.

"Should they let the cat inside?" I asked before we even opened the book, and Olive knew to answer "No!" because he would cause all sorts of havoc as soon as he got inside the house.

"Don't let the cat inside!" I yelled, tapping the Cat in the Hat as he stood on the stoop outside the kids' house. Every page of these masterful books can prompt interactive reading questions, especially for a two-year-old learning new words every day. After many rereadings, Olive started to follow my lead, telling the kids not to let the cat inside before we even opened the book.

Olive especially loved Thing 1 and Thing 2, two misbehaving imps stuck in the cat's mysterious box. "What's in the box?" I'd ask, pointing to the oversized red crate with a giant hook that held those two characters. Olive never got tired of telling me that Thing 1 and Thing 2 were inside. She even held up one and two with her fingers, proud to make her digits work, straining to hold them.

Both books climax with an enormous mess inside the house: books knocked down, chairs overturned, carpets stained, and fishbowls spilled. Every time the cat wrecked something new, we would shout "Oh no!" Olive particularly hated messes in her life, and she always celebrated when the cat returned to clean up the destroyed house.

The Cat in the Hat even ends with a built-in interactive moment, the kids turning to the readers and asking if they would confess to their mother that the cat had visited the house: "Well would you?" The hypothetical question can trigger all sorts of kiddie storytelling. I kept asking Olive that question at the end of the book and her responses grew more detailed each time. Even though that reading session began with a skipped nap, it turned out to be one of my favorite memories of reading with Olive.

Storytelling Lessons: *The Cat in the Hat*

1. Read when your child wants to read, even if it isn't very convenient.
2. Ask warm-up questions about the book.
3. Interact with the characters in the book.
4. Explore the intricate illustrations together.
5. Ask your child what he or she would do.

I'd also recommend that you keep some of your child's favorite books solely in the imagination, even though there may be digital books, apps, TV shows, or movies inspired by the book. No matter what, don't let digital tools replace these interactive print book experiences. These close, cozy encounters are key for young children.

Another problem about reading to a two-year-old is finding enough questions to ask about a book while reading interactively. Kids' books appear fairly simplistic on the surface and your toddler doesn't have a vast enough vocabulary to be a literary critic. After running out of questions to ask my daughter, I created the Born Reading Playbook to make sure I never ran out of interactive questions again.

The American Academy of Pediatrics offers this extra advice about shaping questions for a young reader: "Ask your child to show you all the things in a picture that are alike in some way. You can say: 'Can you find all the blue things?' or 'Show me all the things that can fly.' Point out colors, shapes, numbers in their books. . . . Count pictures and wait for your child to repeat the numbers after you."

If your child doesn't respond well to open-ended questions, try asking multiple-choice questions. My wife mastered that silly art, asking Olive questions like: "Is that a monkey? Or is it a dirty sneaker?" You laugh together at this silly choice, and suddenly things are interactive again; this works best when your kid is being stubborn or quiet, trying to avoid your queries. A couple silly multiple-choice questions can lead to a full-fledged conversation during a book.

Beyond these simple questions, you can dramatize most of your toddler's books and they will learn from you. For example, lunchtime can be interminable if you have a slow eater, but it will pass more quickly with a couple of spare books.

One lunchtime favorite during this period was *Maya Makes a Mess* by Rutu Modan. It is a comic book–style story for kids, telling the tale of a curly haired girl who enjoys spaghetti with ketchup and eating with her hands. After arguing with her parents about her bad table manners, Maya is whisked away by a queen to a fancy state dinner where her manners are truly tested.

Olive loved watching Maya squirt ketchup on pasta, and she demanded both ketchup and mustard whenever we mentioned the book at dinnertime. The book pokes fun at the social conventions your toddler is starting to learn. During one reading, Olive stopped and asked: "Manners, what is that mean?" The abstract question caught me off guard, but the book provided plenty of extra examples: people eating with their hands, feeding dogs at the table, or slurping soup straight from the bowl. Suddenly, this book had created an entire discussion about manners, food, and table vocabulary.

No matter what time you read a book with a child, pretend to eat the food that the characters are eating. It is a simple way to dramatize the story and will always prompt an interactive reaction from your child.

Olive would ask for *Maya Makes a Mess* constantly for a few weeks. If your child is asking you to read a book over and over, you should use this as a chance to play. Move beyond the paper book and show your child how a fun concept works in the real world.

After a few months, Olive started to invent her own games for another favorite book: *Hop on Pop* by Dr. Seuss. This is another great book for two-year-olds. The story involves a series of gags that only last for two or three pages, showing a variety of cute characters enduring minor comical dramas. The book stars Pat, a fuzzy bear-type creature that has a knack for sitting on cats, bats, and cacti.

Every afternoon, we would pass a cactus on the way home from day care. One day Olive asked me, "Where Pat cactus?" and it took me a minute to figure out she was talking about the cactus in *Hop on Pop*. "NO, PAT, NO. Don't sit on that!" I yelled, quoting the book. As we passed that cactus every week, she started to repeat the line.

The book had become a part of her real life. Olive remembered both the story and the context. Using interactive reading, we dramatized Pat's struggles by yelling "ouch!" every time Pat sat on a cactus and cartoon pain lines shot out of his butt. Dr. Seuss never even used the word cactus in the book (too complicated of a rhyme perhaps) but we always explained the illustrations to her.

Eventually the characters in *Hop on Pop* became her imaginary friends. At least once a day, Olive would grab me and ask what they were doing. I had to invent minor little dramas and tasks for them to perform, the book became a real and rich part of her life.

Born Reading Playbook:
Compare the story to personal experiences.

Help associate the book with the experiences that obsess your child. This is how human beings understand the world—it is a crucial skill to apply something in a book or app to real life.

Conversation starters: *Do you remember that cactus we saw by school? How did you feel when you fell off your bike like Curious George?*

Our favorite book-related game was patterned after *The Bear Detectives* storybook. In the Berenstain Bears classic, the bear children wear Sherlock Holmes hats as they mount a cheesy hunt for a missing pumpkin.

Olive would ask for the book over and over, so I turned it into a game. One slow, early Saturday morning, I gave Olive a hat and wandered around the house hiding a purple ball in fairly obvious places.

I would pretend to weep like a private detective client in the old noir movies, asking her to help me find my missing ball. Olive loved chasing me to find the ball and the game continued for months. Soon, Olive could actually ask me simple questions like a real detective, and I could find more complicated hiding spots.

This was co-play applied to books, a way to bring a favorite book into our lives and spark ongoing conversations about losing things, finding things, and most importantly for me, it was an introduction to the world of detective fiction.

As a lifelong reader of Raymond Chandler and Dashiell Hammett, I harbor my own pretend world where I can one day open a private detective agency with Olive. Most of all, I want her to be as fearless as teenage detective Nancy Drew crashing through a den of thieves. It never hurts to practice.

While I probably should keep my day job, I love replaying my favorite games from childhood with Olive.

Storytelling Lessons: *The Bear Detectives*

1. Reenact your child's favorite book moments in real life.
2. Turn the book into a hiding game with an easy-to-spot object.
3. Pick a special hat to attach to the game.
4. Encourage your child to retell the story while playing.
5. Ask to play "The Detective Game" when your child needs distraction.

You've probably found yourself doing what I did, bringing the fictional world of a book into the real life of your child, through make-believe games or stories that continue outside the pages. Storytelling is a basic foundation of our brains, and we need to encourage these developments from the very earliest moments of life. Books can model all sorts of activity.

In 1996, child development researchers Janell P. Klesius and Priscilla L. Griffith wrote an essay called "Interactive Storybook Reading for At-Risk Learners," exploring how interactive reading techniques such as those found at the foundation of this book can help children who struggle with reading or who lack experience reading with parents.

The study trains teachers to read *The Pig in the Pond* by Martin Waddell and Jill Barton using interactive reading techniques. The study also reveals how crucial these lap-reading experiences are for your child. As the teachers in the study read the storybook in an interactive fashion, the kids (many of them lacking the at-home reading experiences that Olive had) started reaching out to feel the book and talk about the illustrations.

The researchers wrote: "The children were observed to gradually move their chairs closer and closer to the reader. At times they knelt directly in front of the reader. At other times, individual children could be seen standing next to the reader with a hand resting on her shoulder."

Kids instinctively respond to these storytelling techniques. If you ever wonder how much your two-year-old actually understands, ask him or her to read a favorite book to a stuffed animal. I loved asking Olive to read bedtime stories to her menagerie of dolls, elephants, penguins, and Mickey Mouse. It was adorable and fascinating to watch—I was always startled to find how much of the book Olive had actually absorbed even as a very young reader.

Born Reading Playbook: Read together.

Make co-play a part of your daily routine, and that includes reading books. Make sure you play games and read together every single day.

Conversation starters: *Do you want to pretend to be a fairy? Could we bake a cake like the bunnies did in the book?*

Using Books and Apps Together

The best part about this year is that you can begin to use both books and devices together. As your child nears three years old, you will have plenty of time to introduce the early markers of literacy. We bought a big bag of plastic bath toys, a buoyant and bright colored set of letters and numbers. For months, Olive just liked to play with these toys, but by the middle of her second year, she started to identify the letters by name.

We created a series of games in the tub, prompting her to name letters as she washed them, stacking towers of letters or hosting a bath-time diving contest—shouting the names of the letters as they leapt into the water. By the time she could identify most of the letters in the tub, Olive started to sing the ABC song completely unprompted as she strolled around the house.

Dr. Seuss's *Hop on Pop* was another big literacy milestone. The book ended with the narrator explaining how her baby brother could read little words like "IF" and "IT." The illustrations highlighted these words in giant letters and suddenly, reading was a game for Olive.

Oceanhouse Media has created app editions of countless classic children's books. If your child enjoys a particular print book, you can explore their digital offerings to discover letters together. They have a digital edition of *Hop on Pop* read by a professional, but your kid can touch the individual words to watch them rise off the screen—encouraging the youngest readers to follow along.

Despite these digital additions, Oceanhouse Media marketing manager Natalie Aller reminded me that these features do not absolve parents from reading. "Parent-child interaction is key in using storybook apps," she explained. "Parents should sit with their kids and read through the story, encouraging early readers to tap on words and pictures. As with print books, asking kids questions about the story helps build reading comprehension."

At the same time, the app does enable parents, grandparents, and other loved ones to create a personalized digital edition of the book. Aller outlined this tool that's included on the *Hop on Pop* app and many other Oceanhouse apps: "With the app version, parents can record themselves reading the story so children can hear their parent's voice at bedtime even if their parent is travelling or lives far away. In addition, parents can use the record feature to capture precious memories of their children reading along to their favorite story."

Around this same time, Olive began playing Endless Alphabet, a brilliant app that works with your child on letters and phonics. The game opens with a word on the screen in giant capital letters. A crew of cute monsters barrel across the screen and knock the letters out—leaving a space shaped like the letter. Using the letters like puzzle pieces, your child can put the letters back and spell the word.

When the kid touches the letters, they come to life, wiggling and making their individual sounds as your child moves them. The app comes loaded with a wide range of 25-cent words for every letter of the alphabet.

Olive learned the world "recycle" with this app. We thought all the words zoomed over her head, but she blurted out "recycle!" in the middle of the afternoon, prompting a whole discussion about family recycling. Olive loved the degree of control she had over these wiggling letters, and the puzzle of moving them into the right spots charmed the part of her two-year-old brain that needs that sort of stimulation to grow.

At the same time, I needed to supervise as much as possible because she would repeat the same words over and over, not to learn something but to watch the animation again.

I used it in concert with our whole letter-learning campaign. When Olive struggled to identify a certain letter in the tub, I would choose that letter on the game. The lovable monsters use words that start with the chosen letter, so Olive was able to learn the troublesome phonetic letter sounds at the same time as she learned which letter it was.

Life became a book that we could read together, and she was so proud.

Children's author Peter H. Reynolds published *The Dot*, a short book about a little kid learning how to paint in class. The clever book models the joy of creation for your child, encouraging him or her to pick up pens, paints, and paper as soon as he or she finishes reading.

Reynolds has also built a flourishing career as head of FableVision Studios, a company that designs web apps for some of the best children's groups around. I asked him for recommendations for parents looking for more resources online, especially some places he had worked with in the past: kid-focused websites for Jim Henson Productions, PBS, *Sesame Street*, and the National Wildlife Federation.

"Find out who is behind the resource," he said. "Stick with trusted brands and organizations that have shown a commitment to serving children (vs. selling to them)." He also offered advice for using anything you discover for your child online: "The web is daunting and not a safe playground for kids, so the usual rules apply for parents and caregivers. Stay close to your kids. Be involved. Be their guide. Teach them how to navigate safely and, depending on their age, be with them while they access the web."

Just as with anything your child is exploring, Reynolds urges parents to vet everything that a kid has access to. "A better approach is to use apps that you choose and test first. Choose apps that connect with a child's interest. I also recommend any app that inspires creative thinking and making."

It's also fun to make the connections between the images your child sees in an app and those in real life. After a few weeks of using the Petting Zoo app, Olive entered a porcupine phase. She would tap the screen endlessly on the simple drawings, watching the porcupine quills rise and fall with magical sound effects. After a few weeks of talking to imaginary porcupines, I showed Olive a video of a porcupine eating a corncob on YouTube. Olive giggled as the porcupine nibbled the corn with enormous sharp front teeth, extending this storybook creature into real life.

The best books, eBooks, and apps work like a blank canvas, letting your kid imagine the details instead of showing everything like television or a video. I think the combination of book and app helped those porcupines cross over into our lives.

It is easy to fill your kid's devices with apps that drill him or her on counting, phonics, letters, and rote memorization. But don't forget the context—could the app help your child bridge something between books?

I spent too much time trying to limit how much time Olive spent on the iPad, but I should have been more concerned about the kinds of things she was learning. If Olive spent 20 minutes learning about porcupines for her imaginary games, that would be infinitely more useful than letting her do a meaningless app for a limited time.

Use your devices to help your child follow his or her interests; that's what makes devices infinitely more useful than traditional kinds of screen media.

Parents need to drop the idea of a device as a babysitter, and instead treat it as a powerful tool. Pairing print books with digital experiences will be more satisfying than simply letting your kids read an animated book and make your print reading even more interactive. And the more interactive reading you do with your child, the easier it becomes to share stories together.

If you take the time to read and play with your child, you will be amazed by the kinds of books he or she will tackle. These little brains can do amazing things with the right kind of help.

Print Recommendations for Two-Year-Olds

I Want My Hat Back by Jon Klassen
A dimwitted bear tries to find his lost hat in this black comedy set in a forest. Your kid will appreciate the grim joke at the end and

once you've read the book a few times, your kid will always spot the missing hat hiding in plain sight.

Jenny's Birthday Book by Esther Averill
This one is a classic kitten tale from 1930s New York City. The simple illustrations compose a love poem to Manhattan, and your kids will love these super stylish cats having a birthday soirée in the park.

Alice the Fairy by David Shannon
Many toddlers go through a "fairy" phase (mine sure did), and this book provides plenty of ideas about how to turn your everyday life into a more magical place—hours worth of make-believe games that you can play with your kids.

The Cat in the Hat by Dr. Seuss
This is Dr. Seuss's most famous book for a reason. Dynamite writing combines with gorgeous art as a very bad cat entertains two children left home alone. Every picture is filled with details to analyze and we enjoyed yelling at the kids trying to convince them to not let the very bad cat in the house.

Where the Wild Things Are by Maurice Sendak
One of the most beloved picture books; you will remember the lush painted pictures of the Monsters for the rest of your life. Use the growls, howls, and voices of the Monsters to bring the story to life. Also try the bombastic audiobook with some great sound work.

Too Big by Ingri d'Aulaire and Edgar Parin d'Aulaire
This classic kids' book was recently republished by New York Review Children's Collection. As your kid outgrows clothes, this

book becomes an easy way to talk about getting older. You will be asked to read this simple story over and over.

Harold and the Purple Crayon by Crockett Johnson
A dreamy book about a young artist's adventures scribbling with a crayon on a blank page. Over the course of an entire night, he sketches adventures in the ocean, the city, and the mountains.

We're Going on a Bear Hunt by Michael Rosen and
    Helen Oxenbury (illustrator)
This picture book seems simple on the surface, but the quiet refrain and rhymes will stick in your head forever. This book will show you how to have an imaginary bear hunt with your kids, a glorious adventure with participatory sound effects.

Interlude: The Joy of Homemade Books and Projects

Olive was two and a half years old when she made her first book at the Los Angeles Times Festival of Books. In one corner of the kids' tent, grade-schoolers colored inside pre-made books with pink cardboard covers and a few folded sheets of paper inside.

Olive saw big kids writing words in the books, so she grabbed a couple markers and started to make her own book. She made one page of yellow scribbles, and switched markers to fill the next page with scribbles in a different color.

Homemade books will help your kids stay creative for the rest of their lives.

My friend Ethan Minsker is an author and zine maker in New

York City. For years, he's created homemade magazines with other writers, artists, and East Village characters. He even published one of my stories many years ago in one of his homemade magazines.

When Minsker had a baby girl, he did not stop making zines. Instead, he decided to get his daughter involved. He shared his secret recipe with me one evening. . . .

Ethan Minsker's Recipe for a Homemade Book

1. Take sheets of copy paper, whatever size. Fold it in half and staple in the crease. Now you have a book. I suggest starting with four sheets. The content could really be anything.
2. Take photos that tell a story. Print them out. Paste them in the pages.
3. Take Wite-Out or an eraser and make word or thought bubbles so you can add your own text.
4. You can take other kids' books that have been ripped or broken and cut out the images to create a new book with your own words.
5. Add photos of your kid so they become part of the story. Same thing applies to any magazine your child might like. Your child can draw in the pages, then you can add the text. Or have your child tell you the text and come up with a new story.

"I would date each one for storing. Then over the years you can track your child's progress with writing and art," Minsker suggests. "They might like to see what they did as a kid. I have comics I made when I waited for my father at his work. Those comics inspired me to make my own books."

Using digital tools, you can also create a personalized book about your family. With Apple's iPhoto, I created a hardcover book with photos of all our loved ones as a gift for my wife. I unwrapped the package with Olive, preparing to hide it from my wife. It was a rainy afternoon and we curled up in her reading chair with the book, tearing through the pages like great literature.

Olive and I read the book together, and every page riveted her. I originally intended the book as a gift for my wife, but Olive commandeered the book and added it to her bookshelf.

You could even make a book for your baby before they are born. You can collect photos of all the relatives and caregivers who will play a role in your baby's life. You should include plenty of close-up faces, framing your family members in a simple way. Shoot new pictures, if you need to.

You can mix in high-contrast black-and-white imagery and baby faces, both popular illustrations for babies. If you want to get really fancy, include snatches of your favorite poems or songs, introducing your baby to some great writing very early.

Don't worry about the paper pages; babies will chew and rip, but this book is meant to be loved, not archived. If your friends or family have babies, add pictures of them as well. You can also find pictures of your favorite animals. This homemade baby scrapbook will help ease your child into reading and show him or her how to find him- or herself inside the pages of a book.

As soon as your child is old enough to wield a crayon or rubber stamp, you can start doing literary projects at home. One morning Olive and I made extremely simple storytelling masks. It gave us something to do on a slow Sunday morning, allowing us a little extra reading time and a fun new way to make it interactive. We drew happy, sad, angry, and scared faces on paper plates. Then we glued popsicle sticks to the back so she could hold them in front of her face.

I would read Olive her favorite book or tell a story, pausing often to ask, "And how did they feel?" She would hold up one of those masks to show the emotion of the character. You would be surprised how many different stories evoke these simple emotions.

Mark Frauenfelder co-founded the popular blog Boing Boing and edits *MAKE*, a magazine dedicated to creative projects you can do at home. Frauenfelder wrote a book called *Maker Dad* filled with 24 projects for making stuff with your kids, projects ranging from building skateboards to making astronaut ice cream to making electronic musical instruments. "I think the best way is to start making things in front of them," he told me. "Kids are naturally curious and will want to try using tools they see you using. When I make electronic stuff my kids ask about the components and how they work." He also recommends that parents visit DIY.org for more inspiration or read the book *Unbored: The Essential Field Guide to Serious Fun* by Joshua Glenn and Elizabeth Foy Larsen.

Ethan Minsker has a few suggestions as well. "I find a lot of inspiration by seeing artwork at galleries and museums," he told me. "It's a fun activity for the entire family. But the best way is to watch what your kid interacts with. If she is more interested in the box a toy came in, then provide her with more boxes. Build a fort or a car out of them. You don't have to be talented; your kid's imagination will make up for that."

As your kid gets older, you can make homemade digital books

as well. Apps like My Story or StoryKit turn your child's drawings into a digital book. You can use the simple drawing programs inside of these applications or you can upload photographs or scan your child's drawings and plug them into the digital book.

Draw and Tell is a fantastic tool to help your child make artwork and digital stories. The app lets you make drawings and add audio recordings explaining the artwork. Duck Duck Moose co-founder Caroline Hu Flexer explains the idea behind her company's bestselling app: "An adult may not actually see all the nuances of what their kids are thinking about when they are drawing. If they are able to record their voice and talk about what that drawing is about—that's really powerful. We've heard that parents and teachers think it is really fascinating to be able to hear what a child is thinking about. I think the recording is one key thing." She suggests that parents let kids use family photos in the app to create artwork or cards for relatives. Whether you print these creations or share them digitally with your family, they make great presents to share with loved ones and will give your children something to hold on to and remind them of a particular time in their lives.

If your child loves comic books, you can use TOON Books' free Cartoon Makers app online. With a few simple swipes of a mouse, your kid can arrange three panels into a simple story. A parent can help type in dialogue, designing a cartoon strip starring favorite characters from TOON Books. "Say 'Okay, tell me a story!'" publisher Françoise Mouly explains, outlining the storytelling lessons behind the app. "You can do beginning, middle, and end. In talking about this with your kids, it's really a eureka moment when they understand that simple idea."

Finally, always remember that you are the most important

influence on your child when it comes to arts and crafts. "Be a role model," children's author Peter H. Reynolds urges parents. "Show them what it looks like. Show them how to bravely sing, draw, cook, wrap, dance—without giving in to the temptation to diminish your efforts. I hear teachers and parents say rotten things about their own art in front of kids. Kids soak in those comments for later use about their own art—their own work and thoughts," he concluded.

So start by trusting your own creative powers, and you will inspire your child to follow in your footsteps.

Chapter 5

Three-Year-Old Readers

Reading Print Books with a Three-Year-Old

As Olive neared her third birthday, we discovered a shared love for the Nate the Great series. When I was a boy, I was thrilled by the adventures of Marjorie Weinman Sharmat's pint-sized private detective. I thought the series was over Olive's head, but I showed it to her anyway while writing this book.

Intended for second-grade kids learning how to read, the Nate the Great series follows the adventures of a kid detective as he finds missing paintings, stamps, or toys. The series uses a simple vocabulary that both preschoolers and grade-school readers can master.

To my surprise, Olive kept asking for more books about the boy detective who constantly eats pancakes (instead of drinking Scotch like a grown-up detective). While adult detectives fall in love with dangerous women, Nate the Great dutifully writes letters to his mother as he goes out on a case. The book contains short and simple sentences, a style mimicking the hard-boiled private detective writers of the 1930s and '40s. This tough-guy style works amazingly well as a kids' book.

It was by far the longest book Olive had ever attempted, but she kept asking for more. If you read the book in a sing-song voice, it sounds like a bad version of the Dick and Jane books from the 1950s with dull, repetitive sentences. But I liked to read the book in a private detective growl, punctuating words like "dog," "Fang," or even "pancakes" with a little bit of hard-boiled menace. The series has a fun set of audiobooks as well, complete with a film noir saxophone and a narrator who can sound tough when he needs to. Olive sat on her floor and listened to the entire *19-minute-long* audiobook.

Exploring the American Academy of Pediatrics list of cognitive milestones for this age group, I realized that three-year-old kids spend life like detectives. They will constantly ask you "why" about everything, trying to decode adult behavior, understand social rules, and investigate how everything works.

Your child will start to grasp time during this year, another parallel to Nate the Great. His adventures follow a simple routine, the time of day and transitions between scenes painstakingly outlined in his narration. He always solves his simple cases, and there is something very reassuring about that—reminding kids they can eventually solve the mysteries of preschool life.

The Academy also recommends that parents refer kids to books when they struggle to answer "why" questions about life. The first Nate the Great book answers questions like "How do you make the color orange?" *Nate the Great Goes Undercover* answers the question: "What happens while I'm sleeping?"

Of course, Nate the Great won't appeal to every three-year-old. When your child starts asking tough questions, you can find kids' books at your local library or learning apps to answer most of them. Show your child how to be a real detective.

I also adapted the Academy's recommendations into a few simple techniques you can use while reading during this inquisitive year.

How to Read to a Three-Year-Old

1. Make "mistakes," like misnaming a character or saying the wrong color. Wait for them to correct you.
2. Let them read the book to you or ask them to recount a favorite book while out and about.
3. Have them categorize things in books—how many balls are red? Do you see any circles in this picture?
4. Ask your child to list his or her favorite books and tell people about them.
5. Interact with your child's favorite characters in real life. Make up stories about these fictional characters or pretend to talk to them in the real world.

Before Olive showed up, I never cared what another person thought about a book. I simply trusted my own taste in books. If I loved an author, I would avoid all book reviews or essays, so I could judge it without being swayed by somebody else's opinion.

With Olive, I had to explore a whole literary world I had avoided for years. She became my research assistant as I brought hundreds of books and apps into our house. But it really didn't matter what I thought about a particular kids' book. I discovered very early on that her opinion trumped everything. If Olive loved a particular book, I wanted to read everything that author ever wrote. She loved books I would have never even touched at a bookstore.

Not So Fast Songololo by Niki Daly is a great example. It tells the story of a South African kid shopping with his grandmother. After a colorful day at the market, the young protagonist gets a pair of brand new red sneakers from his grandmother. The generous gesture lights up the boy's entire face, pure joy of a kid with a simple gift. The story felt refreshing in a picture-book market crowded with princesses, movie tie-in toys, and a casual attitude about materialism.

I would have never picked the book, but Olive immediately latched on to the elegant illustrations when she found it at the library. It contained some of the most beautiful and loving portraits of the aging body you'll ever find inside a kids' book. The book reads like a brief and imagistic short story you could analyze in a college course: the relationships between young and old, rich and poor, the careful depiction of everyday life, and the quiet resolution as grandma and grandson laugh at the bus stop.

Not So Fast Songololo is perfect for talking about emotions with your child, an important skill as you endure mood swings, temper tantrums, and daily displays of three-year-old defiance. The characters in this book wear the most vivid expressions, each face shaded with lines and shadow. There is no great lesson, just a little story that captures the beauty of everyday people. The grandmother and boy laugh together on the last page, their faces so lovingly drawn that Olive smiled along with them every time we read the book.

You can also use books to talk about the trickiest emotional topics, exploring things like fear, anger, or even death. During one of Olive's more willful periods, we read a copy of *Marvin K.*

Mooney Will You Please Go Now!, a lesser known Dr. Seuss book. The book involves an unseen narrator telling Marvin to go away, while our hero refuses to leave.

Olive responded to his stubborn expressions and started to mimic them so well that I laughed out loud. The storybook character's expertly drawn frown communicates volumes: "Hmmmm. I know YOU want me to go, but after much thoughtful consideration, I don't want to go," in a single glorious scowl.

After reading the book twice, we started acting it out in real life, a game that lasted all afternoon: "Olive Boog, will you please go?" Olive would respond by making her brilliant impression of that defiant frown and yelling "Hmmmmm. No! I do not want to!"

Dr. Seuss had distilled the essence of a three-year-old's tantrum, responding to a disembodied adult telling you to do something *you* don't want to do. It was both therapeutic and instructive for Olive to act out that book in real life.

Born Reading Playbook:
Help your child identify with the characters.

Start by talking about simple emotions. These conversations will scale as your kid gets older, when you can ask more complex questions.

Conversation starters: *Why do you think Marvin does not want to leave? Have you ever felt mad like Marvin?*

Kids are inexplicably scared during these early years. Olive could fearlessly face Halloween masks and books about ghosts, but she would wail every time she saw a disembodied limb: a foot scrubber shaped like a foot, shoes with realistic-looking toes, or a skeleton hand at a Halloween pumpkin patch.

You should be aware of what scares your particular kid, but do not get bogged down in age limits or self-censoring books. Let your kid explore and respect those boundaries. You can skirt the edges of scariness without showing your kid a horror movie. You'll find that the best kids' books explore fear and death with a light touch.

Ghosts in the House! by Kazuno Kohara is a simple Japanese picture book that takes a lovely look at the supernatural. A little girl and her cat move into a haunted house, but instead of being terrorized by the spirits, she catches them and washes them. Olive laughed every time she saw ghosts drying on the clothesline, potentially scary creatures turned into blankets, curtains, and table cloths once they were washed.

At the same time, Olive thought a decidedly adult gag book called *All My Friends Are Dead* was hilarious, laughing at black humor cartoons poking fun at mortality, deforestation, extinction, and human loneliness. She especially loved a cartoon zombie with a dangling limb, unfazed by cartoony gore.

As you build your child's library, don't be afraid to share slightly tougher stuff with your kid. The world is filled with harmless and dull kids' books, and you don't want to bury good books under fluff.

From fairy tales like *Little Red Riding Hood* to *Outside Over There* by Maurice Sendak, the violence and uncertainty lurking at the margins of the story are a thousand times more compelling (for both parent and kid) than dull stories with easy morals for kids. I shy away from books that explain everything at the end. I prefer books filled with wonder and confusion.

Because that is what it is like to be a kid.

Born Reading Bundles: Combining Books and Digital Resources

Balance is the key to a healthy media diet, no matter what kind of access you give your child to digital books, apps, or television.

Mother and author Laura Overdeck developed her popular *Bedtime Math* series as an email meant to be shared out loud, then as an app, and then a book. You can explore the series later in this book. But Overdeck made an important point about making decisions about digital and print reading for your child.

"It's part of a diet. You want all your food groups and you want the same thing with how your kids get content," she told me. "I think a little bit of apps is fine, but it's also nice for kids to spend time with their parents and be read to. And it is great for kids to go read books. But it's also fun for parents to read to them, because they can read them something harder and kids also get interested in things when they're getting attention from their parents or whatever important adult is in their life. That's why kids grow up with fond memories of pleasure reading, because they have fond memories of their parents reading with them."

Now that your child is three years old you can create what I like to call "Born Reading Bundles." These are basically a combination of print books and multimedia activities you can share with your child, making sure they have a balanced media diet. The next few chapters will include a few ideas for Born Reading Bundles, and you can design your own as well.

You can turn a book into a complete learning event, much the same way a teacher would design a thematic lesson for a class. Using a combination of print and digital media will ensure that your child never gets bored with books and that they don't overdose on digital devices.

Lynn Schofield Clark teaches in the Media, Film, and Journalism Studies department at the University of Denver. She published a book called *The Parent App: Understanding Families in the Digital Age*, analyzing the effects mobile devices have on family relations around the country. She endorses the idea of learning experiences across mediums. "We know from research that it is important for us to be able to develop young people's imaginations and their ability to engage with stories in a variety of different ways," she said. "Try to think about stimulating young people across different platforms. That helps them to tell stories in different ways, and that helps them to tune into differing aspects of stories. For instance, print media can help young people get a really good sense of detail and grasp the fullness of words. When you are looking at something in terms or film, television, or YouTube, it helps young people to engage with the emotional level of a story."

If you do not want to use digital materials in these Born Reading Bundles with your child, you can skip all the multimedia material and just read the books.

I discovered the concept while we were reading *Cosmo and the Robot* by Brian Pinkney. The book captivated Olive from the very first reading. It showed the adventures of Cosmo and his sister, two astronaut kids living on Mars with their parents. They explored the Red Planet, saved a broken robot, and used a variety of space tools in their adventures.

Extending our interactive reading of the book, we literally acted out the book in her room. We turned her bedroom reading chair into a spaceship, counting down "5-4-3-2-1" and blasting into space. She wore a bicycle helmet as her space helmet and steered the ship all the way to Mars. As a kid riding the bus to school, I used to turn my homesick ride into a spaceship game.

We built space tools: toilet-paper-roll binoculars, a toy space phone, and a Mars rock collection bag. Olive wandered around her room, picking up toys and examining moon rocks. I pretended to be a broken robot on Mars, and she loved fixing me with her toy tools.

Continuing the adventure, I began to build a Born Reading Bundle. We read a few more books: *The Berenstain Bears on the Moon* for more space adventures and a look at a rocket ship flying. We read *Tool Book* by Gail Gibbons so Olive could see how the real tools Cosmo used worked on Earth.

On the visual side of things, we watched clips from "The Magic School Bus Gets Lost in Space" episode, letting Olive see some of the other planets in the Solar System with the popular kids' cartoon. Looking online, I found a whole collection of fun *Magic School Bus* lesson plans and free extras at Scholastic.

We also checked out a copy of the Dr. Seuss–inspired *There's No Place Like Space!: All About Our Solar System* book. Oceanhouse Media also created a digital version of this book, complete with a telescope and interactive constellations in the nighttime sky.

Born Reading Bundle: *Cosmo and the Robot*

1. Make toilet-paper-tube binoculars, a bedroom spaceship, or other pretend toys from the book.
2. Read *The Berenstain Bears on the Moon* and *Tool Book* by Gail Gibbons.
3. Visit the library to find more books, audiobooks, or resources about space.
4. Watch part of "The Magic School Bus Gets Lost in Space" or go to the *National Geographic* Space and Science website for more videos.
5. Download the *There's No Place Like Space!: All About Our Solar System* app.

Instead of letting your kid watch random television or forcing them to read books they don't care about, a Born Reading Bundle respects your child's interests. It will help your child learn how to explore the library and the Internet to find more information.

Child development expert Gordon Wells dedicated his professional career to showing teachers how to follow a child's particular enthusiasms. But he reminded parents that the real work begins at home. "My campaign for the last 25 or more years has been to work with teachers to help them to see that the most effective way of teaching is to be responsive, not to be didactic. And that applies to parents too," he said.

These skills are so crucial for twenty-first-century kids. They have more information at their fingertips than any generation in history, but they need to understand how to explore it. Teach your children these valuable skills early. Show them that eBooks, apps, and videos are not entertainment passively consumed on the computer, they are living and breathing stories that can be part of your life.

Think beyond just the pages of books as you have interactive reading experiences with your child. If they love a particular animal, find a wacky viral video about that creature. If they love a book about construction, take them to a real construction site. If they obsess over fairy tales, check out different editions of the same story at the library to compare.

The list goes on and on. Don't let your children's favorite books end when the book closes. Keep reading and researching until they are ready to chase a new obsession.

Digital Problems with Interactive Solutions: How to Evaluate Digital Products for Kids

When your child turns three, you will face a new set of digital dilemmas about how much time your kid should spend watching DVDs, YouTube videos, or regular old TV.

The problem began in our house when we started to let Olive watch *Sesame Street* videos. We let her have little three- to five-minute snippets of classic educational TV on the iPad, but she never wanted to stop. Once we forced her to stop, she would throw a massive tantrum.

Despite involving a host of new devices, these problems are as old as television itself. In 2013, a Northwestern University study showed that mobile use is rapidly expanding in American families. They surveyed 2,300 parents with kids eight years old or younger. Of the surveyed parents, 71 percent had a smartphone and 42 percent had a tablet. Only 35 percent had both types of devices in the home.

The study divided families into three categories based on screen time in the individual homes. "Media-centric" families made up 39 percent of the survey, letting kids spend an average of 4 hours and 40 minutes of screen time every day. "Media moderate" families composed 45 percent of the responses, allowing children to spend an average of 2 hours and 51 minutes of screen time every day. Finally, "media-light" parents composed 16 percent of the survey, limiting their children to an average of 1 hour and 35 minutes of screen time every day.

Once your child passes the two-years-old mark, the American Academy of Pediatrics suggests two hours or less of screen time for kids. But even two hours of screen time is an enormous amount of time to spend with devices, television included.

After watching Olive spend extended periods of time with the device, we could see the effects. She would huddle with the iPad, slack-jawed, limp, and sometimes even drooling if she used these magical devices over a prolonged period of unsupervised time.

Special education teacher and Teachers with Apps co-founder Jayne Clare shared an invaluable tip for striking a balance between reading time and digital device time. If her kids want to play a game on the computer or device, they must read a book for the same amount of time first. One hour of reading gets one hour of video game time, for instance. "Then it's much easier for you because they have the motivation that they want to do something else. It's dangling the carrot, but it works for me," she says.

After grappling with Olive for a week over her iPad usage, we decided to only let Olive watch half an hour or less per day of unsupervised screen time during these early years. But screen time doesn't have to be a dirty word.

Grover Whitehurst, the founder of the dialogic reading techniques that guide this book, told me: "I think there is a way to adapt digital materials to make them interactive." Whitehurst described an educational video fad that swept parenting in the 1990s, an unfortunate trend that didn't have the same kind of interactive value for children. "It's much better to have digital materials that engage the child in interaction than what it would have been years ago, just somebody reading the story on a videotape for a child to listen to," he concluded.

Nevertheless, this new device time adds up, and it may even be disrupting our bedtime reading. The survey conducted by Reading Is Fundamental and Macy's that came out in the summer of 2013 revealed a frightening statistic. Out of 1,000 parents surveyed, only one in three read to their children every night.

These are heartbreaking statistics. We don't need very much to fix it; it only requires one parent reading one book every night. In terms of intellectual and emotional growth, story time is as important as feeding your child healthy food. I caught up with the experts at Common Sense Media to find out more. Founded in 2003, the nonprofit guides parents with all kinds of media, from children's books to television to apps to eBooks.

"There has never been a study showing that digital devices or screen time is better for healthy development than an intimate relationship with a loving caregiver. That relationship is absolutely primary to all of the aspects of development: cognitive, social, emotional, physical," Common Sense Media's parenting editor Caroline Knorr told me.

Still, she sees plenty of digital opportunities for parents.

"There are some great age-appropriate quality media that can show their kids when they need a certain amount of time to take a break, put dinner on the table, and all of that. We're not as strict as we used to be around guidelines, but we do encourage parents to understand why it's important to choose mindfully, have time limits, and provide a balance of activities," Knorr said.

The lines between digital books and apps is a blurry one, changing in between devices, marketplaces, and operating systems. Ultimately, it comes down to a personal preference. The first thing you have to decide is what devices you want to use.

There are two major players in the world of digital media: Apple and Android. Apple users have the iPad, iPhone, and iPod Touch for digital reading. Android users can use a much larger collection of devices: Samsung Galaxy Tab, Kindle Fire, and more. Microsoft, Blackberry, and a few other players also offer tablets or eReaders, but we'll focus here on the most robust marketplaces.

Apple has a clear advantage in the world of apps, with hundreds of thousands of offerings in its crowded App Store. Still, Android is growing, and many Android customers feel offended by the media's constant focus on Apple devices.

If you feel limited by the selection of Android apps and eBooks mentioned in this book, I recommend you explore Oceanhouse Media's website. They have a massive list of classic kids' books adapted for Android devices, including beloved series like Dr. Seuss, the Berenstain Bears, and Little Critter.

"Most Android marketplaces have curated kids' collections where parents can find a wide variety of digital book apps and other children's content," Oceanhouse Media marketing manager Natalie Aller says, urging parents to search places like Amazon Appstore, Google Play, or Barnes & Noble's Nook store for more

Android reading material. "Searching for your kids' favorite characters or hobbies can also be a good avenue to discover apps they will really enjoy," she concludes.

In this book, you'll find material from both of these worlds to make sure families with both kinds of devices have resources, but our own family usage depends on the iPhone and iPad. So, many of the apps recommended in this book were tested on Apple devices.

The next question you need to ask yourself is this: How much interactivity and how many games do I want included in a digital book for my kids? You can find digital books where every element on the page can be manipulated like a video game at the push of your child's finger. On the other hand, you can also read many eBooks like straight-ahead texts on a digital screen. Your child will only have to turn the digital page.

A number of the digital offerings I discuss here are not within the bounds of traditional reading. Olive and I traveled fairly freely and between digital books, apps, and games as we explored educational content on these devices.

Some of my digital suggestions tend toward imaginary play rather than traditional reading. I am not offering any of these resources as substitutes for books. They are meant to enhance the creative and literary experience for your child. Books will play a crucial role in your child's life and in our education system for years to come. You can use eBooks, apps, and games to encourage deeper conversations about the books you're reading and the topics you are exploring together.

As long as these apps and eBooks are part of a healthy diet of traditional books, they can be productive. If you spend a few days reading a great storybook app like *Little Red Riding Hood* with your child, you will see the amazing possibilities inherent in these new technologies. "Kids don't really see the difference in multiple formats like we do," librarian Cen Campbell told me. "The difference between a book and a game or text versus pictures. It's all the same thing. Information. And that is what their literacy looks like as opposed to our black-and-white concept of literacy."

In the end, it doesn't matter what we think about digital literacy. The world has already changed, whether we like it or not. Olive and her generation will not make the same distinctions that we make about media. By the time she graduates from high school, the boundaries between eBooks, apps, and other technology will have crumbled.

Olive truly benefited from some of the apps we used while I wrote this book. I outlined her fascination with Endless Alphabet in the last chapter, an alphabet-learning app led by a crew of lovable monsters.

One morning, Olive put these letter-recognition skills into practice. She was scribbling in a notebook with a pen, carefully filling every page with one-word squiggles. She told me she was writing "mommy" and "daddy" over and over. After a while, she decided to draw a monster.

She drew a giant oval and put a couple of stray lines on top, explaining that was the hair. Then she drew two stick arms and two stick legs, calling them arms and legs in the very first representational drawing she'd ever produced. I felt like a hiker stumbling upon caveman paintings in France.

I believe the app helped to trigger her writing and drawing impulses that morning, combining her interaction with letters and the lovable monsters in Endless Alphabet. I witnessed the beautiful and simple creativity milestone, and I felt so lucky to be the person who happened to be there at the kitchen table at that moment.

Computers, tablets, and smartphones also give parents some much-needed time to do things around the house. As long as you follow the expert recommendations in this book and fill your devices with quality material, these can be useful tools for your child.

Common Sense Media's Caroline Knorr sums it all up: "If you do need to use a device to occupy your kid while you're working, choose age-appropriate, high-quality programs mindfully. Then you know that your kid is getting a good experience out of that and it's not just a waste of time."

Reading the Alphabet: Recognizing Patterns and Letters

Three-year-old readers will spend a lot of time wrestling with the alphabet. ABCs are not something you can pinpoint in time; some kids get it faster than others. Still, most Born Reading babies will start analyzing letters early.

I once watched Olive read a 26-minute-long audiobook edition of *Curious George Learns the Alphabet*, the ideal book to read when your child is ready to tackle the alphabet and the early mechanics of reading. At first, George struggles to decode squiggles in a book, miming the experience of a kid learning how to read.

George and the man with the yellow hat spend the rest of the book painstakingly studying the alphabet. The man draws the letter, then traces an animal around the shape. The big "A" becomes the jaws of an alligator or the little "d" becomes a one-humped camel. The book tackles both upper- and lowercase letters, showing kids how to rearrange the letters into simple words. Over the course of this repeated epic reading experience, Olive started to understand the fundamentals of reading along with her monkey friend.

If you are looking for a shorter reading experience, try *Dr. Seuss's ABCs*. The classic book teaches both lowercase and uppercase letters, all mixed in with his charming wordplay.

Olive and I watched a string of *Sesame Street* videos when she started to tackle the alphabet. These free and legal YouTube videos provide a three- to five-minute viewing experience, making it easier for parents to keep screen time under control.

In my favorite alphabet-driven video, droll comedian Ricky Gervais sings a lullaby for Elmo about the letter "N." After singing a sweet acoustic verse about "N" words like "nighttime" "neighbors" and "nightshirts," Gervais screamed "N-N-N-N-N" like a punk rock singer. His screaming highlighted the phonetic sound of the letter "N" and woke up the sleepy Muppet. That was the first joke that made Olive and I both laugh at the same time.

As I tucked Olive into bed, it dawned on me I could use the song with *any* letter of the alphabet. For the next few weeks, I sang the silly lullaby using highly phonetic letters like "B," "M," or "S," shouting the sound at the end of the song. Olive would make me sing the song endlessly, and I had turned mindless TV time into a learning experience.

Born Reading Playbook:
Continue the conversation.

Don't stop talking about a book or digital reading app after you've ended the reading experience. Reference the book in real life and keep asking questions.

Conversation starters: *Do you want to sing Elmo's alphabet song? What shape did Curious George draw for the letter "A"?*

The best kids' apps take this into account as well. Tom Bonnick from Nosy Crow explains how kids can discover letters and reading inside his company's apps. "For pre-literate children there's a lot that you can get out of them. We've included features like text-highlighting, so that every word lights up as it's read aloud, which is a good tool for attaching sound and meaning to written words in a child's mind when they're learning to read."

While watching *Sesame Street* videos, we met Harvey Kneeslapper. When I was a kid, this scruffy Muppet always made me laugh with his super corny jokes. Olive laughed out loud at his first alphabet-themed pun: "Can I take a picture of U?" he asked a bald-headed man. Without losing a beat, he slapped the letter "U" on his victim's bald head and took his photograph.

After watching the video, I cut out a paper "U" and chased Olive around the house. We took turns sticking the letter on each other and making the same joke. She loved it.

The best crafts are that simple: taking something from a book or TV show and cutting it out with construction paper. Olive loved the activity, and it brought some real educational value to the passive activity of watching television.

Born Reading Bundle: *Curious George Learns the Alphabet*

1. Make cut-out letters or draw pictures like Curious George.
2. Listen to the audiobook edition.
3. Read *Dr. Seuss's ABCs* and ask your librarian to recommend an alphabet book based on your kid's favorite things.
4. Watch *Sesame Street* videos about letters, play the Ricky Gervais or Harvey Kneeslapper game.
5. Visit PBS Kids' "Alphabet Games" section online. It is filled with lovable characters exploring the alphabet.

Reading Your Way through Potty Training

At some point during this momentous year, most parents attempt potty training. This seemingly endless process requires lots and lots of children's books.

According to the American Academy of Pediatrics, it takes between 10 and 12 bathroom successes before a kid is potty trained. That can take a LONG time. You will spend hours crouched beside your toddler and you will need something to do during these painfully dull moments in the bathroom waiting.

During our potty training process, we built a bathroom library with four books: *Once Upon a Potty* by Alona Frankel, *Potty* by Leslie Patricelli, *It's Potty Time* by Roger Priddy, and *Potty Time with Elmo*.

You can visit a bookstore and make your own collection, giving your kid a chance to pick out a special book. They will grow tired of a single book eventually, so I recommend throwing in a few more titles for variety.

My favorite book was Patricelli's *Potty*. Olive had picked it out months before our successful potty training efforts. The lovable baby from all of Patricelli's books will walk your toddler through the act of potty training. We read it over and over, and I think it helped Olive ultimately make the decision to try potty training.

My least favorite book was *Potty Time with Elmo*, a simplistic potty training title saddled with an electronic gizmo and push buttons that triggered annoying sound effects of toilet flushes, sink washing, and the red Muppet cheering "Elmo can use the potty!" Your toddler will push that button so many times that Elmo's catchphrase will haunt your dreams.

Frankel's *Once Upon a Potty* has been handed down between generations since the 1970s. The book offers a more detailed look at the physical mechanics of potty training, with an edition for both boys and girls. The vintage clothing and charming illustrations will keep parents reading. This book is especially helpful for guiding your children through the names and functions of their body parts.

As you add new potty books to your library, you should compare the books' vocabulary with your family's lexicon of bodily functions and body parts. Your kid will notice the difference while you are reading. Olive would correct me during potty time reading: "We don't call it wee wee. We call it pee pee," she reminded me.

Both Frankel's book and Elmo's book have app editions. Frankel's app comes in both a boy and girl edition, complete with a potty song and simple interactivity. Elmo's app simply increases the interactivity of the push-button print book. It even includes a few potty songs. Now "Elmo can use the potty!" will haunt both your dreams *and* your smartphone.

Every family will strike their own balance, but I recommend having a nice stack of books in the bathroom and *lots* of other ways to entertain and distract your kid as he or she perches on kiddie toilets. This is not a fast process and will require reading, singing, playing, and lots of waiting. But there's never been a better time to practice your interactive reading.

You must be gentle and supportive during this emotional time for your toddler. After one unsuccessful day of potty training, Olive looked up at me and asked in the sweetest voice: "I getting better, Daddy?" And I said "Yes!" and gave her the biggest hug—almost weeping at this little creature looking for a little extra encouragement. Later I realized that she was quoting *It's Potty Time* by Roger Priddy. At one point in the book's potty training process, the narrator looks straight at your child and proudly states: "I am getting better!" It melted my heart, seeing how this little phrase wove its way into her life, how much of an effect it could hold on her.

The Priddy book also includes a free chart and magnetic stickers. You can hang it on the bathroom doorknob, letting your child choose a sticker for every successful potty training moment. When Olive collected five stickers (more or less), we'd take her for a blueberry muffin at the local deli. These little encouragements make a big difference, helping toddlers cope with this scary, daunting, and decidedly difficult task of being a big kid.

Born Reading Playbook:
Compliment your child as you read.

Reward your child for simple responses, cuddle them after a reading session, and praise them for choosing good books or apps.

Conversation starters: *You are such a big girl now, just like the kid in this book! Great job! Do you want to choose a sticker?*

Reading to Inspire Sports and Movement:
Exercise for Bookworms

Believe it or not, the daughter of a skinny writer with thick black glasses was not particularly enthusiastic about running, jumping, or kicking balls around the backyard. Hoping to give her a little athletic stimulation, we enrolled Olive in a toddler soccer program at the YMCA.

Olive got her own adorable orange jersey and learned to deliver a high five. It took two more classes before she could kick the ball and run at the same time. She generally toddled at the back of the pack during these short soccer classes, but she learned all the basic moves: passing me the ball or kicking a goal into a kiddie soccer net. At home, she started running and jumping.

I was proud of my little girl, polishing the non-literary side of her life. But I kept trying to find ways to extend the learning from a six-week soccer class into her daily life. We checked out a stack of books about soccer at the library, but only one book inspired Olive: *Madlenka Soccer Star* by Peter Sís.

The book follows a little girl who lives in an unidentified country as she kicks a soccer ball around the block. Using the powers of her imagination, she dodges some fantastical opponents: a mailbox, parking meter, and a dog magically transform into soccer players.

Suddenly, an everyday walk around the block becomes a thrilling soccer match. The book ends on a crowded soccer field filled with neighborhood kids playing the beloved sport. Olive loved naming these kids after her friends on the soccer team. It was so easy to make this book interactive. We could kick the soccer ball around the house or pretend parking meters and mailboxes could come alive during our daily walks.

Storytelling Lessons: *Madlenka Soccer Star*

1. Practice celebrating a goal in the most theatrical way possible, shouting "GOAAAAAAL!" and running around the room.
2. Act out running, jumping, and sports from books.
3. Turn your daily walks into imaginary games based on the book.
4. Talk about coaches, teams, and sportsmanship in everyday life.
5. Reward your kid with high fives.

Even if you can't go outside, books can inspire all sorts of movement and other active games. "Any thing that you can incorporate that involves physical activity, even if it's an outgrowth of the book or you're making it up, it's okay," Caroline Knorr, the parenting editor at Common Sense Media, suggests. "We encourage parents to make up activities that connect the book or think of things that the kids are already doing: tumbling, jumping, those kinds of things. Make some kind of connection between online activities and offline activities. I think a lot of books nowadays are offering those types of activities. Take advantage of those."

Shira Lee Katz, the director of digital media at Common Sense Media, adds this example that works for any book about dinosaurs (or other animals, for that matter): "Parents can say, 'Let's do all the motions that the dinosaurs do. Pretend you are a Tyrannosaurus Rex or pretend you are a brontosaurus.' Have the kids role-play some of the characters. Combining some sort of physical play or activities. It solidifies some of the ideas. The book is about characteristics of different dinosaurs, let's say. You're reinforcing that by having kids pretend to eat leafy greens or pretend to eat meat."

Another sports book that Olive loved was *Little Yoga* by Rebecca Whitford. We live in Los Angeles, a place where it is pretty easy to see somebody doing yoga at the gym, the park, or chanting in the middle of an apartment complex. Babies have a profound connection to yoga; some of the primary poses were drawn from the movements of these flexible creatures. *Little Yoga* will give any parent enough yoga background to do simple poses with his or her kid. The poses are all tied to animal names and movements, making it easy for your kid to read.

Reading is a visual process for these Born Readers; they learn everything from sign language to colors to movement from your interactive reading experiences. Whether you choose baseball or yoga or ballet for your kid, these will encourage daily movement, focus, and a lifelong love of exercise.

As the world moves online, these habits cannot be under-estimated. Like most of my peers, I spend long hours hunched in front of screens for work. If we model this behavior, our kids will live digital lives following our own bad habits.

Reading with Audiobooks: Have You Listened to a Good Book Lately?

I loved audiobooks as a boy. My parents let us use a battered record player to play 45s with giant holes. We needed a special attachment to play our kid-sized records.

My favorites were all science fiction: a *Star Wars* book, a kiddie adaptation of *The Black Hole*, and a few others lost to the movie tie-in dustbin of history. I loved the *Star Wars* book so much that my parents would make me recite it at parties. I could reel off the entire record the way more cultured children of other generations could recite one of Shakespeare's sonnets.

At our library, Olive and I discovered the audiobook section together. She couldn't resist the corner filled with books in plastic bags and CDs in shiny cases. We found *Charlie Parker Played Be Bop*, a kids' book introduction to 1940s jazz. Chris Raschka captures the historic moment when jazz bands moved away from crowd-pleasing dance numbers into solo-driven and complex arrangements. Bebop helped create our rich jazz history, and the book makes it simple enough for any toddler to grasp.

The audiobook edition is actually read by a jazz musician and is set to Charlie Parker's classic rendition of "Night in Tunisia."

Over the course of different tracks, the narrator reads the book with the music, switches to a rhythmic reading, and ends by singing the book like a jazz solo. From two years old and onward, Olive knew what bebop sounded like and could spot saxophones in music.

The best way to find an audiobook that your child will love is to start with a book they already like. For example, if your child is obsessed with Curious George books, check out your local bookstore or library for their accompanying audiobooks. Once you find something your child loves, he or she will likely listen to the audiobooks for weeks straight.

Or you can be like my parents and find a book based on your kid's favorite movie. Almost every popular kids' movie comes with a host of tie-ins. If you can't find audiobooks at your library, visit the publisher's website or an online bookseller to find MP3 audiobook editions of your family's favorites to download to your devices.

"I've had a really great experience with audiobooks," Caroline Knorr told me. "One of the best applications is if you are sick or if your kid is sick. If you don't want them watching TV or a computer all day, audiobooks provide an entertaining experience. There are studies that show that developing those aural skills is great for kids, and it is one of the building blocks of their education."

When Olive got closer to turning three years old, she would sit in her bed and read audiobooks by herself. We could get dressed in the morning while she sat with an oversized edition of a Curious George book. Olive would turn the pages by herself, yelling "Daddy, where we at?" when she needed backup. She also adored the audiobook edition of *Blueberries for Sal*, an old-school audiobook packed with 20 minutes of extra songs and activities for kids to perform along with the book.

Listening to audiobooks with Olive, I had the most vivid memory of wearing headphones and listening to an audiobook in grade school. Recess had been canceled for some thunderstorm and my classmates were wreaking havoc in the classroom around me.

In my memory, those same warm voices from *Blueberries for Sal* were reading the story and singing. I did not want the story to end. In the safe story space inside those headphones, I could escape the crazy classroom. Very early on, books were cozy that way for me, a place where nobody could get to me.

For better or for worse, I still feel that way in a subway or on the bus with a book. I'm always searching for the next book that's powerful enough to put me back in that same cozy spot where I have been hiding since I first learned how to read.

You can read this book to make your kid smarter, more verbal, or more creative, but you can also show your son or daughter a perfect, serene place in the middle of him- or herself where he or she will always be safe. As children grow up, they will learn how to cope, heal, and grow inside that safe place.

Audiobook Recommendations

Blueberries for Sal by Robert McCloskey
A classic kids' book about a boy picking blueberries with his mom in the 1940s. They encounter two bears on a mountaintop,

complete with great sound effects and stunning illustrations. The audiobook edition has some great music and games to get your child involved in the story.

Madeline by Ludwig Bemelmans
The classic book about a French girl who gets into trouble at boarding school. The impressionistic illustrations will fascinate your child, and the audiobook editions include French kids' songs and some language lessons.

Curious George by Margret and H. A. Rey
Immortal kids' book from the 1940s that still feels familiar even in the twenty-first century. I recommend starting with the very first book and moving through the earliest books in the series. The stories unfold at a surreal pace that three-year-olds appreciate.

Pete the Cat by Eric Litwin and James Dean (illustrator)
This book will charm kids of any age, but this first book in the series will make any three-year-old yell out colors and predict what happens next. Visit the website for a free MP3 version of the book sung in a bluesy melody.

Charlie Parker Played Be Bop by Chris Raschka
One of the most abstract books you can read to your child, but little kids respond to the ratatat rhymes and kinetic illustrations. Track down an audiobook copy for a recording of Charlie Parker playing "Night in Tunisia" to give your kid the complete experience.

Born Reading with Poetry

Poetry is the backbone of children's literature. The oldest picture books simply mixed simple verse for children with attractive illustrations. If your child can understand picture books and the nonsense language of Dr. Seuss, then they can appreciate great poetry.

We started with wordplay and dramatic readings. Once, Olive and I were reading *Let's Go for a Drive!*, a Mo Willems book packed with fun onomatopoeia—action words as the little pig dashes on and off the page going "zip" and "zoom!"

"Just like Cat in the Hat," she exclaimed, connecting the wordplay to the climactic moment in Dr. Seuss's *The Cat in the Hat Comes Back* when the cat unleashes his magical power: a gigantic "VOOM!" that fills two pages and cleans up some dirty snow. Olive loved that text-based explosion, bouncing in her seat every time we read the book with a 5-4-3-2-1 countdown before turning the page to see the magical "VOOM!"

I introduced Olive to *Poetry Speaks to Children*, an anthology collecting famous poems in a fun package for kids. The book comes with a CD so kids can listen to the poets reciting their work. Olive's favorite poem was "Gas" by C. K. Williams. Composed for kids, the poem explains how "farting is forbidden" in France. Olive gleefully repeated the word *fart* while we read the poem.

I spoke with publisher Dominique Raccah to find out more about the best-selling anthology. "One of my frustrations with life in general is that people love poetry until they get to high school. And then we beat it out of them," she explained. "We torture poems and we force kids to think there's so much deep meaning that they can't just enjoy it."

This book will introduce your child to poetry before school can ruin it for them.

Raccah concluded: "Kids want to play with words. They're at that stage where everything is new. Everything is learning for them. Learning is not a bad word for them. It's their job and they actually like it! They want to be bigger and know more and be more in control of their environment."

One afternoon when Olive stayed home sick from school, I produced the poetry anthology for some nap-time reading. We discovered a Robert Louis Stevenson poem about a boy staying home from school and playing with his tin soldiers in his bed. It was breathtaking to watch Olive instantly connect with a kid in a 100-year-old poem. Despite the outdated vocabulary and the formal poetry rhythms, the cozy illustrations helped Olive connect with the story—a timeless bridge between children's authors.

Olive also loved an excerpt from Sylvia Plath's "The Bed Book." Plath wrote the book as a goodnight poem for her own children. She imagines a whole variety of beds, large, small, and magical. The quiet rhythm gradually sends your kid off to dreamland.

Raccah thinks this is a crucial part of your child's mental development. "Language is one of the ways that we learn how the world works. This is going to sound really old-fashioned, but I would say having kids memorize poetry is actually a gift. . . . I memorized a lot of poetry because I came to the U.S. as a child and didn't speak any English. Poetry was short. As a result, I learned a lot of poetry during those very dark times when I couldn't speak the language and was trying to figure my way out."

If you explore *Poetry Speaks to Children*, I recommend you

find a few poems that discuss activities your child loves to do already. There's plenty of material in this book, everything from sports to dinosaurs to temper tantrums.

If your child really loves poetry, I recommend finding public domain digital books for free online. You can track down countless free books of children's verse from the old days or even newer poetry. On my Born Reading website, I link to more free poetry resources.

You can find free books with gorgeous illustrations, ranging from Mother Goose to Robert Louis Stevenson stories. Using the My Story app, you can actually create a digital book preserving your child's favorite poems. They can draw illustrations on paper or make digital sketches, saving the pictures with the poems.

Born Reading Bundle: *Poetry Speaks to Children*

1. Read books with lots of wordplay: Dr. Seuss, Mo Willems, or any book with lots of musical language.
2. Read *Poetry Speaks to Children* while listening to the CD together.
3. Download free poetry books online.
4. Have your child illustrate his or her favorite poem, just like in *Poetry Speaks to Children*.
5. Use the My Story app to make a digital poetry book collecting all of your child's favorite poems. Give the book to family members as presents.

Three is an amazing age. Your kid gets taller in the blink of an eye, and all your reading work will blossom as they craft more complicated sentences. Olive loved to flip through family photo albums at this age, learning the names of her cousins in distant corners of the United States. One night we cuddled on the couch, browsing a photo album with photographs of my grandparents, great-grandparents, and great-great-grandparents. I felt like a time traveler, watching my little daughter meet these people who had passed away years before she was even born.

"And they lived happily ever after," she said before turning every page, blessing these photographs of her ancestors and bearing their memory for another generation. Storytelling wasn't just an activity stuck in dusty old books anymore. Olive had learned how to tell a story—however sweet and simple—about her own life. That is the magic of interactive reading and a life filled with stories.

Book Recommendations for Three-Year-Olds

Not So Fast Songololo by Niki Daly
This gorgeous book tells a simple story about a boy shopping with his grandma in South Africa. Perfectly drawn characters will spark conversation about emotions, family relationships, poverty, and Africa.

Bedtime for Frances by Russell Hoban and Garth Williams (illustrator)
Pitch perfect reconstruction of a preschooler's reluctant bedtime ritual. Even if the book brings back traumatic memories of bedtime tantrums, it will help your kid talk about sleeping and why he or she won't go to sleep sometimes.

Madlenka Soccer Star by Peter Sís
A deceptively simple book about a little girl who loves soccer. We follow her as she kicks the ball around her neighborhood, inspiring a combination of motion and imaginary play with everyday objects.

Poetry Speaks to Children edited by Elise Paschen
An inspiring collection spanning generations of great poetry. Celebrated poets like Rita Dove, Seamus Heaney, and Billy Collins are included, introducing kids to accessible and fun poems.

Truck by Donald Crews
A wordless glimpse into the world of transportation, a stylized view of a truck traveling. The perfect way to introduce young readers to the world of nonfiction, exploring a familiar and evocative sight—these massive semitrucks.

Cosmo and the Robot by Brian Pinkney
Following the adventures of two kids on Mars, this book encourages children to study space and play with tools. Olive carried cardboard binoculars and collected Mars rocks for weeks, turning the book into a fun science game.

The Big Honey Hunt by Stan Berenstain and Jan Berenstain
Hypnotic first book in the Berenstain Bears collection, edited by Dr. Seuss into a gentle, rhymed journey through nature. While Dr. Seuss books focus on hard, crisp rhymes, this book has a smoother style.

Pete the Cat and His Four Groovy Buttons by Eric Litwin and James Dean (illustrator)

This sequel to *Pete the Cat* tells the story of a hippie cat that learns counting and patience while showing off his shiny buttons. You can download a free MP3 of the song, one of the best parts of this series. You will be humming his songs for the rest of your life.

I Read Signs by Tana Hoban

A classic nonfiction book for kids with vivid pictures of the signs they see every day. They will recognize these signs, but the book will help you talk about them and learn how to read the letters.

Ghosts in the House! by Kazuno Kohara

This Japanese picture book follows the adventures of a little girl and her cat in a haunted house. Instead of being terrorized by the spirits, she catches them and washes them.

App Recommendations for Three-Year-Olds

Toontastic Jr. by Launchpad Toys

If you feel like your child spends too much passive time on a device, this game will let him or her create pirate-themed stories with an easy interface. I recommend that parents participate to make use of all the fun tools in the app.

Available in the Apple App Store, but only works with iPad and requires iOS 5.1 or later.

There's No Place Like Space!: All About Our Solar System
   by Tish Rabe, Aristides Ruiz (illustrator), and Oceanhouse
   Media
This digital book app extends the Cat in the Hat series, adapting a
book written by other authors using Dr. Seuss's characters. In this
installment, the Cat in the Hat takes his friends on a tour of space.

Available in the Apple App Store; works with iPhone, iPod Touch, and iPad.
Needs iOS 5.0 or later.

Bizzy Bear on the Farm by Benji Davis (illustrator) and
   Nosy Crow
A lovable storybook bear takes your kid on an animated tour of
a farm. The book maintains a simple storybook structure, but allows your child to steer a tractor, collect eggs, and feed the pigs.

Available in the Apple App Store; works with iPhone (3GS, 4, 4S, and
5), iPod Touch (third, fourth, and fifth generation), and iPad. Requires
iOS 3.1.3 or later.

Toca Tea Party by Toca Boca
A fun app to augment your child's imaginative play. If they love
hosting or reading about tea parties, this app provides a safe way
to do it. Stuffed animals, imaginary friends, and parents can be
arranged around the iPad, making an interactive alternate to TV.

Available in the Apple App Store, but only works with iPad and requires
iOS 4.3 or later.

Draw and Tell by Duck Duck Moose
A charming drawing app that lets your kid color, draw, or illustrate
photographs. The app includes some inspiring music and should

keep young artists busy for years. Ask your child to illustrate a favorite book page or digitally color a beloved family picture.

Available in the Apple App Store; works with iPhone, iPod Touch, and iPad, but requires iOS 4.2 or later.

Once Upon a Potty by Alona Frankel and Oceanhouse Media

This classic potty-training book gets an eBook update with editions for both boys and girls. Without adding too many bells and whistles to the story, this digital edition brings music and interactive reading to the book that has helped generations of kids.

Available in the Apple App Store; works with iPhone, iPod Touch, and iPad. Needs iOS 3.0 or later.

Available in Google Play for Android devices.

Available in Amazon Appstore for Android devices.

The Cat in the Hat by Dr. Seuss and Oceanhouse Media

Another classic kids' book gets the digital treatment. Oceanhouse added a professional reading to the app version, but you can also record yourself reading the book and share your recording with other people who have the app.

Available in the Apple App Store; works with iPhone, iPod Touch, and iPad. Needs iOS 5.0 or later.

Available in Google Play for Android devices.

Available in Amazon Appstore for Android devices.

My Story—Book Maker for Kids by HiDef Web Solutions

A slick app that helps kids make digital books. The easy interface lets them draw, color, and add photographs, and they can share the digital book with family and friends.

Available in the Apple App Store, but only works with iPad and needs iOS 5.1 or later.

Road Trip Bingo by Bright Bunny
A digital device can be a life saver during long car rides, but you can also melt your kid's brain with mindless entertainment. This game lets kids play bingo by looking out the window, turning device time into an interactive experience.

Available in the Apple App Store; works with iPhone, iPod Touch, and iPad. Needs iOS 3.0 or later.

Toca Band by Toca Boca
Kids will love this app and so will all of your adult friends. The game offers you a set of musical cartoon characters, a wiggly accordion, an opera diva, and a kid plucking a mandolin. Put them together to build your own catchy song.

Available in the Apple App Store; works with iPhone (3GS, 4, 4S, and 5), iPod Touch (third, fourth, and fifth generation), and iPad. Needs iOS 5.0 or later.

Interlude: Why Your Kid Should Read Comic Books

In grade school, I literally dissected the full-color Sunday morning comic pages in the *Detroit Free Press*. I would cut out *Bloom County*, *Garfield*, *Calvin and Hobbes*, and other classic comics, pasting the strips into photo albums like rare artwork.

I moved on to comic books a few years later, collecting *Wolverine*, *Spider-Man*, *X-Men*, and a few other series with my allowance. I'm excited to share these comics with Olive someday, but in the meantime, I've found some amazing comic books for kids.

New Yorker art editor Françoise Mouly has championed comic book creators for most of her professional life. She co-edited the legendary *RAW* comics anthology with her husband, *Maus* author Art Spiegelman. She told me that too many parents have a bad attitude about comic books. She traced this prejudice back to the legacy of an old anti–comic book crusade that profoundly changed the landscape of American children's reading.

"There was a moment in the 1950s where 94 percent of kids growing up in America, boys and girls, were reading comics," she told me. Then, in 1954, a doctor named Fredric Wertham published *Seduction of the Innocent*, a nonfiction book that blamed comic books for juvenile delinquency and prompted a congressional crackdown on the medium. "They did the same thing with rock and roll and they did the same thing with video games. It's something that scares the grown-ups and the parents when all of the kids are absorbed for hours with a medium," Mouly said.

Pushing back against anti–comic book forces, Mouly founded TOON Books in 2008. This Candlewick Books imprint specializes in gorgeous editions of comic books for kids. Her husband once summed up the simple power of a great comic: "Comics are a gateway drug to literacy." Using great artists from around the world, TOON Books bridges the gap between picture books and superhero comic books.

Olive discovered her first TOON Books title at the library when she was one and a half years old. She grabbed a copy of Art Spiegelman's *Jack and the Box*, a screwball comic about a kid meeting a crazy jack-in-the-box toy. The comic book panels are simple and vivid, perfect for an early reader. As Olive got older, she graduated to other favorites like *Silly Lilly* by Agnès Rosenstiehl and *Luke on the Loose* by Harry Bliss.

Mouly shares a few tips for reading comics with kids:

How to Read a Comic Book with Your Child

1. Find a comic book that you like to read. "Anything that you do with your child in your lap and that you enjoy is going to have the right effect."
2. Guide your child through the different panels. "Keep your finger on the character that is talking, but make sure you don't block out the speech balloon or facial expressions."
3. Have your child guess the sound effects. "Their guess is as good as the artist's guess as to what sound the character makes."
4. Let your child help dramatize the story. "You can actually assign parts in the comic book, you can have the dialogue and the back and forth."
5. Ask your kid to tell his or her own version of the story. "If

you had an adventure with Luke, what would happen if
Luke goes on vacation with his parents to the beach?"

But these books do much more than introduce your child to comic books. "We live in an increasingly visual culture," explains Mouly. "If they know how to read comics, then they will know how to watch television and they'll know how to look at YouTube videos on the net. Because they'll see the visual narratives in a very grammatical way. It's really good training for any kind of building block of understanding storytelling and narrative."

Comics can literally teach your child how to follow a story on a page, a valuable skill for kids figuring out how to decode books. One-year-olds can handle *Silly Lilly* or *Jack and the Box*, the pages filled with simple frames and a small series of actions.

But don't let age limits slow you down. As a two-year-old, Olive obsessed over *The Shark King* by R. Kikuo Johnson, a folklore-inspired story about a shape-shifting shark man. Even though the book was intended for much older kids, Olive loved the fairy tale imagery and didn't blink at the magical plot.

Olive also devoured *The Big Wet Balloon* by Liniers, a book about two sisters exploring their backyard during a summer rain. At the end of the book, the author includes a photograph of his real-life daughters with a homemade drawing that inspired the story.

That picture prompted Olive to make her own drawing as soon as we finished the book. Those little girls were real to her; she could imagine their adventures beyond the pages. "The goal is for somebody to make the story happen in their head when they are given the book," Mouly summarized. "Comics are a very good starting point for that."

Disney Interactive editor in chief Catherine Connors reminded parents not to worry about formats: "Some kids respond to comic books, some kids respond to stories presented in a more interactive form," she said. "If you can use that as a gateway into the stories and more traditional media, you basically lure them in with the power of the narrative itself while worrying less about what the form is that it is being presented in."

Comic books are perfect for practicing early literacy skills. Parents can point out short, capitalized letters inside comics. Phrases like "Bang!" "Ha," or "Yaaaa!" punctuate action scenes inside these adventure books, and your child will love reading the letters out loud on the page.

You can see these exuberant comic book fonts in the work of Mo Willems too. In *Pigs Make Me Sneeze!*, Willems's elephant sneezes for 30 pages. The running gag is that his "a-a-a-a-a" presneeze gets longer and the mighty "CHOO" gets louder every time. The letters get bigger and bigger as the book gets sillier and sillier.

While taking a bath, Olive reenacted *Pigs Make Me Sneeze*. Surrounded by bubbles, she giggled like crazy going "Ah-CHOOO!" as I pretended to be blown away by her sneeze. By the time my wife tucked her in that night, Olive had no problem identifying these letters written in cartoony fonts.

She was reading.

Born Reading Bundle: *Luke on the Loose*

1. Read *Luke on the Loose* by Harry Bliss. If your child likes it, find other books Bliss illustrated at your local library.

2. Ask your child to continue the story: What would happen if Luke went to the beach? What would happen if he went to the mall? Draw, paint, or color these stories on paper.

3. Turn the story into a game, pretending to lose your child on the sidewalk, in the park, or at the store. They will giggle as you chase them around town, and you can talk about the book.

4. Visit Harry Bliss's website, and check out his cartoons organized by theme. Many of these are for adults, but kids will appreciate the animals and silly scenes. Compare them to the book.

5. Use TOON Books' CarTOON Makers tool online to help your child make a customized Luke cartoon.

Chapter 6

Learning with Four-Year-Old Readers

Reading with a Four-Year-Old

It is hard to explain exactly why Mo Willems's books appeal to kids.

Browsing at a bookstore, an adult might flip past the deceptively simple drawings and stories inside. But when you sit with a child on your lap reading that same book you will see those pictures light up like they were plugged into a light socket.

In Willems's Elephant and Piggie series, the dialogue hops around all corners of the page, the letters shaded and punctuated dramatically like a flashing neon sign to help you read the book out loud. It doesn't take a degree in literature to figure it out: When the letters are big and bold, you need to yell. When the characters get weepy, you need to wail like the world is going to end.

Once a parent starts following Willems's punctuation roadmap, your child will giggle all the way through the books. They are the perfect books to learn how to read with a four-year-old.

During this year, your child will grow into a fully functional kid. Dramatic books like these—those that portray strong emotion and allow you and your child to echo those emotions—are a great teaching tool to allow your kid to experience these feelings in a safe context.

According to the American Academy of Pediatrics milestones, your child will also learn the art of socializing with other kids at this age. Your child will start to make friends and work to make his or her friends happy. Books can play an invaluable role in talking about all these emotional states with your kid.

"So much of the foundation of a young child is identifying your own feelings and understanding that other people have feelings," Shira Lee Katz from Common Sense Media told me when talking about this crucial period in a kid's emotional development. She said that the right mix of books and apps can model "good ways to treat people" for your children.

Model Emotions

In my efforts to be more interactive I began to imitate the facial expressions of characters in Mo Willems's *Should I Share My Ice Cream?*, one of the Elephant and Piggie favorites in our house. In the book, the characters make all sorts of exaggerated eyebrow, forehead, and eyeball movements to telegraph their feelings. Until then, I never realized how complex facial expressions are in kids' books.

In a number of Willems's books, one character will make the devious expression that we know so well from comic book and movie super villains: the narrowed eyes and locked fingers of a bad guy saying "Heh heh heh" as they scheme an evil plan. (Obviously, I added the requisite "Heh heh heh" to our readings.) Olive mimicked my expressions, raising her eyebrows, frowning, and laughing along with the storybook characters.

These emotion-modeling reading techniques work with kids of any age, but four-year-olds can actually have a conversation about what they mean—invaluable ways to discuss tricky social issues.

Mimic emotions as you read. It's a great way to dramatize the story, but also helps your child understand emotions and other people's expressions. And it will come in handy the next time your kid throws a tantrum—you can use the books as a way to discuss overwhelming feelings.

Draw What You Read

At the same time, your child will take great artistic leaps this year. Your child will be able to draw shapes or sketch people with simple bodies. You can use this art time to sketch letters, numbers, or more advanced shapes too.

I asked Willems how to turn his books into a full-fledged interactive experience with my daughter. "Draw with her. You don't have to tell her it's cool to draw: if she sees you doodling away, she'll know." he replied. He even suggested turning dinner into a drawing experience. "At Chez Willems, we have a big roll of butcher paper that we use as our dining cloth every night so that we can have a big old family draw after dinner. I'm sure it has all sorts of developmental and social benefits besides being great fun. The important thing is that it's great fun," he said.

How to Read to a Four-Year-Old

1. Your child can hold conversations with longer sentences; start asking questions about books that require longer answers.
2. Your child can start recounting longer stories, so test him or her on what happened in favorite books.
3. Your child can sing a song or act out a story, so be sure to dramatize every reading experience.
4. They can start writing at least a few letters; point out those letters in books and keep paper handy for writing.
5. Friends are very important during this year of growth; use books as a chance to talk about his or her relationships.

Revisiting the Born Reading Playbook

When your child turns four years old, it's time to brush up on the Born Reading Playbook. Reading with a four-year-old is a radically different experience than reading with a one-year-old, even if you are still using the same techniques.

If you have been using interactive reading techniques for your child's entire life, by four years old you should be able to have rich and involved conversations about books with your child. As he or she gets older, you need to expand the range and difficulty of the questions you ask while reading.

To find out more I caught up with Grover Whitehurst, the researcher who pioneered these groundbreaking interactive reading techniques in the 1980s. I asked him where parents can look for more guidance on his methods. He suggests that parents actually watch videos of other parents doing interactive reading: "The best way to learn how to do this is to see other parents doing it. In our original videos, we had examples of parents doing a good job and we also had examples of parents screwing up—stepping all over the child's talk lines or not rewarding the child for having said something or not expanding. Learning by observation is really a great way to do this."

If you would like to see some videos about these techniques, visit the Fred Rogers Center. The Center's Early Learning Environment page has a dialogic reading video playlist, a set of short tutorials showing trained teachers reading interactively with kids. I've watched a number of these videos and learned a lot about applying these techniques with young readers. In one video, a teacher asks kids what they think about a character's decision, quickly inspiring the kids to shout out answers—the deceptively simple question generates real passion. Most importantly, you will see how easy this kind of reading can be. These teachers are not trained actors or hyperactive kids' show hosts. They read in normal voices and ask simple questions, but they manage to convert a room filled with quiet kids into spirited readers.

You can copy their questions, responses, and mannerisms to polish your own readings with your four-year-old.

In 2001, the U.S. Department of Education gave WETA public radio and television in Washington, DC, a major grant to build the Reading Rockets project. The multimedia project includes DVDs, books, podcasts, video interviews, and lots of free digital resources. The site includes worksheets that break down dialogic reading into easy-to-remember acronyms. If you visit the Born Reading website, I've linked to many of these worksheets and pages. These materials are still useful after all these years, and Whitehurst urges parents to explore them for more guidance. At the same time, Whitehurst stresses that anyone can learn these techniques.

"It's not complicated," Whitehurst says. "The basic light bulb that needs to switch on is understanding the difference between reading the story to the child and having the child eventually be able to read it to you. That kind of role reversal is a critical part of dialogic reading."

These techniques transcend socioeconomic and literacy boundaries, Whitehurst explains. "A lot of our focus was on low-income parents, some of whom were illiterate. They couldn't read themselves, but nevertheless, could figure out pretty quickly how to share a picture book with a child and have a conversation about it in very productive ways. It is pretty easy for parents to do, and once they're doing it, it's pretty hard to go back to a straight reading of the book." I think you'll notice a similar change in your reading life.

If you have not yet been using the Born Reading Playbook for interactive reading with your child, then there is no time like the present to start. Go back to the introduction and read over the guidelines. The basics are easy to implement, and you will notice the difference in your child's engagement within weeks. Remember, the benefits of interactive reading are almost immediate, and lasting, which is especially important as your child nears kindergarten.

Upping Your Reading-Aloud Game

Another thing you'll notice at this age is that your child will be an even more demanding audience. Many parents of four-year-olds quickly learn that they need to step up their game when it comes to narration. Your kid is going to demand different voices for different characters, lots of lively inflection in your voice while you read, and possibly an even higher level of engagement than before. As they become a more discerning audience, there are ways parents can keep up.

As a book reader, my greatest inspiration was LeVar Burton, the great actor and *Reading Rainbow* host. That PBS show peaked during my childhood, showing me a whole world of new books as a kid living in a small town in Michigan. I learned from his example: use a warm voice, careful inflection, enthusiasm, and act out the voices. Burton offers a few more suggestions for being a lively narrator when you're reading a book aloud: "When you interact with a narrative as a storyteller, you're playing all the parts. A good children's book gives you all the tools you need—words and pictures! All you have to do is be in the moment and engage. That's all the child is looking for." But still, he says, storytelling involves a bit of showmanship—don't be afraid to have some fun with it when you're reading to your child. "You've got to market it right! Those kids are savvy. They've got people selling to them all the time. You have to offer them a value proposition that's going to be worth their investment in time. . . . You're not just going to read a book together, it's going to be a storytelling *experience*."

If you need help learning, check out old episodes of *Reading Rainbow* or download the *Reading Rainbow* app. The show and the app both feature great professional storytellers. After listening or watching a few pros, you can be a master reading to your own children as well.

Beyond that, YouTube has *thousands* of videos of parents, teachers, and authors reading their favorite bedtime stories into a webcam. You can look up your child's favorite book on YouTube, and get inspiration from other readers. Never underestimate the power of enthusiasm. Children study your actions and your interests very closely. If you show enthusiasm for a new book or digital app, a child will follow your lead. Some grade-school teachers stick Post-it notes inside of the book as they read it out loud to the class, reminding themselves of key moments for questions or interactions. Sticky notes will probably distract your child as you read, but you could make a single note to yourself at the beginning of favorite books—reminding yourself of the interactive games, questions, and discussions your child loves while reading that particular book.

Digital Reading with a Four-Year-Old: Interaction Is Key

Now that your young reader is even more engaged in the reading process, you can make even better use of digital tools like apps, eBooks, and audiobooks. But remember that just as before, it's crucial that you, the parent, are present and engaging with your child as he or she is using these devices. Don't ignore interactive reading when thinking about digital reading.

We live at a peculiar moment in history, I realized while watching Olive plunking away on the iPad. These seductive devices could potentially wipe out interactive reading altogether:

they read the book for you and give your child addictive games to play.

No matter what, do not let mobile devices and digital books replace good old-fashioned interactive reading with your kids. The evidence has been undeniably clear for 30 years: interactive reading is a crucial activity that should be part of every parent's daily routine. Whitehurst highlights the most dangerous side of digital reading: "It loses the emotional component of sitting there with your mother or your dad and they're sharing time with you— which makes the activity, for most kids, all the more valuable, interesting, and motivating."

We don't need to wait until more research is gathered to know that an app can never replace a parent. None of the app developers I interviewed thought parents should stop reading traditional books with their kids. While working in this brand-new medium, they discovered the same thing: apps and eBooks enhance learning and enrich a kid's reading, but they are no substitute.

At the same time, you should apply Born Reading Playbook techniques and all this enthusiasm to your digital reading too. Sharing reading experiences together is a crucial part of Born Reading. Whether you are reading a print book or playing with an app, it always helps to do it together. Grover Whitehurst stresses this point: "What I would encourage parents to do until the child is clearly hooked on reading (whether digital or in print), is to be a part of the interactive experience. Rather than turning the child loose with the app, be part of that. Be sitting there with the child, taking turns and reacting to what the child is doing."

Fred Rogers Center director of education and research Michael Robb offers tips on how parents can make the app experience an interactive one rather than passively playing (or worse, letting your child play unsupervised). When you're working through an app with your child, he says, "It is good to label something. To say, 'What is that?' If there's a good chance to ask a why question, or a prediction question: What do you think is going to happen next? What do you think will happen if you fling the Angry Bird in one direction versus that direction?"

Born Reading Playbook: Guess what happens next.

These questions will reinforce a sense of narrative and enhance reading comprehension.

Conversation starters: *What do you think will happen to Little Red Riding Hood in the forest? What if you tickle Elmo?*

It's these kinds of questions—even when playing a fun game rather than an educational digital app—that can hone the kinds of critical thinking skills that are necessary for a child's future success. Robb says, "One thing that we always encourage is even after you ask, 'What do you think is going to happen?,' is follow it up with, 'And why do you think that?' When you are saying 'Why do you think that?' or 'Why might that be?' you're encouraging children to provide evidence and use some critical thinking skills to get some rationale for what they are seeing or they are hearing. That kind of critical thinking—with any kind of media, TV, or app or otherwise—is a really important twenty-first-century skill. That's a big part of getting the kid to be digital media literate."

When using apps based on your kid's favorite books, you need to make sure the digital material supplements, rather than replaces, the experience of reading your kid's favorite storybook. The only way to do this is to sit with your child, helping to tell stories with the digital stickers or pick up the print book once the device is turned off.

This chapter began with the print books of Mo Willems, but like many kids' book authors, the award-winning writer has built a few apps. In our household, we spent hours playing Pigeon Presents Mo . . . on the Go!, a digital collection that translates his print book characters into iPad material: it includes a bus-driving video game, a doodle game, a collection of digital stickers that lets your kids tell new stories with his characters. It was tempting to let Olive play this silly app by herself, but I started dropping in to play with her whenever I could. With my help, she could have more fun with the digital sticker storytelling and she could experiment with the creative doodling functions. With a few extra minutes, I turned a passive experience into an interactive one.

The app company Nosy Crow has created a number of best-selling apps for kids, but they always build in features that encourage parents to join their child in the experience. "There are also activities in every app that are a lot of fun to take part in together," Nosy Crow's digital projects and marketing manager Tom Bonnick explains. "Some of the most popular forms of interactivity are the things that parents and children get to *share* in: blowing into the iPad microphone to blow down the houses in our *The Three Little Pigs* app, making faces in front of the front-facing camera and appearing in a magical mirror in our *Cinderella* app, and copying a musical tune by playing different instruments in our *Little Red Riding Hood* app."

When you are choosing the best apps for your kids, look for similar features. Will the app encourage your child to interact with you? What moments should you share with your kid in a digital reading experience? But always keep interaction in mind.

"Some of the multimedia books provide so much, they add a lot to the experience in terms of motion graphics, audio files, and pop-ups and things like that," Caroline Knorr from Common Sense Media cautions. "What the studies have shown is that those multimedia experiences can actually limit the interaction between the child and the person they are reading with. Those interactions as the two people are reading a book are what help comprehension and improve a child's reading ability. Parents should make sure that they are providing a balance of those types of reading material."

No matter if you are reading a digital book or a print book, talk about the shared experience. Let your child recount what happened while you are driving, walking, or waiting in line. I asked these follow-up questions ever since Olive was a toddler. At first Olive did not respond or offered a simple "yes" or "no" answer. But by the time she was two and a half, a magical thing happened: she would say, "Remember that book daddy?" as we walked, telling me about her favorite books.

Researcher Lesley M. Morrow identified a correlation between children being asked to recount a story and their eventual understanding of that same story, urging teachers to include the technique in interactive reading sessions. You can build this kind of question into your everyday life, asking your child to retell stories at dinner, in the grocery store, or during long car rides.

These interactive discussions teach your child how to be a

great conversationalist in general. A young child who can discuss the plot of a favorite book or describe what happened in a digital storybook will also describe what happened at school, tell grandma how much he or she used her birthday present, or explain symptoms at the doctor's office.

Born Reading Playbook:
Encourage your child to recount the story.

This is the perfect way to reinforce a reading experience and teach storytelling.

Conversation starters: *Can you read that book to your teddy bear? What happened after elephant dropped his ice cream cone?*

What began as a cute little game to pass the time had become a way of life. Thanks to our daily interactive readings, Olive had integrated these books and her experience. "We read that book long time," Olive would say back then. It roughly translated to, "Our family has not opened that particular book in quite a few months."

She began marking the passage of time with books. They helped her understand the world and these memories surfaced at moments—reminding her of things she learned in the pages of books. This kind of critical thinking is absolutely crucial in school and in life, and I was proud to see it so early. The older she got, the more complex these literary discussions became.

Fairy Tale Reading: Turning Story Time into Playtime

Apps are another way to bring stories—especially familiar stories like fairy tales—to life on the page in a way that deepens a child's understanding of the material. Particularly for well-known fairy tales, you'll find a wealth of apps (some great, some not) that you can use to supplement your reading. For example, my daughter read *Little Red Riding Hood* on the iPad before she ever found the fairy tale in a print book.

The Nosy Crow app read Olive the story, but allowed her to take her own path through the forest. As Little Red Riding Hood traveled through the forest, little interactive flourishes let Olive play simple games to collect items that would play a role in the story. She could add things to her basket like pond water, honey, flowers, or a flute by interacting with different animals in the story.

No matter what she collected, she always ended up at Grandma's cottage, battling the big bad wolf to save Little Red Riding Hood's grandmother. The climax took subtle turns depending on what Olive had gathered in the forest, but Little Red Riding Hood always used these items to save Grandma. It was a fascinating twist on a well-known and well-loved story, and it kept Olive engaged because the story unfolded slightly differently each time. We could talk about the differences and discuss what actions she took to affect the outcome of the tale.

Once your kid gets intrigued by a story, keep feeding his or her interest. At the library, Olive discovered a whole fairy tale storybook section that included five different versions of *Little Red Riding Hood*. We flipped through all five until Olive settled on the one she liked: James Marshall's *Red Riding Hood*. While reading that book, I also explored Spotify and discovered a massive playlist of people playing the classic Disney tune, "Who's Afraid of the Big Bad Wolf?" Although that story talks about the wolf that terrorized the Three Little Pigs, Olive adored the song. We cycled through a long list of artists playing that same tune—Duke Ellington's jazz version, a squeaky chipmunk voice cover, and my favorite, a matronly Broadway star from the 1950s belting out the tune with a whole orchestra.

In short, we turned a fairy tale into a complete multimedia reading experience.

"I love the idea of blending reading of print and digital books with kids—especially familiar stories," Carisa Kluver told me. "Folktales are by definition found in many different forms, so they are among the ideal subjects for this." Kluver founded Digital-storytime.com, a resource for librarians and parents looking for the best reading apps for kids. She talked about how she integrated both print and digital reading in her household. "My child often points out [that] the books at school or in the library are the same as the ones he loves on the iPad (and vice versa)," she said. She offered the Dr. Seuss, Berenstain Bears, and Little Critter series as examples of books that can encourage your kid to explore the same book in multiple formats.

She concludes: "I can see why studies show that kids who read eBooks read more print for fun, because they are simply jazzed about reading, period, and want to find out what might be different or the same in versions across formats. I often ask my child what he notices and it provides another level of engagement with the narrative."

After all this digital and print reading, I thought it might be time to take the story out of the pages of a book (or a device), so we started playing Little Red Riding Hood in real life. This can be a good way to break the "iPad trance" that kids often get into. Even though we set strict limits on her digital device time, sometimes Olive would emerge from her limited time on the device in an iPad fog, begging for more time to play. To avoid a tantrum, we'd quickly transition into a game about whatever we'd been reading about—for a while, it was always Little Red Riding Hood. Bringing the game into real life never failed to snap her out of a digital trance. We opened her dress-up box, filled a basket with flowers, and I lay on the couch like the big bad wolf.

Thanks to endless time on the game, the script was burned into her head already. "What big teeth you have!" Olive would yell, learning the script through repeated readings. "All the better to eat you!" I cried, chasing her around the living room. The combination was enough to keep her off the device the rest of the day.

The Born Reading Playbook techniques work with both print books and great storytelling apps. They also highlight the radically different skills used in both kinds of play. The app can teach a story, charm, and even produce a creative trance. But imaginative play reinforces the all-important movement, the vivid drama of spoken storytelling.

It's easy to turn any exciting book or app into a game—just reenact the story with some simple props. Your child's imagination will do the rest of the work.

Born Reading Playbook: Dramatize the story.

You can mime sweeping when you see a broom or pretend to eat the character's food. This will help your child match the concepts to the words, a pillar of the interactive reading experience.

Conversation starters: *Do you want to be Little Red Riding Hood? What would the big bad wolf wear?*

Too often, parents see books and digital books as a competition, worrying that one reading experience will overwhelm the other.

By the time Olive tackled the Little Red Riding Hood story, she didn't see the story as something limited to a single format, device, or art form. With a classic story like *The Three Little Pigs* or *Little Red Riding Hood*, you can explore a whole range of storytelling options: apps, storybooks, or a family game.

"Personally I'm not sure that print books and apps *are* in competition with each other, even when they're based on the same stories," Nosy Crow's Tom Bonnick replied when I asked about the digital library divide. "When a child picks up an iPad, our apps are not competing with physical, printed books for that child's attention, they're competing with every other form of media available on the iPad—films, games, music, the Internet. That's why we try and make our apps as compelling and exciting as reading experiences as possible: we don't want reading to be the 'boring' option. I also believe that reading books and using apps offer fundamentally different experiences for children, and I would never want to replace the printed book (particularly given that we also publish them!)."

If your child responds passionately to a fairy tale, you should expand the experience beyond books, apps, and games.

Online, I found a host of free digital versions of classic fairy tales. If you are looking for more story ideas or different digital books to explore with kids, you should look at these options as well. On the Born Reading website, I've laid out a number of free fairy tale links for you to explore.

Born Reading Bundle: *Little Red Riding Hood*

1. Find a few different versions of the classic story at your local library. Read them all and have your child pick a favorite.

2. Download Nosy Crow's *Little Red Riding Hood* app. If your kid enjoys it, the *Three Little Pigs* app will also be popular.

3. Turn the story into a game, dressing up like Little Red Riding Hood and the big bad wolf. Dramatize the story as much as you like.

4. On Project Gutenberg, download free digital copies of *Household Stories by the Brothers Grimm* and *Grimms' Fairy Tales* to find more fairy tale stories.

5. Explore classic fairy tale songs on Spotify like "Who's Afraid of the Big Bad Wolf?" I've built a special Spotify playlist you can listen to on my Born Reading website.

Music and Reading: Putting Stories to Song

Olive has always loved music. She could pick out a Bob Dylan song at two years old and belted out "Happy Birthday" and the ABC song in the bathtub countless nights as a toddler. She could sit for 15 minutes straight watching street musicians play. She would sit on her grandma's piano and flip the pages of the children's song book—"Read me this one," she'd say.

I know how to read music and plunk out one-handed tunes on the piano, so I could help her "read" the songs. It was a different kind of literacy, but a very important part of our lives.

If your child enjoys pounding on buckets, plunking piano keys, or strumming a guitar there are many different books that can help your child learn how to talk about music.

We found *Ben's Trumpet*, a gorgeous picture book by Rachel Isadora filled with stylized pictures of jazz instruments. Olive would scrutinize the individual instruments, learning the shape of each one.

We continued to follow her music obsession with *This Jazz Man* by Karen Ehrhardt, a brilliant kids' book that fills the old "This Old Man" nursery rhyme with jazz musicians. I used this book to introduce Olive to great artists like Cab Calloway, Charlie Parker, and Bill "Bojangles" Robinson.

Olive also liked *Violet's Band* by Angela Johnson and Laura Huliska-Beith. The book follows the adventures of a little baby who grows up playing music on everything she can find. Eventually, she connects with a few other cool kids and builds her own band.

You should share all kinds of music with your kids, from

classical to rock to jazz to rap. All these genres have something to offer a growing mind. The poet Nikki Giovanni edited *Hip Hop Speaks to Children*, a classic music-related book. Following the model of Sourcebooks' *Poetry Speaks to Children* anthology, the collection explores the glorious history of hip hop. It exposes kids to Langston Hughes, the Sugar Hill Gang, Kanye West, and Gwendolyn Brooks in an eclectic mix. The book contains a CD, introducing your kids to some classic rap and poetry. You can use it to transition into your own hip hop favorites while driving in the car or hosting a home dance party. When I asked Giovanni about her collection, she compared hip hop to opera.

"I think it's quite fair to say the basis of opera is gossip and jealousy and love. The things ordinary people talk about," she explained. "Opera is classic because of the universal themes that got expressed. And I think it is safe to say hip hop will be classical one day for the same reason: hip hop is the vernacular of the people. This is a sound, like jazz, that has gone around the world. It speaks to the legitimate concerns of all people in all languages."

Hip Hop Speaks to Children will give both parents and kids an education in the roots and growth of rap. Exploring these lyrics on the page will convert even the staunchest hip hop critic. These songs are a new kind of poetry, carrying a host of musical traditions into the future.

What can a kid learn from hip hop? It is storytelling, plain and simple. And you will go crazy if you spend your life only listening to little kid music. Share the music and songwriting that you appreciate with your kids. It will make car rides and home dance parties so much more enjoyable.

"You don't always teach by preaching," Giovanni concludes. " 'Do as I say, not as I do' is a cliché, but a lot of parents live by it. We all learn by observing what people actually do. If parents enjoy poetry, storytelling, hip hop, or anything else, that joy will spearhead to the kids. It's always fun to memorize. I know a lot of people don't believe in it but it's a good way for kids to catch the drift even if the politics aren't always clear. A lot of hip hop is nonsense (like a lot of fairy tales), so memorizing is fun. Enjoy the ride yourself and the kids will squeal with you."

As Olive got older, I started to add more media into the mix. We downloaded ABC Music, a slick app that really showcases the young research potential of tablets. The app mixed letter identification, simple games, and music, helping her learn the sound, shape, and use of a huge variety of instruments from harmonica to bongo to rain sticks. The app let Olive surf between a huge range of instruments seamlessly, and she mastered the alphabet button interface quickly. Within the app, Olive could see the individual instruments, read the letters that spell them, and watch a simple, short, and safe video about them. We all learned a lot about musical instruments using the app together, like how rain sticks were made in South America by pounding cactus needles into a dried cactus trunk.

Olive extended the app into real life, pounding on upside-down buckets in the tub like bongos, hitting a tin cup, a little cup, and a big blue bucket like a full drum kit. She screwed her eyes shut in the bath, splashing water out of the tub as she pounded her two-handed beat.

The app showed her all the percussion instruments from around the world, traveling from bells to drums to rain-sticks to gongs. One video showed a gong master playing his enormous collection. She got an advanced music appreciation course before she even entered kindergarten.

Born Reading Playbook: Show your child the world outside your neighborhood.

Even if your child hasn't seen France or New York City or Guatemala or the Pacific Ocean, books can show him or her these places. Make sure you choose books that explore diverse places, cultures, and stories, and follow your child's interests when he or she loves a setting.

Conversation starters: *Do you want to know about Antarctica? Should I show you where France is?*

Online music subscription services like Spotify, Google Play Music, or Rhapsody give parents access to vast libraries of music on digital devices—ideal music educational tools. While reading *This Jazz Man*, I introduced Olive to Cab Calloway's "Minnie the Moocher" and Louie Armstrong's "Oh When the Saints Go Marching In" during a particularly long car ride. Olive could call out the names of her favorite instruments in the back seat. I could scroll through 70 years of jazz history in a couple minutes.

As we've discussed, the best way to keep the conversation going is to supplement any interest with more exposure on different media. So to further our jazz discussions, I could show Olive a video of Armstrong blowing his horn and another video of Calloway singing and dancing in *The Blues Brothers* back home on the iPad. This kind of time travel between musical eras and media would have been unimaginable even just ten years ago. Olive will have the power to shuttle through endless libraries for the rest of her life. Her generation can chase obsessions in ways we never dreamed.

You can teach your child how to be a new kind of detective. Just like reading a book is a learned set of motions, so is creativity and exploration. These early trips through virtual libraries of music will prepare children for research papers, novel writing, work memos, legal briefs, speeches, or songs. This early education will serve them well wherever they travel.

Born Reading Bundle: *Hip Hop Speaks to Children*

1. Read *Hip Hop Speaks to Children* and spend some time talking about words, music, and instruments with your kid. Play the CD over and over, letting your kids attach the music to the words.
2. Check out more music books like *This Jazz Man* by Karen Ehrhardt or *Violet's Music* by Angela Johnson. Talk about your favorite instruments.
3. Download ABC Music or another music-related app. Let your kids explore instruments at friends' houses or the music store.
4. Play your favorite music. Use Spotify or other digital music services to quickly jump between eras of music in the car or when dancing at home.
5. Watch videos of your favorite musicians with your kids on YouTube or DVD. Talk to your kids about the performances.

Reading Rainbow and Literary Television: Making Choices Count

As your child gets older, they can start to entertain themselves a little bit more. But while this can be a relief to parents, it also brings a new set of problems.

Specifically, your child will start to get ever more strident opinions about what he or she wants to watch . . . and you won't always agree with his or her choices. As she got older, we started to give Olive a bit more input on what she wanted to watch during her digital device time. But whenever we let Olive browse with the iPad, she starting enjoying the process of flipping through all the various content choices (going quickly from one to the next, focusing on nothing in particular) rather than sticking with a single learning tool and exploring it with us. If a great app didn't offer enough selection, she would switch to some other piece of entertainment instead. Soon, she was wasting too much time shuffling through stupid children's videos and had lost interest in many of the digital books that we put on her device.

This was a terrible habit and is an unfortunate side effect of digital tools—for both kids and adults. Think about your own viewing habits: with millions of websites, eBooks, and videos at our fingertips online, restless browsing has crippled our reading. We've all lost some of our ability to focus.

But it doesn't have to be that way. We rehabilitated Olive's mindless browsing with the *Reading Rainbow* app. The app is free, but if you pay a monthly or six-month subscription fee, your child can access a library of more than 300 digital books from a variety of publishers. The selection ranges from classic picture books to nonfiction wildlife books to nursery rhymes.

The app offered Olive a seemingly endless collection of choices, but instead of choosing between one annoying kids' video and another annoying kids' video, she browsed a library hand-picked by LeVar Burton. "The whole point of the app is that it is a mobile library of books and videos so that the child can be the master of their own journey," Burton told me. "Look what technology offers: you can have a library of books on a tablet computer these days. You can travel with virtually a library of books. That is a miracle only made possible in the modern era by technology."

It's a maxim Olive's mom and I are trying to follow in our own lives. When we switched to streaming video through Netflix, we stopped watching traditional television. Instead of making mindless TV choices based on limited availability, we could browse through a larger selection to find the kind of movie we wanted to watch. The *Reading Rainbow* app provides the same experience for young readers.

One of the first books Olive discovered on the app was *What Will You Be, Sara Mee?* by Kate Aver Avraham and Anne Sibley O'Brien. It tells the story of a Korean American family holding a traditional ceremony for a toddler. The little baby sits in front of a table filled with symbols of different professions: ink for a writer, a book for a scholar, a brush for an artist. The baby's older brother narrates the book and explains the ceremony. The baby's choice points toward her future profession. Olive carefully read the entire book, and could ask questions about what those relatively abstract symbols represent.

That was the best thing about the *Reading Rainbow* show. It always showed kids a diverse, educational, and entertaining selection of books—a tough balance to strike, I discovered while researching this book. The app also includes educational videos just like the *Reading Rainbow* show, as LeVar Burton tours interesting locations from the insides of a submarine to the White House to a remote island.

The app can help break a child's bad Internet habits. You can sample five books for free on the app to see how it works. In our house, that alone was worth the price of admission. If your child is a reluctant reader, I recommend you try the *Reading Rainbow* app for a month. Whether your child is reading a digital book or watching a video inside this ecosystem you will know that they are exploring safe and useful material. Parents can access a reading log on the app, seeing what books their kids like and how long they read them. This is invaluable intelligence if you are looking for more books or activities to offer your child offline. The app adds a new book and video every week, keeping your child's reading list fresh. Burton notes that this is especially important for families. "The conversation never gets stale. We are what we read."

Beyond this app, there is a virtually infinite supply of videos for kids online. But kids need your help.

Watching free videos on YouTube can seem like an attractive choice for parents. Google will feed your child an endless stream of age-appropriate videos with characters that they love. But you will quickly see the destructive power of the Internet, providing entertainment so vast that a child could spend weeks tabbing through three-minute videos. Even worse, if you start with a quality kids' video on YouTube, Google's search algorithm will churn out some cut-rate alternatives. Within a few minutes, your child will be watching videos with bad animation, terrible music, and the barest hint of educational content.

If you let your child watch videos on a tablet device, you should check out the PBS Kids app instead. The free app contains an amazing collection of videos without commercials, including lots of videos that can supplement books you are already reading in print: Dr. Seuss, Curious George, or *Sesame Street* characters. PBS Kids gave us a small library of free videos we could trust Olive to browse.

Finally, remember to constantly refer your young reader back to books, even when you're working with a great educational app. Every family must strike its own balance for media, but for us the carefully curated digital collections at places like PBS Kids and *Reading Rainbow* gave us an easy way to tie Olive's TV time back to books. If Olive watched a Curious George or Dr. Seuss video, I always broke out a copy of *The Cat in the Hat* or *Curious George Takes a Job* later that week to remind her of the original books. Revisit the source material as often as possible. We need to draw very clear lines in between these types of experiences, making sure twenty-first-century kids understand the value of both mediums.

PBS Kids App Shows with Print Book Counterparts

Show: *The Cat in the Hat Knows a Lot About That!*
Related Books: *Why Oh Why Are Deserts Dry?*, *Ice Is Nice!*, and *Safari, So Good!*

Show: *Curious George*
Related Books: *Curious George Flies a Kite*, *Curious George Goes to the Hospital*, and *Curious George Gets a Medal*

Show: *Arthur*
Related Books: *Arthur's Nose*, *Arthur's Reading Race*, and *Arthur Writes a Story*

Show: *Dinosaur Train*
Related Books: *Dinosaur Train, I Am a T. Rex!*, and *Hey, Buddy!*

Show: *Sesame Street*
Related Books: *Baker, Baker, Cookie Maker; Elmo Loves You;* and *Shake a Leg!*

Reading Math Books with Your Child: Make It Fun!

Even if your little one is tiny, you probably have a few ABC books on your shelf. But if you are going to spend these early years reading to your kids, you should think about including some math and science in your reading diet, too. Many American kids suffer from math or science anxiety, and these early years provide the perfect opportunity to instill a lifelong sense of comfort with these tricky subjects.

After earning a degree in astrophysics from Princeton and an MBA from the Wharton School of Business, a young mother named Laura Overdeck vowed to help kids cope with math. She founded the *Bedtime Math* series as an email newsletter, giving parents simple and fun math problems to share with their kids before bed.

"I think our country has a culture around math that is not entirely positive," she told me. "There's a small crowd that loves math and they're enthusiastic. There are kids in school who pick up math easily and they really love it. But for a lot of people, that is really not the experience. We have a lot of adults with math anxiety and what happens then is, as parents, they cede that to their kids inadvertently. It's not on purpose, but kids' first teachers are their parents."

While reading math and science books will help your kids in school, there are far more important things at stake. Overdeck called it "an emergency," explaining how it affects the health of our very country. "We are not breeding the talent we need to have innovation. If someone is going to cure cancer or build a better iPhone antenna, somebody's got to understand technology and you need to understand math. We all as a society are responsible for fixing this."

She turned her *Bedtime Math* project into both a book and an app that you can share with your kids. As she entered the book market, she was appalled to discover that ABC books vastly outnumbered math books in the educational arena. "There were three times as many ABC books and they were way more fun, about Bob the Builder or *A is for Zebra* [by Mark Shulman]," she recalls. "But the more disturbing thing was that the math books were all workbooks. Every single one, drill drill drill. We have to look at ourselves as parents and say, what are we teaching our kids about math? It's very different from how we teach the alphabet."

Her words shocked me, but she was right. Like most parents, I spent much more time playing with the alphabet with Olive than I did with numbers. You can make a conscious effort to familiarize your child with numbers, even from this early age. Try to use the same strategies you employ to teach your child his or her letters. While reading a book with easy quantities, you can stop to count them. If a book has a spaceship countdown, you can use your fingers to do the counting in real life. Well before Olive knew her numbers, I would tell her the correct count of objects on a page and guide her finger to count small quantities.

Researchers call this "scaffolding," when you share the right answer with your child, guiding him or her beyond what they already have learned and preparing him or her to eventually answer correctly. In 1990, Lesley M. Morrow, currently the coordinator of the literacy program at Rutgers University's Graduate School of Education, published "Assessing Children's Understanding of Story through Their Construction and Reconstruction of Narrative," a paper describing a number of interactive reading techniques in greater detail. The paper stresses the importance of scaffolding in the classroom, but it is valuable whenever an adult reads to a child.

Born Reading Playbook: Guide your child beyond what they already know.

As often as possible, guide book reading into new material.

Conversation starters: *Do you know why his car did not work? Should I tell you how he cooked the soup?*

You can make math a part of everyday life. Following Overdeck's advice, we made sure Olive could do very basic math while performing one of her favorite tasks: cooking. Gradually, she became aware of quantity and measurement.

"With my kids, I started pretty early, asking them to help me bake chocolate chip cookies. What kid doesn't want to help do that?" asks Overdeck. Even fairly advanced concepts can be introduced by incorporating math into everyday activities. "If you're working with fractions, ratios; when you multiply a recipe, what are you doing exactly? How do you work those numbers? You can get as sophisticated as you want with your eight-, nine-, ten-year-old with the math. Even with three- or four-year-olds, you can have them count out how many scoops of chocolate chips. They're happy to do that and they are actually learning math without even realizing it."

If your kids respond well to this kind of early math, you should take a look at apps like Park Math or Montessori Numberland. These two apps take kids through a number of simple math concepts and work for a whole range of preschool learners. While the Park Math app teaches kids key concepts for school, the developers at Duck Duck Moose made sure that fairly young children could play it.

"Park Math aligned with Kindergarten Common Core Standards from a math perspective, but we've designed the interactivity so that even a two- or three-year-old can play with it," Duck Duck Moose co-founder Caroline Hu Flexer told me. "Just like when they are playing with blocks in the real world, they start getting a number sense from just interacting with things. In our Park Math app, for example, you can move ducks up a slide and start counting that way or start understanding some concepts of addition and subtraction. We've really worked with educators to see how children are developing those early numeracy concepts and tried to reflect that in our apps."

What makes a good math book? Overdeck spent a lot of time reading through early math books and discovered that the majority of books don't let kids have fun with the numbers. She outlined the contrast between fun math problems and drilled math problems. When you are looking for math books for your kids, be sure to weigh the fun factor:

"[In textbooks] it's worksheets, it's really dry. Then they get into word problems, and it's still really dry. It's like adding pencils and pens. The freedom we have at *Bedtime Math* is that I can write math problems about ninjas and roller coasters and candy. No school textbook will talk about candy, because that's like a bad word. But kids love candy and I can write about candy. I can write about ninjas and their weapons. You could never put that in a textbook." Because apps are freed from some of the decision-making-by-committee that constrains school districts and textbook manufacturers, apps can be a bit more playful and a lot more fun for kids. "Part of the problem is that our committees that write these textbooks beat all the life out of it," Overdeck laments. "The results are very dry, and it's not making it appealing for kids when it can be. You don't *have* to have candy and ninjas in there. Kids like flamingos, they like roller coasters. That's what our math problems should be about."

Born Reading Bundle: *Bedtime Math*

1. Get a print copy of *Bedtime Math* or subscribe to the email newsletter. Read these problems with your kids every night. They have different age levels, giving even little kids a chance to participate.
2. When reading books, ask math-related questions: How many penguins are on this page? Could two giraffes fit inside the garage?
3. Make math problems in real life. While cooking, building, walking, or any other daily activity, look for ways to make simple math problems. How many cars do you think can fit in that garage? How many cups of flour did we put in the pizza?
4. Download some math-oriented apps like Numberland, Park Math, or *Bedtime Math*.
5. Watch *Sesame Street* videos on YouTube. You can search by numbers or characters. Start with The Count; he'll give your kid plenty of exciting counting in a silly package.

Reading Science with Your Child:
Take It Beyond the Book Pages

The great physicist Neil Degrasse Tyson explained it in a famous speech: "Kids are born scientists." Just watch your kid discover an anthill or pour water between buckets in the tub. Everything they do is an experiment, but our cultural focus on tests and memorization can destroy kids' sense of curiosity and exploration.

Black Out! by Ginjer Clarke was the first kids' science book I brought into our house. The book opens with a simple premise: "Do you ever wonder what happens at night when you are asleep?" After battling with your child over going to sleep for a few years, you will understand why a kid might wonder this.

The book catalogs strange, dangerous, and awe-inspiring animals, accented with vivid nature drawings by Pete Mueller. We saw razor-toothed fish at the blackest bottom of the ocean, cute bug-eyed bush babies hunting lizards, glowworms snaring moths in shimmering silk traps, and the bizarre face of the star-nosed mole with 22 pink feelers wiggling on his face as he chased worms. It focuses on scary predators without gore, the pictures capturing the moment before gobbling up the prey. The book has a simple vocabulary that is punctuated by advanced science terms like "nocturnal" or "echolocation."

I asked Ginjer Clarke for suggestions about using interactive reading techniques with her books. She explained how recent updates from her publisher actually built participation into the books. Her editor includes a set of suggested activities and thoughtful questions for parents at the start of each book. "There are several types of activities similar to those you would see used in classrooms to enhance reading comprehension, such as Compare/Contrast, Make Connections, Comprehension, Creative Writing, Research, and Vocabulary," she explained. While some books come with these questions and activities baked in from the publisher, any parent can start to expand on the ideas in a science book with his or her own kid.

Clarke shared two sample post-reading questions with me. While your four-year-old won't be writing down an answer to these questions yet, they could prompt a post-reading discussion or drawing.

Here's a writing prompt from *Freak Out!: Animals Beyond Your Wildest Imagination*: "At the end of the book, the author asks a question: 'Have you ever dreamed of an imaginary animal?' Write a paragraph about an animal you imagine. What makes it strange, insane, crazy, bizarre, or amazing?"

Here's a post-reading activity from *Baby Elephant*: "At the end of the book, the author writes, 'Baby elephants are a lot like you!' Discuss why this statement is true."

You can use her model to fashion your own science-related questions.

"Nonfiction is great for providing a jumping-off point for further discussion and looking up additional facts about the animals or other material that is being presented," Clarke adds. "Once parents get comfortable with the type of questions that most intrigue their specific children, they can translate that new skill to enhance reading comprehension with all kinds of books."

Her books encourage interactive reading, loaded with nice sounds to repeat like "swoosh," "poof," or "snap," dramatizing science facts with plenty of action like swooping, pouncing, and chomping predators. The book is very easy to act out. Your kid can soar like a barn owl chasing a mouse or snap like a sleek shark in the ocean. You can also extend these science conversations into your life, discovering what kind of creatures live in your neighborhood at night.

But don't let the activities end with books. If you are looking for a hands-on activity, Clarke added a great example of a home science experiment you can use after reading *Black Out!* "I created a recipe for Owl Barf Balls, which is yummy no-bake candy that looks like owl pellets (the food they regurgitate) but tastes great." (Kids this age are starting to really respond to the gross-out factor, so this would be a big hit in most preschools.) If you want to take it a step further, she urged parents to buy real owl pellets for sale on science education websites. "Parents can help their children dissect the pellets with tweezers to find the bones of the last meal the owl ate and try to determine what that animal might be," she said in an email interview.

Black Out! also gave us a chance to talk about the coyotes around us in Los Angeles, wildlife prowling at the corner of our lives. Once a coyote crossed in front of our headlights on a late-night drive. I shivered a bit as the coyote crossed, just like you will shiver when reading about unlucky mice, moths, and worms gobbled by predators in the book.

Many kids gravitate to these somewhat brutal nature stories, and Clarke caters to our primal fears with other books like *Gross Out!*, *Freak Out!*, and *Bug Out!* You can extend the conversation into your backyard, park, or museum. Clarke offers these suggestions: "Science is a basic fact of everyday living if we just take time to notice it. Go outside and pick up rocks to see what bugs live underneath them. Look up in the trees for nests and listen for birds. Stay up late one night and see what other types of animals come out after dark. Talk about that day's weather. It's amazing what you can discover (and rediscover) when you try to see the world through your child's eyes and attempt to explain how the world works."

When your kid responds well to a particular book, you should head straight to Google for more information. Most authors and publishers have web pages dedicated to their children's books, usually packed with free material for kids.

For instance, Clarke has a huge collection of extra science resources for kids, including projects you can do at home. I urge you to look up all of your child's favorite authors and find some extracurricular activities online—it will make your job much easier and make playtime a little more interesting. If parents want to explore more online resources, Clarke recommends the National Geographic Kids website and World Wildlife Fund's "Games" section for children. If you look online at the Born Reading website you can see some YouTube videos of their pages and extra resources to explore with some of my recommended books.

As your kid gets older, Nosy Crow's Rounds: Parker Penguin app is perfect for exploring the world of preschool science. It dramatizes the life cycle of a penguin with a series of interactive storybook pages. Your kid helps the penguin waddle, slide, and swim in an uncluttered frozen world. The swimming was my favorite part: it was relaxing to steer the creature through a blue, hushed sea. Eventually you can help your penguin eat fish, a twenty-first-century version of *Pac-Man* embedded in a digital storybook. Once you eat, your penguin emerges from the ocean and barks to attract his mate. Your child will help make a love connection and care for a penguin egg. When the baby is born, it grows up and the story starts all over again. The gentle book is filled with solid science vocabulary and facts about penguin diet, lifestyle, and life cycle.

The scenes are catchy enough to charm a video game–hungry kid, but the smooth action won't have you worried about violence or overstimulation. These tools were designed as a cross between a book and a digital education tool, as Nosy Crow's Tom Bonnick explains: "The Rounds apps are our first entry into 'educational' storytelling—they're still narrative driven, with characters and a story, but they're also filled with a lot of facts about animals and the environment. The apps are also a good starting point for broader discussions about life science, I think—we made them hoping that they would spark an enthusiasm for biology and encourage curiosity in children."

Children will uncover many of these facts by reading and playing with the app—the characters reveal bits about their biological lives as the story unfolds. You can follow one teacher's lead and turn the app into a whole learning experience. "One teacher created a whole lesson plan around Rounds: Franklin Frog, and had his class narrate the story themselves, draw other animals in the same circular style, and write their own animal life cycles," Bonnick told me.

Reading-related questions are vital during this time in your child's life, helping him or her process more complex books and practice responding to tougher questions. In 1977, Boston University reading and language professor James E. Flood wrote a paper about "Parental Styles in Reading Episodes with Young Children," stressing how parents, teachers, and caregivers need to ask questions throughout the reading process. According to Flood's study, the best interactive reading sessions should be filled with questions: before you even open the book, during the reading, and after the book is finished. These science materials are perfect for posing questions before, after, and during the reading experience.

Born Reading Playbook:
Ask lots and lots of questions.

Questions are the foundation of interactive reading, and should continue as long as you are reading with your child. Be sure to ask questions before, during, and after the reading experience.

Conversation starters: *Before we start, what do you know about penguins? Now that we have finished reading, could you draw a picture of a penguin?*

Ultimately, you will be preparing your child for an educational system that is placing more value in the ability to process nonfiction texts. Children's author Melissa Stewart explains how these reading habits can serve your kid in school eventually. "To prepare students for more exposure to nonfiction at school, parents should bring more of these titles into their homes," she said. "Many nonfiction picture books make wonderful read-alouds. The key is to choose titles in consultation with your child. Find out what topics he or she is interested in or what he or she would like to learn more about. Then head to the library or bookstore and pick up a selection of books on those topics."

Reading for discovery can change the course of your child's life. You can help him or her maintain a natural curiosity throughout school. This precious flame of scientific curiosity can be snuffed so easily. Don't let your child lose that sense of wonder. Follow up science books and apps with zoo visits or natural science museum trips. Make sure part of your home library is dedicated to science, gross or scary as it may be.

Don't let that fire go out.

Born Reading Bundle: *Black Out!*

1. Read a print copy of *Black Out!* by Ginjer L. Clarke.
   Discuss all the reading questions at the end of the book.
2. Draw, paint, or use clay to explore themes in the book.
   Have your child make a wiggly worm or fluttering moth.
3. Download science-related apps like Rounds: Parker Penguin or Rounds: Franklin Frog.
4. Watch National Geographic Kids and World Wildlife Fund videos online. Look for videos of your child's favorite animal.
5. Go outside and look for animals. Let your child take pictures, draw, or measure the wildlife in your backyard.

Book Suggestions for Four-Year-Olds

Black Out!: Animals That Live in the Dark by Ginjer L. Clarke
Gorgeous scientific illustrations of nocturnal creatures mixed with evocative facts about some strange, dangerous, and gross animals. A great introduction to science at any age.

Hip Hop Speaks to Children edited by Nikki Giovanni
This glorious anthology mixes Langston Hughes poetry with Queen Latifah songs, a unique blend of music education, history,

poetry, and storytelling with a killer soundtrack the whole family can appreciate.

This Jazz Man by Karen Ehrhardt and R. G. Roth (illustrator)
This book uses the "This Old Man" nursery rhyme to introduce jazz musicians. We used this book to meet great artists like Cab Calloway, Charlie Parker, and Bill "Bojangles" Robinson.

Gorilla by Anthony Browne
Beautifully painted book about a sad single parent and his imaginative daughter. A safe and evocative way to explore intense emotions about family, loneliness, and fears of abandonment.

The Shark King by R. Kikuo Johnson
This is a comic book retelling of a Hawaiian folktale. The book features stunning action sequences, magical transformation, and a story Olive wanted to hear over and over.

Tar Beach by Faith Ringgold
This book is literally a work of art based on a story quilt that the artist, illustrator, and writer made in the 1980s. It is now part of the Guggenheim Museum's collection. It helps children explore complex themes like dreams, city life, poverty, and their parents' work lives.

George and Martha by James Marshall
A book about the adventures of two sincere but slightly dim-witted hippos. The book unfolds in small chapters, stories perfectly plotted for reading with a kid. If they love this book, there are many more and some elegant audiobook versions as well.

Little Red Riding Hood by Jerry Pinkney
A longer look at the classic fairy tale. The author doesn't sugarcoat it, but has a light touch with dark corners of a great story. The intricate illustrations can spark plenty of questions.

The Munschworks Grand Treasury by Robert N. Munsch,
  Michael Kusugak, Michael Martchenko (illustrator),
  Hélène Desputeaux (illustrator), and Vladyana Kyrkorka
  (illustrator)
An enormous collection of kids' stories by a writer with an unmistakable style. The book is filled with surreal adventures of kids who attempt to fly airplanes or fight dragons, every story filtered through a kooky sense of humor.

I Broke My Trunk! by Mo Willems
One of a long line of Elephant and Piggie books, this title follows the adventures of two highly animated friends. Elephant appears with his trunk in a cast, and he tells a long, convoluted story about how it happened. Olive laughed out loud for the entire book.

App Recommendations for Four-Year-Olds

Alien Assignment by Fred Rogers Center
One of the only apps that actually *requires* parental participation. Kids use a smartphone as a scientific device, taking pictures and exploring the backyard as part of a cosmic scavenger hunt.

Available in the Apple App Store; works with iPhone, iPod Touch (fourth and fifth generation), iPad 2, iPad (third and fourth generation), and iPad Mini. Needs iOS 4.3 or later.

Montessori Numberland HD by Les Trois Elles Interactive
A simple app for teaching numbers and simple math concepts. It shows kids how to recognize, count, and trace with the numbers 0–9. It all follows Montessori school principles as they learn.

Available in the Apple App Store; works with iPhone (3GS, 4, 4S, and 5), iPod Touch (third, fourth, and fifth generation), and iPad. Needs iOS 4.3 or later.

ABC Music by Peapod Labs
This inspiring app teaches kids the alphabet by showing them pictures, videos, and puzzles about a wide variety of musical instruments. You'll learn a lot by just playing along.

Available in the Apple App Store; works with iPhone, iPod Touch, and iPad. Needs iOS 4.3 or later.

Bedtime Math by Bedtime Math Foundation
An app meant to expand upon the *Bedtime Math* book or website, introducing math in a fun context for the littlest kids. The founder recommends not using devices at bedtime, so use the app as a digital supplement to night math.

Available in the Apple App Store; works with iPhone (3GS, 4, 4S, and 5), iPod Touch (third, fourth, and fifth generation), and iPad. Needs iOS 5.0 or later.

Little Red Riding Hood by Nosy Crow
A gorgeous digital retelling of a classic story. The new interactive material is captivating and your kid will want to read and play more after reading this book. Use with other versions in print.

Available in the Apple App Store; works with iPhone (3GS, 4, 4S, and 5), iPod Touch (third, fourth, and fifth generation), and iPad. Needs iOS 4.3 or later.

Toontastic by Launchpad Toys
This big-kid version of the storytelling app lets kids write, record, and share their stories with other kids. They can choose from a huge variety of online characters and a whole range of stories.

Available in the Apple App Store, but only works with iPad and requires iOS 5.1 or later.

i Learn With Poko: Seasons and Weather! by Tribal Nova
This science app shows little kids the basics of weather, seasons, and the calendar. These will all be important topics as your kid heads to school, so the app gives a valuable early introduction to these fun topics.

Available in the Apple App Store; works with iPhone (3GS, 4, 4S, and 5), iPod Touch (third, fourth, and fifth generation), and iPad. Needs iOS 4.3 or later.

PBS Kids Video by PBS Kids
A video app that contains ad-free short videos for kids. Many of these shows are based on beloved kids' books or TV shows like *Curious George*, *Sesame Street*, or Dr. Seuss. Scroll through individual shows to choose the right content for your kid, rather than random TV or YouTube browsing.

Available in the Apple App Store; works with iPhone, iPod Touch, and iPad. Requires iOS 4.3 or later.

Available in Google Play for Android devices.

Available in Amazon Appstore for Android devices.

Sid's Science Fair by PBS Kids
Based on PBS's *Sid the Science Kid* TV show, this science app covers many of the common childhood science-fair themes in a

digital frame. Your kid can learn how to examine, sort, and organize chronologically.

> Available in the Apple App Store; works with iPhone, iPod Touch, and iPad.
> Requires iOS 3.2.2 or later.
> Available in Google Play for Android devices.
> Available in Amazon Appstore for Android devices.

Pigeon Presents Mo . . . on the Go! by Mo Willems
This digital collection supplements the storybooks of Mo Willems, encouraging your child to doodle inside the app or tell new stories using sticker versions of the characters from his books.

> Available in the Apple App Store; works with iPhone (3GS, 4, 4S, and 5), iPod Touch (third, fourth, and fifth generation), and iPad. Needs iOS 4.3 or later.

Interlude: Mastering the Art of Storytelling

As Olive got older, we started telling her goodnight stories, the final step after her bath and bedtime book in our laps. Her mom and I both invented a whole series of stories to tell her, and Olive always asked for more until we finally slipped out of her bedroom.

My favorite story was called "Party at the Library." In this story, I woke up Olive in the middle of the night and we rode the bus to a huge party at the Santa Monica Public Library. Olive ate all of her favorite foods, ending with a big slice of cake. Then Bob Dylan showed up and sang my favorite song ("Shelter from the Storm") and we danced with all her friends. On the way home, Olive got to drive the bus by herself. I always ended the story by tucking her into bed once again.

Any parent can build bedtime stories like stacking LEGO bricks. You take a few of your child's favorite moments (library visits, parties with cake, or favorite songs) and you stick them together into a simple journey. As Olive got older, she would ask me to add other people or events from her life. The framework was so simple, I could add almost anything to our nighttime visit to the library.

Storytelling is about making sense of the world, one of the most crucial skills your child can learn. By telling stories, you show your child how to turn his or her experiences into a (more or less) coherent narrative. These skills will be absolutely crucial in school, helping your child to do everything from answering questions in class to writing term papers in high school. The earlier your child learns the skills of storytelling, the richer his or her creative life can be.

Toddler storytelling does not require a parent to be a great writer like J. K. Rowling. You can spice up your stories with spaceships, ghosts, or treasure hunts, but you have to start with raw materials that are familiar—favorite toys, beloved characters, repeated rituals, foods they love, and settings they have memorized after days and days of repetition.

I adapted the great science fiction film *Planet of the Apes* as "Planet of the Cats," a space adventure starring Olive and her friend. But you don't even have to be that fancy. My wife would let Olive give her a simple set of story ingredients at bedtime: "making bread" or "visiting grandma," and my wife could always spin a story out of the request by making a few silly things happen in the course of these mundane events.

Olive loved mundane stories. For months, she would make us retell the story of a brunch we had with our friend Tyler, reciting the food we ate, seating arrangement, and weather like it was a great adventure.

By the time she turned two and a half, Olive could tell simple stories if I asked her to recount a favorite book or memory. The stories got more complicated every single week.

I found a whole suite of digital apps for kids to extend their storytelling.

Olive and I spent a long time playing with My Story, a digital storytelling app that works well for younger kids. It includes basic tools for writing a digital story, including drawing tools, audio recording features, and the ability to import personal photographs into the piece of digital art.

"The maximum value comes in for both [parent and child] when they can work with an adult," My Story creator Azin Mehrnoosh told me. He suggested that parents pick a simple theme for their child while using the app, something like "let's tell a story of your summer vacation" or "tell a story about you as a ninja in space." "We feel that having this guided experience creates better bonds, and really reveals amazing value in getting kids to express themselves," he explains. When they finish, he says parents should export the story and share it with loved ones. But don't let this digital art replace good old-fashioned crayon, marker, and paper story art.

"I think there's tremendous value in the traditional print activities," he concludes. "We've even seen My Story used as a recording app to simply take pictures and record audio over a story that the child has created with traditional media to capture the moment and send it to a loved one, or as an assignment in class."

As your child nears kindergarten you also might want to try Toontastic. This is a combination video puppet/storytelling platform that actually allows your child to share stories with other kids. Your child can make a story for free or you can buy certain add-ons to make the story more elaborate. But your child can actually include his or her own drawings and photographs within these short movies. The opportunities are limitless, but the toolset is simple enough that most kids can pick it up pretty quickly.

Once your kid figures out the app, creator Andy Russell has this advice: "Take a step back and let the kid shine. Once that kid starts creating something, once he or she hears their voice and they start to see their story come together, it's like this magical moment. If you hit it right, they'll tell stories forever. Once they see how powerful it is to be a storyteller and be a performer, it's addicting. It's like a runner's high. The only thing that can really derail a kid at that point is if the parent gets in the way."

Toontastic also has a great recording feature, letting your kid narrate his or her adventures while using the digital puppets within a story he or she has created. Toontastic teaches your child how stories are built with setup, conflict, challenge, climax, and resolution, ultimately helping him or her understand how a story works.

Russell has some noble goals for his creation: "We're training kids how to be storytellers. That means storytellers in the oral tradition of sitting around the campfire; storytellers in photography, in creative writing. The most important thing for me is not that kids get really good at using our animation tools or that kids get really good at using our template specifically. The ideas inherent in Toontastic—set up conflict, climax, and resolution, the idea of the story arc, the idea of breaking down stories into character and setting and emotion—these are tenets of creative writing."

Our children are fortunate to be born in a generation with

seemingly boundless sets of storytelling tools, from digital books to blogging software to smartphones. They are armed with a professional set of tools that would make any twentieth-century storyteller jealous. Someday, this generation will tell stories in ways that we cannot even imagine yet. They have all this fabulous possibility for creation, but the most popular children's apps focus on mindless games, rote memorization, or passive viewing of popular TV shows. You need to introduce digital storytelling tools early and often to fight these digital trends.

Librarian Cen Campbell limits her son to creation on digital devices, rather than mindless television. "My child has very limited access to technology," she says. "The access that he does have is about content creation as opposed to content consumption."

I don't need jet packs or trips to the moon to feel like I'm living in a science fiction story. It makes me so excited to see these digital tools that Olive can use to tell stories. I can't even imagine what I would've created if I had these tools back then.

When Olive neared three years old, I retold my famous "Party at the Library" story one fateful evening. She'd been listening to that story for more than a year and I'd added a few flourishes: the Cat in the Hat made a cameo, there was birthday cake, and Bob Dylan stopped singing so he could give Olive a hug. She loved to extend a story as long as possible, but I'd mastered the art of coaxing my daughter to sleep at this point, adding sleepy-time cues inside the story. "Goodnight, Bob Dylan," "Goodnight, Cat in the Hat," I said, ending with "Goodnight, Olive," and a kiss on her head. I started to edge out of her room, but Olive had another surprise that particular night.

"Then there was a knock at the door!" she yelled, extending

the story all by herself with a technique that storytellers have used for centuries to draw out a narrative.

I was flabbergasted. My little girl had rewritten my own story so she could stay awake longer.

I took a deep breath and we finished the story together.

Born Reading Bundle: Storytelling

1. Take your child's favorite book and retell it as a bedtime story. Let him or her help you rewrite the story as you tell it.
2. Use an app like Draw and Tell or StoryKit to turn your digital photographs into simple artwork—scribbling, editing, or changing favorite pictures into a new story.
3. Take these pictures and make a digital book using the My Story app. Share it with your family.
4. Download a free copy of *Andersen's Fairy Tales* by Hans Christian Andersen at Project Gutenberg. Pick a favorite fairy tale and have your child illustrate it.
5. Have your child retell the fairy tale before going to sleep.

Chapter 7

Kindergarten and Beyond

How to Prepare Born Readers for School

Your child never looks smaller than he or she does standing outside the preschool gate.

You just want to protect your kid; you want to keep him or her out of the big-kid world filled with bullies, insults, grades, tests, and the million other stressful parts of school. You have to navigate a confusing world of preschool options and prepare your kid for a major environment change. And every step of the way, you worry that you are bungling your child's future.

I can't make it easier to let go of your cute little child, but if you follow the Born Reading Playbook, you will have prepared your child to be creative, critical, and comfortable in school. If you have been reading books, asking questions, and talking with your child, they will be ready (as much as anybody can be ready) to flourish in the current classroom environment.

To find out more about easing born readers through the school transition, I caught up with first-grade teacher Karen

Lirenman. "It's important for parents to help kids make connections to what they're reading," the award-winning educator explained. "The kids that have come in that have been talking about the books they read, they have a better connection to reading and it is more meaningful for them."

She can see the difference between kids raised with interactive reading: "It becomes more a part of the kid when they've really connected to the story. When you just read to a kid for the sake of sharing a story, you're only seeing it at one level. But the higher levels and deeper thinking you get [with interactive reading], the more it becomes a part of them, it becomes something they can't live without."

By the time your child reaches five or six years old, they will head to kindergarten. In its materials for parents, the American Association of Pediatrics (AAP) lists a number of emotional and intellectual milestones necessary for school. Reading is at the very top of this list: "Remain attentive and quiet when being read a story." The AAP recommends reading to your child throughout the early years to meet this goal, so just by reading this book, you have helped your child take a crucial step toward school.

The list also includes being able to go to the bathroom without help, the ability to handle buttons and zippers on their clothes, and the memorization of your address and phone number. Finally, your child needs to be able to play and interact with other children peacefully, from recess to classroom time to reading time.

Instead of looking at reading milestones during this busy year, I wanted to look at the new model of evaluation being adopted by public schools around the country. Over the course of this year, your child will learn a variety of new reading skills and apply them in a group setting.

Even though your child is only in the first year of official school, there are a few standard measures used by kindergarten teachers as part of the Common Core Standards—a curriculum adopted by 45 states to hold children to a new shared standard. We will discuss these ideas more in the conclusion of the book, but you can make sure your child is comfortable with the "English Language Arts and Literacy" skills required by these new educational standards in kindergarten.

Common Core materials for teachers require a number of reading skills, beginning with "Key Ideas and Details" about a book. Your child must be able to respond to questions about a story and ask his or her own questions about parts of a book. Your child also needs to be able to recount a story that he or she enjoyed. Teachers will ask your child to talk about the elements of a book, including people, places, and important plot points.

The next set of skills relate to "Craft and Structure." The teacher will quiz your child about new words in a book or story. Your child should be familiar with different genres, ranging from poetry to storybooks. The teacher may also ask about the author or illustrator of a particular story, discussing what these people do in a book.

The next stage is "Integration of Knowledge and Ideas." Your child should be able to discuss how pictures and stories work together, talking about what happens in a particular illustration. Your child should also be able to compare different books or contrast characters across books.

Finally, and perhaps most importantly, your child will be evaluated on his or her ability to "actively engage in group reading activities." If you have been reading to your child throughout these early years, you will have prepared him or her to share this activity with others in class.

You can extend this kind of interaction to apps and other digital materials as well. Caroline Knorr from Common Sense Media has some important advice for parents preparing their kids for school. "Around four or five is when kids begin to need to learn social skills like sharing, cooperating, working with a group. They are going to need all of those social skills when they actually get into kindergarten."

Knorr recommends parents seek out books and apps that highlight these particular skills, especially as kids prepare for school. "They prepare kids for the types of digital experiences that are going to be a crucial part of their development going forward. You can read about how kids can have a difference of opinion and solve a conflict. A lot of storybook apps have modeled really good social interactions between characters. The more you can see kids solving problems, diverse kids and kids from different backgrounds, we really support that."

If you are looking for more suggestions, schoolteacher and Digital-Storytime.com founder Carisa Kluver thinks parents should check out *Hurray for Pre-K!* by Ellen B. Senisi and *The Kissing Hand* by Audrey Penn. Both books specifically tackle the emotional process of heading to school and are available in digital and print editions.

Kluver adds that parents should look for book apps that automatically help children learn how to read by highlighting words as the audiobook narrator reads them. "Book apps with highlighting word-for-word with the narration are particularly useful for building a strong visual connection between the way a word looks and how it sounds."

Caroline Hu Flexer from Duck Duck Moose actually built school readiness into the company's collection of apps, collaborating with teachers as her team constructed the digital tools. "We have an advisory board of teachers who are using our apps in their classroom and have been very supportive of us," she told me.

The company also consults directly with Jennifer DiBrienza, a former New York City public school teacher with a PhD in elementary education from Stanford. "She'll come into our offices and sit with our project teams really early on in the process and explain to us, 'Okay, if you want to do a math app for kindergarten kids, these are the things that are covered typically in kindergarten. These are the Common Core Standards.' Most importantly for us, she explains how the concepts are actually taught and what the nuances of the curriculum are."

Another tip, say experts: don't focus on a single kind of reading material at this wonderful age. Babble editor in chief Catherine Connors told me how she learned to look at *how* her kids were reading, rather than what kind of device they were using for reading, and if they were getting good, interactive learning on an iPad then she was OK with that. "If you are directing them toward apps that are engaging them in some beneficial way, then I'm inclined to be a little more permissive about it because I regard it as just another medium for my kids to dig into narrative and stories."

Early educator Anne Rachel co-founded Teachers with Apps, a resource for teachers using digital tools in the classroom. Even so, she has some cautionary advice for parents about using devices at home. "There's a lot of interaction in those books and apps. Sometimes too much because they are usually set up so the child could use them on their own," she says. "But if a parent wants to sit down with them in the same way—that's very important. iPads should not be a babysitter. Whether you're reading a hardcover book or an app book with your child, you should be asking questions. You should be raising conversation."

Finally, first-grade teacher Karen Lirenman reminds parents that *your* personal reading habits are just as important as your child's desire to read. "The parents have to like to read themselves. If you're always reading to your kids but you're never modeling reading yourself and you don't have the love for reading, it's a lot harder for your kids to get the love of reading. If you value reading and your kids see that you value reading, there's a good chance that they'll start to value it as well."

If you cared enough about your child's reading to get this book, chances are you've already passed along your own love of reading. But don't forget to model a balanced media diet by showing your child that you read print books, magazines, and digital books.

Read to Learn: Preparing Born Readers to Master Informational Reading

Olive obsessed over Dr. Seuss's *The Lorax* for a few weeks straight, a substantial book by the master that introduces everything from ecology to biology to pollution. Following the Born Reading Playbook, I decided to keep chasing this newfound interest in ecology.

At the library, I grabbed a nonfiction book called *A Tree Is a Plant* by Clyde Robert Bulla. We read the book for the first time at breakfast, exploring Bulla's cozy illustrations of different trees.

Olive made me catalog every single tree in the book, learning new words while munching on cereal. When one illustration showed roots spreading out underneath a lovely apple tree, we went out to the yard barefoot to look at tree roots.

If you used this book and books like it during your child's early years, then you have already introduced him or her to a number of great science and math texts. You followed your kid's interests, experiences, and questions with inspiring reading material.

But as your child enters kindergarten and grade school, these nonfiction books will be reframed as part of the educational experience. As part of the Common Core Standards sea change in American education, nonfiction books about all kinds of topics will be emphasized as "informational texts."

Children's author Melissa Stewart has published scores of science books for kids and helped me understand how our education system will change with this new curriculum. "Traditionally, teachers have focused most of their instruction on fiction. But the main goal of the people who developed the new standards is to prepare students for college and the job market. They believe students need to be better at reading and writing nonfiction. So in the elementary grades, teachers are supposed to focus half of their instruction on nonfiction. By high school, nonfiction should be an even greater focus."

Stewart thinks this change will revitalize children's literature. "Nonfiction for children has been undergoing a quiet revolution over the last 10 or 15 years. In the past, nonfiction books were often a bit dry and didactic. But now, nonfiction authors are creating titles that delight readers as they inform them. The books are lavishly illustrated and the writing style is lively and engaging. Parents will probably be surprised by how different today's nonfiction is from the nonfiction books they remember from childhood."

At the end of this chapter, I have listed a number of these informational texts, great books in their own right. As you read them with your child now, you should keep in mind how teachers and the educational system will use those books in the classroom. Drawing on materials from the Common Core Standards, I will guide you through key evaluation questions that teachers will pose about books in this new system. While reading these great books, you can actually practice school questions and comprehension questions with your child.

It will help them master new reading material and proudly answer questions when they start school. Most of all, don't let the new school focus overwhelm the joy of reading. Follow your child's own questions and interests again, show them that these books can still be savored like a book at home.

If one "informational text" piques your child's interest, find more books, eBooks, apps, videos, and art projects that can extend that book into his or her life. Do everything you can to help him or her enjoy these books, not just to be better students, but to become better human beings.

The Common Core materials explore Bulla's *A Tree Is a Plant*, asking kids to "identify the reasons Clyde Robert Bulla gives in his book in support of his point about the function of roots in germination," a challenging way for any kid to think about this book for the first time. When your child reads a book like this for the first time at home, use the Born Reading Playbook to ask more fun questions.

The "text exemplars" section also looks at *Starfish*, a gorgeous book examining the life and biology of the titular creatures. The sample question asks kids to talk about Edith Thacher Hurd's role as the book's author and Robin Brickman's role as the book's illustrator. Instead of introducing this book as homework, try visiting the beach or aquarium first. *Starfish* will answer many questions kids have about fish and the sea, great conversations to have before they end up studying them in school.

Another "sample performance task" involves *National Geographic Young Explorer*, a print magazine with a large free database online. You can actually peruse back issues of *Young Explorer* in full color on the website. The Common Core "text exemplars" section singles out one issue entitled "Garden Helpers." The sample question asks kids to "demonstrate their understanding of the main idea of the text—not all bugs are bad—by retelling key details." Children will be expected to answer questions about these high-resolution photographs of spiders, ladybugs, and worms in the classroom.

This raises a bigger point—think of ways you can use informational texts in your child's real life. Many local fire stations welcome visits from parents, for instance. Your kid will leave a short visit with the firefighters filled with stories about trucks, gear, and giant tools. You could follow up this neighborhood visit with Gail Gibbons's *Fire! Fire!*, another exemplar text.

While reading the book, have your child explain different parts of a firefighter's job and share favorite moments from the book. Suddenly, your simple field trip has met one of the Common Core Standards' key requirements—"answer using key details from the text." Kids raised with the Born Reading Playbook have been practicing this particular skill for years.

During this period, children will also be asked to learn and process more complex science terms from these informational texts. With some help from a parent or teacher, these young readers should be able to illustrate key concepts from these books. The Common Core materials online use Fran Hodgkins's and True Kelley's *How People Learned to Fly* to illustrate this particular skill, asking kids to reenact the "arm spinning" experiment described in the text—literally demonstrating how "drag" works as an airplane soars through the air.

Finally, your child will begin to explore the mechanics of books during the first years of school. The "text exemplars" section uses *Earthworms* by Claire Llewellyn to illustrate this, asking kids to use "headings, table of contents, glossary" to find "key facts or information" inside a book.

Olive used to love choosing Curious George stories from a hardcover omnibus collection of some of his adventures. After reading one section, she forced me or my wife to go back to the table of contents so she could pick the next story. As long as you hold open, child-guided readings, your born reader will learn the same way.

Olive learned from a very early age—even before she could read the words herself—how to control a book. There are very few things a young child can control in this world, but a book is a simple and perfect place to start.

Reading these suggestions for teachers, you might feel some school anxiety of your own as your child's pure love of reading transforms into yet another skill to be evaluated during the schooling process. But born readers will have explored many of these structures already during a lifetime of reading at home.

Author Ginjer L. Clarke has this advice for the transition to school, helping parents work Common Core science themes into children's lives without taking away the joy of discovery. "I think the basic concepts covered are generally: the five senses, seasons and weather, and a basic knowledge of plants. These topics can be covered in everyday conversations by just talking about how our bodies work, observing changes in seasons, and discussing where food comes from."

She adds: "Simple science experiments with water can be a lot of fun too. I think the most important quality to encourage in children is curiosity. The only way you can learn about new things is by wondering, asking, and answering questions. Even though it can be exhausting as a parent, try to support your child's natural curiosity by asking questions yourself and making an attempt to answer theirs accurately. Let them see you reading, read together from a young age, and foster reading as a recreational activity."

Informational texts will be a larger part of your child's life as he or she continues through school. By introducing them at home, you can make sure your child feels comfortable with this new kind of text at school. You can have productive conversations about these new books and make sure your child is ready to field teacher's questions about the same kind of reading material.

If your child is comfortable talking to you about these informational texts, he or she will have a much easier time in the classroom. At the end of this chapter I recommend a long list of these texts that will come to play a crucial role in your child's education as they move to grade school.

Customized Interactive Reading Experiences:
Tailor a Story to Your Child

In the 1980s, my great aunt bought me a customized *Sesame Street* book. The simple story follows Big Bird as he joined an alphabet-themed scavenger hunt around the neighborhood. Throughout the story, Big Bird would speak to me personally at key moments. The book also includes personalized tidbits like my favorite food or color.

That book meant so much to me as a kid, and I rediscovered it by reading it to Olive. I simply substituted her name, her address, and her favorite foods instead of the fill-in-the-blank answers that I had as a kid. Just looking at the drawings now brings back vivid memories of being little—the characters so real I can almost touch them.

Anything you can do to customize a book will help keep your born reader fascinated with books during this period.

You can personalize any book with a little bit of literary graffiti. *Battle Bunny* by Jon Scieszka and Mac Barnett, and illustrated by Matthew Myers, is a great example. The authors defaced an imaginary and cheesy kids' book about a cuddly bunny's birthday party. They doodled eye patches, explosions, and rockets in the book, turning it into an action-packed adventure.

These scribbles convert a cuddly bunny into a rampaging monster that can only be stopped by an adventurous young boy. I remember so clearly doing the same thing with books as a kid, doodling stick-figure battles to add a little bit of adventure to my life. *Battle Bunny* contains lots of stylized, cartoony violence, the kind of mayhem you see in Bugs Bunny or other classic kid's material.

"*Battle Bunny* is the ultimate model for kids interacting with a book," author Scieszka explained in an email to me. "We've heard from teachers and librarians and booksellers across the country who are having kids do the same thing co-author Mac Barnett and I show our narrator doing—taking an old book with a lame story and making it your own by adding and subtracting your own words and illustrations. It is such satisfying fun. And anyone can do it."

Look at your own library—perhaps you can find an old book to customize with crayons, pens, stickers, or paints.

The digital revolution has produced an amazing range of customized and interactive books. I caught up with Sourcebooks publisher Dominique Raccah to find out about Put Me in the Story, the publisher's customizable book series for kids in both print and digital. "When you personalize a book, it becomes more 'mine.' It creates a greater bond with the book itself," she explains.

Raccah also suggests that parents get copies of beloved books in multiple formats. "Kids from the age of two until about four or five, what they want is reassurance," she told me. "They want some kind of stability and control over their environment. Because for them the world is big and scary. There's a certain reassurance for them in that product being familiar across a lot of platforms."

If you want to create a completely digital customized reading experience, try the Story Before Bed app from Jackson Fish Market. You can use the app to record a video storybook reading that a child can watch no matter where you are. The publisher offers books from a wide variety of children's publishers.

You can also create a customized digital audiobook reading for your child with the StorySticker app. It works for iPhone, iPad, and Android users. A parent, grandparent, or friend can record an audiobook using the app, and then stick a teddy bear sticker with a special QR (Quick Response) code inside the book. The kid can build a whole library of personalized audiobooks with the app, using the sticker to access the reading by scanning it with the smartphone or tablet camera.

Raccah says that parents approach books with more enthusiasm when they are customized for the child. "They've got something special, and they know it. They really lean into the experience. Now the child has no knowledge of the book at all, but just notices the way that the parent comes into it and responds differently. That whole beginning creates what I call a 'digital virtuous circle.'"

Experiment with these different formats. If your child responds well to one method, build a library of digital readings. My parents mailed Olive a CD filled with MP3 recordings they created, simple audiobooks that Olive loved to listen to over and over. When a loved one lives far away, these book recordings can create a genuine connection between long-distance family members.

Customized books also fulfill a key purpose for interactive reading, helping kids compare a story to their own lives. Back in 1977, researcher James E. Flood stressed the importance of relating a book to a kid's personal experiences—discovering that this kind of conversation can boost the impact of an interactive reading session. It helps your child remember the book better, along with the vocabulary, concepts, and knowledge inside it.

Born Reading Playbook:
Compare the story to personal experiences.

Help associate the book with the experiences that obsess your child. This is how human beings understand the world—it is a crucial skill to apply something in a book or app to real life.

Conversation starters: *Did you see that kind of animal at the zoo? Did you get mad when we left the park too?*

Teaching Your Child How to Code:
A New Kind of Literacy

As a toddler, Olive never understood my job. At one point, she thought I pushed buttons for a living. Now she knows I tell stories, but it's hard for her to understand what I do working on a laptop, calling sources on the phone, reading new stories on Twitter, or editing a chapter of this book.

Jobs used to be represented by kid-sized vehicles, dolls with uniforms or toy tools, but our virtual economy is pretty hard for a kid to replicate in a game. Many adults spend endless hours working with these digital tools, and it's hard for children to imagine (or emulate) exactly what their parents do.

Throughout my career as a writer and journalist, I have

learned a number of digital skills that helped my career grow: how to post stories I've written online, to hand-code HTML, and to edit photographs, audio, or video for online publication. Most of my contact with sources comes through email, telephone, or Skype—twenty-first-century kids will do all these things and more in their jobs.

Over and over when I spoke with app developers and designers for this book, they were amazed at the amount of time it takes to write and publish a book. In their world, technology can change radically in the space of a few months. By the time your child enters the workforce, they will need a whole set of technology skills we can't even imagine yet. And even though it might seem crazy, you can start to teach kids as young as kindergarteners the basic tech skills they will need to survive and thrive in this new economy.

"We live in a world that is completely constructed around technology," elaborates *Fast Company* journalist Anya Kamenetz. "We're in a transitional period now where there are special people called 'programmers' who run the technology, but it's so ubiquitous and transformative that I really believe in a generation's time it's going to be part of basic literacy. Everybody who purports to be an educated person is going to have to do a little bit of coding in order to make the world around them work in the way they want it to."

She introduced her toddler to the MaKey MaKey kit, an amazing kit that lets creators of all ages attach alligator clips to everyday objects—building a simple circuit to control a computer. Using the $50 kit, you can turn your stairway into a digital piano or convert a banana into a video game controller. It doesn't even involve wiring or circuit board creation. Just use the alligator clips and the simple circuit board provided inside the kit.

"It gets kids started on the idea that they can create interfaces with the world," explains Kamenetz. "They can connect the world to the computer and the computer to the world. It gets them started down the path of figuring out the world around them."

With a suite of apps and books, you can teach your child how to explore this technologically rich world. You can help your child understand the infrastructure that runs underneath our everyday lives. Most importantly you can remind your child that computers and mobile devices are not just toys, they are also powerful tools for creating. That may be the earliest and best lesson that you can give to your child.

Cen Campbell chose to send her kids to a Waldorf School, an educational model that discourages technology use. But she saw the technology divide as a battle for her kids' future. "These babies, their concept of reading is completely different from our concept of reading. There's just so much more that they are going to have to navigate from an information literacy point of view. Trying to handcuff them by restraining them to what we believe to be the best type of literacy is not going to do them any favors. There's going to be two classes of people in the future, those who are manipulated by media and those who can manipulate the media—content creation."

App designer Cristoph Niemann agrees. He introduced his kids to Scratch, another simple coding program. He actually told his grade-school kids: "If you want to play video games, first I want you guys to program something."

He learned the basics of coding along with his kids with the app. "On the one hand, we feel it satisfies their cravings for anything having to do with computers. But on the other hand, it really forces them to think about the structure behind it and be creative together."

"It's literacy for the twenty-first century, in a world that's increasingly dominated by technology," Jocelyn Leavitt told me. She helped develop Hopscotch, a free app to teach kids how to perform simple computer programming. "Now every single person uses smartphones to communicate, uses Internet to get their information, and uses technology in every single industry. Computer programming is really the building blocks of all technology. Learning basic software and learning how software functions on a very basic level gives you the ability to understand how all these things around you work."

Using the Hopscotch app, kids can build simple animations, pictures, games, or tools with these open-ended building blocks. "If you know how to code in one language, then it's not so hard to learn other languages. The basic components of each programming language are the same. Once you learn how to use the basic fundamentals of computer programming, those will translate into other languages also," Leavitt explains. "I think a lot of schools are behind and they are trying to get better about computer programming curriculum, recognizing that computing is much more than how to type or use Microsoft Office. I think schools are catching up a bit."

You can use these tools to combat gender and educational stereotypes as well. Leavitt says: "One of the things that puts a lot of girls off about computer programming is (you hear this again and again) girls are like, 'I like reading, I don't like math.' A lot of people feel that computer programming is just for math nerds. I know several programmers who were not good at math. You don't need to be good at math to be good at programming."

These early experiences can help ease your child into the world of programming and code, mastering skills that will guide what many of the best jobs in America will be by the time your child grows up.

Exploring Social Networks with Born Readers

I signed up for my first social network account in my twenties. During my adult lifetime, I have had accounts with Friendster, MySpace, LiveJournal, and other sites I don't visit anymore.

As a journalist, Twitter and Facebook have become a daily part of my life, powerful tools for interacting with my readers and finding stories to cover. At one point while writing this book, I asked my Facebook community for suggestions of great kids' books; I ended up with a list of hundreds of books that I could include in this collection.

I managed to explore countless networks as an adult, but I can't imagine what it would be like to visit as a kid. My daughter (and all the children of parents reading this book) will grow up in a digital world built on social networks. They will not encounter these new worlds as adults as I did. They will have a level of comfort with virtual experiences that I can only dream of. It will be very useful in both their social and work lives as they get older.

At the same time, social networks will be more dangerous for these children because they will not enter these worlds with the adult perspective that I had when I first entered these communities. Even though your child won't be signing up for a Facebook account as a grade-school kid, you can start teaching them good behaviors and ways of thinking about your online life right now.

In *The Parent App: Understanding Families in the Digital Age*, author and media professor Lynn Schofield Clark explores how kids use these networks across different social classes. "We have to figure out ways to educate them about their digital trail," she told me about this new generation of socially networked kids. "They are going to have a digital trail that exists throughout their whole lives. They're going to need to be much more conscientious about that because there will be consequences for how people review the social media trail that they create."

Despite the fact that your kids won't be full-fledged Facebook members at this age, it is never too early to talk to your grade-school kid about digital citizenship. "There is a tendency for young people to idealize social networks, to some extent, to think 'this is different from the spaces that I spend time with my parents in,'" Clark explains. "It's really important for parents to talk with their young children and to help the child to recognize that online environments and social media environments are not separate from the rest of their lives."

You can look at the Toontastic app where children share millions of short cartoons that they have created in a simple social network. Using this digital tool, kids can create short animated movies using onscreen puppets. Older kids can share their creations on Toontube, the company's online home for kids' creations. As of this writing, over seven million videos from more than 200 countries had been posted on this simple social network.

Creator Andy Russell reassures parents that this is a highly controlled environment. "We actually mandate that parents review everything before it goes online," he explained. "The kid goes in and creates the cartoon and we send an email to the parent and say, 'Hey, can you watch this and make sure that you are comfortable with this?' Because at the end of the day, everyone has their own standards about what's appropriate to share online. We think it is important for the parent to make that call and not us."

Russell called the social media chat an "ongoing conversation" between parents and kids. While he thought some kids were ready to post on Toontastic at four or five years old, he stressed that every family will have to find their own comfort level for these activities. There is no ideal age to start kids on social networks. There is only the ideal age to start on social networks within your family.

The company also monitors the simple social network for profanity or objectionable content. But he also reminds parents to be involved in a child's social media use. "With any network, I just encourage parents to be involved, and not to offload that work to the network developer or the app developer. YouTube doesn't know what's best for your kids. You do. Your kids have to take some responsibility around digital citizenship and, quite honestly, you do too."

Caroline Knorr from Common Sense Media said that her son loved the LEGO site, another place where kids can post their own creations. She spent some time exploring the site by herself first, and advised parents to look for some of these features in a social network: "What I was looking for was that the comments are appropriate. Somebody needs to be on the other end making sure that the user-generated content is acceptable for your kid's age. I look for that. For a young kid, you want it to be moderated."

She also offers these key points: "Look for good privacy settings, make sure you are comfortable with the site's rules and regulations. Make sure that your kid understands those rules and regulations so everybody is playing fairly."

Canadian first-grade teacher Karen Lirenman uses blogs, social networks, and other digital tools inside her classroom, developing some invaluable experience in this uncharted territory. She suggests that parents use Twitter as an early tool to explore social networks with kids. You don't even need to have a Twitter account for your child, they can share yours.

Lirenman suggests that parents use Twitter as a tool to contact your child's favorite authors. If they love a book, send a message to the author or illustrator. "The kids can actually tell, directly through Twitter, what they liked about the book or ask a question," she said. "Typically, the author will tweet you back relatively quickly. That's how powerful that instant feedback and that direct link to the people that inspire you is. That shows my kids that their voice means something."

She also uses Twitter to share simple math problems with her students and had her kids tweet in the voices of characters from *Little Red Riding Hood*—turning the social network into a digital storytelling tool.

All of these concepts of social networks come back to digital citizenship, an important term among child-development experts, educators, and writers. You must show your child how to live safely and happily in online worlds, just as you are teaching him or her to be better citizens of the world.

Lirenman stresses these basics for young kids: "Teach them about personal information: not giving your phone number and address, keeping things that should be private, private. Things that you would only give to people that you trust are the things you should keep off social media." Her students use blogs as "digital portfolios" in her classroom. Blogging is not mandatory, and the kids choose how much they want to share. The teacher monitors the entire posting system, approving everything that ultimately gets published on the class blog.

She says parents could follow her example with a family blog using Blogger, Wordpress, or even Facebook or Twitter. "Their kids could totally have their own blogs that they are doing from home, documenting their learning or what they are creating. Then the parents get a scrapbook as well. It's a digital portfolio."

Sharing these digital activities with your child can help avoid problems later on as your child explores social networks as a pre-teen or teenager. I think that most adults do not understand the full extent of online behavior. Every single day, I see adults offending somebody within their community with a Facebook or Twitter post. Our kids will learn from our social media behavior, and we need to teach them how to navigate these tricky worlds with more care.

Olive grew up watching me use Facebook, Twitter, and other tools for work every single day, but she also saw all my bad online habits as well. As you absentmindedly scan Facebook, constantly post family photos, or obsessively consult your Twitter feed, your child will also model these behaviors.

Don't wait until your child actually has accounts to introduce them to these worlds. I think it is worthwhile to show your children how you use these accounts yourself well before they can use it for themselves. Show your child how you post a picture on Facebook of him or her at a birthday party, or how you ask your friend a question on Twitter.

Clark suggests that parents use their children as guides through digital spaces dedicated to kids. "Put your kid in the role of advising you. Even when they are young, like five or six years old. Ask them to give you a tour of whatever site they are visiting.

We can have conversations with them about those sites and participate with them, which they think is pretty hilarious, usually. They know you are out of place there."

It can be as simple as looking at your child's videos on Toontastic or letting him or her choose a silly picture to post on Facebook. The key is doing the activity with your child, rather than teaching that social network participation is a solitary activity.

"As parents we can express interest in our children by expressing interest in their online worlds," Clark concludes, powerful advice for twenty-first-century parents.

She also reminds parents not to let social networks become tied into your child's sense of self-esteem—a tough topic for twenty-first-century kids when sharing work on LEGO or Toontastic. I can't think of a more important value for them. This problem didn't even exist ten years ago, so most parents won't even think about it.

I see it in my own life. The writing profession has changed so profoundly since social networks were invented. I used to write for an unknown audience, but now I can measure responses to my writing in seconds. Watching readers respond to my work in real time on social networks, I often feel like a failure when something I wrote barely registers online. I can spend too much time looking for validation from these virtual analytics. I don't want Olive to inherit these life-altering habits.

You've probably fallen prey to this, too—maybe watching to see who "likes" a post on Facebook, or getting frazzled and impatient waiting for a return email. Some of this is inevitable in our hyperconnected world, but all of us (parents and kids included) need to look for communities that nurture our work and ideas without making our self-esteem hinge on this online interaction.

Caroline Knorr from Common Sense Media cautions parents about social networks and self-esteem. "What's important is the pride that they feel of having done that work, versus any kind of external validation that they get from the web," she stresses. "We want to train our kids to have that sense of internal self-pride. That's the icing on the cake, that they can share it with other kids." I think most adults can learn from her powerful advice.

It is almost impossible to write about these networks in a book like this because within one year the entire landscape of social networks could change—especially the places where kids love to visit. So instead of focusing on the specific mechanics of individual sites, I think it's better to consider your child and your family's overall strategy for using these networks.

I've included a list of a few popular sites below. You should explore them all yourself and even talk to other parents about what worlds they let their children use. That way you can make an informed decision together with your children.

Social Networks for Children

Club Penguin
http://www.clubpenguin.com/
Founded in 2005, Club Penguin is an ad-free virtual world for kids. Users get a personalized penguin and can interact with other kids through motions, games, and simple chat functions. You can use the site for free, but the company offers a number of paid membership packages.

Toontastic

http://toontube.launchpadtoys.com/

Kids who use the Toontastic tool to create short animated movies can post their work inside this simple social network. Millions of videos have already been posted and parental approval is necessary before a video goes up on the site.

LEGO Create & Share Galleries

http://www.lego.com/en-us/createandshare/

Kids post photographs of LEGO creations and scenes acted out with LEGOs. They receive comments and thumbs-up approval from other LEGO builders.

Everloop

http://www.everloop.com/

A simple social network for kids under 13 years old. They join "loops," or theme-based groups, about topics like sports, crafts, music, or movies.

Surviving in a World of Standardized Tests

As a kid, I always had a queasy, shaky feeling at testing time. The teachers would hand out standardized test booklets printed on brittle paper. I dreaded the whole experience, wondering how I would be judged for my answer sheet dutifully filled out with a No. 2 pencil. Even as a kid I realized that these tests were not helping me learn. They produce anxiety among students and cause teachers to panic.

Fast Company journalist Anya Kamenetz talked about the

unique anxiety presented by these tests and is working on a non-fiction book about their impact on society. "Students are experiencing a lot of stress around these tests," she told me. "They're absorbing the attitude that comes from their teachers and their principals and schools. Very often funding decisions are being made on the basis of test scores. Decisions about whether or not the school will be able to be kept open are being made on the basis of test scores. That pressure comes from superintendents, from governors, and it trickles down to principals and teachers and down to classrooms."

She offered a few examples of this test anxiety: "We hear a lot of anecdotes of students undergoing real intense stress: throwing up, not being able to sleep the night before the test, and these kinds of things."

First-grade teacher Karen Lirenman urges parents to share all these fears with teachers. "I think it's important to get a relationship with the classroom teacher and be working on the same side. I may have a strategy that works at school or you may have a strategy that works at home. If we are both here to help your child become the best that they can be, then we need to work together."

To minimize anxiety about tests and school, she advises parents to provide lots of "positive talk about school and the exciting things that are going to happen." At the same time, you need to "acknowledge those fears, and tell them they are probably not the only person that felt that way. Hopefully the teacher will recognize that and make them feel welcome."

Most importantly, you need to tell your child to communicate with the teacher and other adults in his or her life. "Teach children, if you can, to use their voice," she concludes. "If they're feeling sad, they have to say, 'I'm feeling sad.' Teach them to advocate for themselves." These skills will prove invaluable for coping with the stress and anxiety of adult life as well.

"Make sure you're managing your child's emotional health, that they have methods of dealing with stress, are identifying it when it occurs, and have safe things that they can go to when they are experiencing classroom anxiety," said Kamenetz, making the connection between school skills and adulthood. "It's going to be good for your kid, not just to get through the tests, but all of school and the rest of life."

If you want your child to attend a selective school, you may have to take the Early Childhood Admissions Assessment (ECAA). It is hosted by the nonprofit Educational Records Bureau (ERB), a company that handles testing for almost 2,000 member schools including "independent, public, faith-based, and boarding schools." I will take a little time to explore this test, because it illustrates key concepts your child will need on any early standardized test. I've also included a series of recommended books you can read alongside the test sections. If you read these books together and use the Born Reading Playbook to create an interactive reading experience, then you can help your kid get comfortable with these fairly tough questions.

The ECAA will evaluate your child in four different verbal areas: Vocabulary, Similarities, Information, and Comprehension. The ERB website hosts a fact sheet for parents, including sample questions from each category in the preschool, kindergarten, or first-grade test.

The vocabulary section evaluates "a child's scope of knowledge, learning ability, long-term memory, and degree of language development." One sample question asks the child, "What is a bed?" looking for both a definition and your child's sense of the concept of a bed.

The "Similarities" section tests "verbal reasoning and concept formation" through simple concepts. The sample question might bring back some bad memories of taking the SAT to get into college: "Finish what I say. Flowers and Trees are both _____." Your child should answer "plants," demonstrating a grasp of "auditory comprehension, memory, distinguishing non-essential and essential features, and verbal expression."

Next is the "Information" section, asking questions with more open-ended answers, evaluating your kid's "ability to acquire, retain and retrieve general factual knowledge." The sample question is pretty broad: "Tell me the name of a dinosaur."

Finally, the "Comprehension" part of the test explores more advanced skills: "abstract and concrete verbal reasoning and conceptualization, the ability to evaluate and utilize past experiences, verbal comprehension and expression, and the ability to demonstrate practical information." The sample question could hang up some kids: "What is money used for?"

I survived my own educational experience despite my anxiety about standardized tests. Oddly enough, reading comprehension and English language and literature skills saved me over and over on these tests. If anything, born readers will have a little extra test armor with their excellent reading and verbal skills.

While I would prefer not to have my daughter be part of the standardized testing world, we can't avoid it. Even if you do manage to send your kid to private school, you can never completely insulate your child from standardized tests. The doors to higher education will always be guarded by them. So if you want your child to have a rich educational experience, he or she needs to know how to take a test.

But I hope through this section and the later sections about Common Core Standards, you can guide your child through these rocky experiences safely. The ultimate goal is to have your born reader calmly take these tests, while at the same time maintaining a rich creative life. A lifetime of books, both inside and outside the classroom, will give your child the best chance at achieving that balance.

When Your Born Reader Graduates to Middle-Grade Reading

I watched the great middle-grade author Peter Lerangis speak in front of hundreds of authors at the Society of Children's Book Authors and Illustrators conference in Los Angeles. Every chair in the sprawling ballroom of the hotel was filled, with overflow writers sitting along the walls. They were writing the stories that will someday inspire children around the world.

Lerangis gave a rousing speech about the often overlooked genre of middle-grade literature. The publishing industry stakes the age range of this genre between 8 and 12 years old, but if your young reader has been following the Born Reading Playbook, he or she may be ready for these books even earlier.

Lerangis has written scores of books, including Babysitters Club favorites, Hardy Boys mysteries, 39 Clues installments, and countless other books that middle-grade readers devour every single day.

"Middle grade is forever," he declared, and the whole room

cheered. "They last. Kids are still reading not only Harry Potter, but Madeleine L'Engle, E. L. Konigsburg, and Louis Sachar, generations later," he concluded. All these authors would make a good introduction to middle-grade fiction, when your child is ready.

Can you remember the first big-kid book you ever read?

I made the transition with *Charlotte's Web*. My grade-school teacher read it out loud in class, the longest story I had ever experienced at that point. It was raining, so we had to skip recess while reading the book. But I didn't care, I would have stayed inside to finish that book even if it was sunny.

The first chance I had to read E. B. White's classic by myself, I took. That book led to the Encyclopedia Brown series and *Charlie and the Chocolate Factory*. From there, I tackled some Ray Bradbury short stories and The Hardy Boys, tumbling into a lifelong love affair with fiction.

All of those books are still burned into my head. My heart beat for poor Charlie who couldn't even afford a chocolate bar but still managed to win the golden ticket. The ground shifted beneath my feet when I discovered big-kid books.

Sourcebooks publisher Dominique Raccah reminded me that the transition to chapter books is not tied to a specific age. "It's more a moment when a child starts needing more than pictures. You can see they are looking for more story. You're looking for books with very short chapters and have illustrations built in, so the child feels supported in that transition. If they go from a picture book to a 25-page chapter that's all text, that's going to be impossible. It's about building that confidence."

As your child graduates from picture books, he or she will move into chapter books and the world of middle-grade fiction.

TOON Books publisher Françoise Mouly reminds parents

not to steer their child completely away from comics and picture books, a "puritanical" idea about reading she only saw in America. "My textbooks when I was a kid in France were heavily illustrated, even in middle school and high school. The goal in American education is that your kid is supposed to read chapter books that do not have pictures because it's like training wheels and you have to be able to ride the bicycle. What they don't realize is that reading pictures involves the same processes of inference and deduction and abstraction."

She concludes: "The picture-making in comics is as potent as the words in a poem. In a poem you don't judge it by the quantity of words or the number of syllables, but by how evocative the words are. In comics, it's a matter of having the right distillation."

Ask your parents and friends what they liked to read when they were that age. This is a great time to start reading Harry Potter or other classic books to your child, sharing some magical reading time. Middle-grade reading only lasts a few years, so enjoy it. "They will buy into a book as long as the story is good," author Lerangis said, describing how middle-grade readers will sample anything. "They'll read a book like *The Phantom Tollbooth*, The Chronicles of Narnia series, or *Charlie and the Chocolate Factory* as if it were written yesterday, not rolling their eyes at the old-fashioned expressions or dated fashion references. They're young enough so that they don't care."

Sample as many different kinds of middle-grade fiction as possible, letting your child discover the genres that mean the most to him or her. Digital books can make it easier to share large quantities of these books with your child. Tablets and eReaders make it easy to devour an entire collection of Nancy Drew mysteries or 39 Clues.

In terms of book sales, print books will still dominate this category of readers. While adults have started reading digital books at a rapid clip, eBooks still compose just a fraction of the children's book market.

I caught up with Scholastic's senior vice president Kyle Good to find out more about the school transition. The company has a Storia program—a reading app you can download on your device—allowing you to buy and read a long list of Scholastic books inside the app. "Of course, the adoption of children's eBooks has been far slower than for adults. We currently estimate the market is only about 10 percent of children's book sales if you do not count The Hunger Games series (which sold to many, many adults)," she concludes.

Nevertheless, digital books are spreading more quickly to classrooms. "We have had great acceptance by teachers as they begin to use eBooks in the classroom, and we believe this will continue to increase in the coming years," Good explains. The company targets kids from kindergarten until second grade with the iRead program, helping kids learn how to read with new digital tools. If your child's classroom has the tool, your kid will spend at least 20 minutes a day reading or participating in teacher-led discussions. The app provides digital rewards as your child learns.

You can reward your growing reader with digital books without spending a dime. When I was young, there was a series of books called *Free Stuff for Kids*. I read those books like a monk poring over a sacred scroll, writing companies for free samples of stickers, stamps, and little gadgets. There was something so magical about discovering something free in the book and sending out the letter myself.

I hope that your kids can have that experience of discovery too, even if they aren't mailing letters. But instead of a *Free Stuff for Kids* book, you can help them find vast libraries of free (and completely legal) eBooks they can download by themselves. On the Born Reading website I have created a few lists of free public domain books for different reading levels, ranging from nursery rhymes with gorgeous vintage illustrations to *The Wizard of Oz*, *The Adventures of Tom Sawyer*, or back issues of *Galaxy Science Fiction*. These longer books are perfect for middle-grade kids preparing for a lifetime of reading.

If you follow the links on my blog, you can build a massive children's book library on whatever device you use for reading. If you have a Kindle, download the .MOBI file on your computer. Plug your Kindle into the computer and drag the file from your desktop into the "Documents" folder on your Kindle. If you have a Kindle reading app on your tablet or smartphone, simply download the .MOBI file directly and the device will prompt you to open the file with the Kindle app. You can read it like any book in your Kindle library after that.

If you have an iPad or iPhone, download the .EPUB version of the book and the iPad will prompt you to open the file in iBooks. You can read it like any book purchased through Apple's iBook store. Nook readers will also need to download the .EPUB file. With a little bit of digital practice, you can actually give your child a reading buffet on your device without spending a single dime. Keep your middle-grade reader well fed.

"Middle-grade readers are in an amazing place," Lerangis concluded in his speech for children's book writers. "They're reading on their own, but they still rely on teachers, librarians, and parents to recommend, to buy, to stick conspicuously on the night table next to the bed. The most voracious of them will read anything,"

Kids at this age are developing their own sense of taste, but will sample almost anything along the way. A parent's job does not end with picture books—it is only beginning. As your child enters this crucial phase of the reading life, you should help him or her explore any kind of book that he or she wishes.

Informational and Nonfiction Reading Recommendations

Adapted from the "text exemplars" section of the English Language Arts materials for the Common Core State Standards

A Tree Is a Plant by Clyde Robert Bulla
Warm, inviting illustrations guide this book, cataloguing different kinds of trees and the biology of the trees in your neighborhood. It is easy to make this book interactive, exploring the trees outside your window while reading.

Starfish by Edith Thacher Hurd
The perfect complement to an aquarium visit. This book explores the ocean, sharing textbook-quality illustrations of sea creatures.

Earthworms by Claire Llewellyn
An expert nature photographer takes kids on a tour of the underground lives of worms. The book includes a table of contents and other key features studied in Common Core Standards, so this is a good book to practice with at home.

Fire! Fire! by Gail Gibbons
A classic kids' book about firefighters and fire safety. Fire truck loving preschoolers and older kids can all learn from these detailed, informative, and action-packed illustrations.

From Seed to Pumpkin by Wendy Pfeffer and
James Graham Halle (illustrator)
Soft, painted illustrations show how a pumpkin seed grows, giving a glimpse into the relationship between a plant and the environment around it.

How People Learned to Fly by Fran Hodgkins
and True Kelley (illustrator)
This whimsical exploration of the history of flight doesn't read like a textbook. Instead of offering dull facts in boring old chronological order, this brilliantly colored book zooms along from theme to theme, inspiring as it teaches.

What Do You Do With a Tail Like This? by Robin Page and
Steve Jenkins (illustrator)
This collection of animal close-ups examines the purpose of body parts like tails, snouts, or flippers. The book gives kids a rare glimpse at the bodies of animals, showing the silly and beautiful side of these creatures.

A Weed Is a Flower: The Life of George Washington Carver
by Aliki
A moving account of this great man's life, this book is a quality biography to introduce kids to the genre. The elegant paintings are packed with emotion, giving the quiet prose power.

Amazing Whales! by Sarah L. Thomson
Part of the I Can Read series that many grown-ups will recognize from their grade-school libraries, this book features vivid and kinetic pictures of whales coupled with some mind-blowing facts.

Water, Water Everywhere by Cynthia Overbeck Bix and
  Mark J. Rauzon
Stunning photographs of nature mixed with easy-to-read facts
about water. The prose swims with the beautiful cadence of the
ocean. Children of many different ages can learn from this book.

App Recommendations for Kindergarten and Beyond

Free Books for Children by International Children's
  Digital Library
A free collection of digital books for kids that "spans the globe
with thousands of children's books from over 60 countries." It
will give your kid a safe collection of books to explore, and even
allows readers to sample other languages.

> *Available in the Apple App Store; works for iPad and needs iOS 4.2 or later.*
> *Also available for iPhone and iPod Touch and needs iOS 2.0 or later.*

Rounds: Parker Penguin by Nosy Crow
A whimsical look at the biological life cycle of a penguin, this
app takes your child careening through a beautiful icy world.
The slick interactive reading experience contains loads of facts
about the science of penguins.

> *Available in the Apple App Store; works with iPhone (3GS, 4, 4S, and*
> *5), iPod Touch (third, fourth, and fifth generation), and iPad. Needs*
> *iOS 3.1.3 or later.*

The Kissing Hand by Audrey Penn and Oceanhouse Media
This classic storybook shows a mother helping her young rac-

coon prepare to go to school. The digital edition from Ocean-house Media keeps the interactivity simple, helping your child read along with the narrator and appreciate the quiet story.

Available in the Apple App Store; works with iPhone, iPod Touch, and iPad. Needs iOS 5.0 or later.

Available in Google Play for Android devices.

Available in Amazon Appstore for Android devices.

Storybird
http://storybird.com/
This online community for kids to tell stories is used by 125,000 schools around the world. Kids explore inspiring artwork and share their stories with an online community of young writers.

This free web-based app can be accessed from a variety of devices.

Daniel Tiger's Neighborhood by PBS Kids
Kids join an animated puppet from *Mister Rogers' Neighborhood*, exploring his home and dealing with common experiences: bathroom time, doctor visits, and bedtime. Includes a sticker section so your kids can tell stories.

Available in the Apple App Store; works with iPhone (3GS, 4, 4S, and 5), iPod Touch (third, fourth, and fifth generation), and iPad. Needs iOS 4.3 or later.

Available in Google Play for Android devices.

Available in Amazon Appstore for Android devices.

Montessori Geometry by Les Trois Elles
You may not believe your kid is ready for geometry, but this app introduces concepts in a creative way. Following the Montessori

philosophy of education, this app shows more than 20 shapes with 3D animation and cartoon character guides.

Available in the Apple App Store; works with iPhone (3GS, 4, 4S, and 5), iPod Touch (third, fourth, and fifth generation), and iPad. Needs iOS 5.1 or later.

CarTOON Makers by TOON Books
http://www.toon-books.com/cartoon-makers.html

A free online tool that lets your kid make three-panel cartoons using characters from TOON Books' line of comics. Using a wide range of characters, kids can continue the stories from their favorite comics—printing, saving, or emailing the final product.

This free web-based app can be accessed from a variety of devices.

Super Why! ABC Adventures: Alphabet

Based on another PBS Kids TV show, this app tests lots of skills your kid will need in preschool and kindergarten, from letter recognition to letter sounds.

Available in the Apple App Store; works only with iPad. Needs iOS 4.3 or later.

Available in Google Play for Android devices.

Available in Amazon Appstore for Android devices.

Toca Builders by Toca Boca

This deceptively simple building app can introduce your kid to digital engineering. Using an interface similar to the popular *Minecraft* game, kids can make digital castles, forts, or houses using a collection of building robots that perform specific functions.

Available in the Apple App Store; works with iPhone, iPod Touch, and iPad.
Needs iOS 5.0 or later.
Available in Google Play for Android devices.
Available in Amazon Appstore for Android devices.

Word Wagon by Duck Duck Moose

When kids are ready to work on phonics and spelling, this charming app will guide them with an animated mouse named Mozzarella. It teaches children how to sound out letters, recognize words, and spell simple words.

Available in the Apple App Store; works with iPhone, iPod Touch, and iPad.
Needs iOS 5.0 or later.

Conclusion

How Born Readers Can Thrive with Common Core Standards

Our born readers will enter a challenging new era of education, facing stricter educational evaluations and the dramatic changes of the Common Core Standards.

Fast Company journalist Anya Kamenetz is writing a book about the impact of standardized testing and new standards, but she already has cautionary words for parents. "We're easing into a time period over the next couple of years where parents with kids in public schools are going be to dealing with a really intense barrage of tests," she told me. "The scores are probably going to go down as well, because these tests are thought to be much more difficult."

Tests offer parents, teachers, and the government an easy way to measure performance. But as we discovered by studying the science of reading and storytelling for the last seven chapters, children learn in many different ways. The most powerful educational experiences cannot be measured by filling in bubbles on a multiple-choice test. We shouldn't wait until test scores plunge to have this debate. We should evaluate these new standards now with our fellow parents and with our policy makers.

In terms of reading and writing, children's author Melissa Stewart thinks these upcoming changes will ultimately help our kids thrive in this new century. "I wouldn't characterize the Common Core English Language Arts standards as tougher than previous standards. They emphasize many of the same skills and strategies educators have always focused on—recognizing main ideas and supporting details in a piece of writing, building vocabulary, studying how writing is structured, examining how an author supports points."

Born readers will have already mastered many of these crucial skills, and I think this new emphasis on critical reading and writing will make all students stronger—both in school and in the workplace. But there will be changes, and Stewart has spent a lot of time exploring the curriculum, discovering how it will affect both children's writers and readers. "There are a few new ideas, such as focusing on how visual elements and text work together, which are a great addition for twenty-first-century learners. I also like that there is more emphasis on comparing texts, whether they be print or digital or audio or a combination," she says.

By following the Born Reading Playbook, you've already been practicing many of these skills. Your kid can describe what's going on inside a storybook illustration, compare a Dr. Seuss character to a Mo Willems character, or tell you the difference between the storybook and app versions of *Little Red Riding Hood*. By encouraging your child to compare, elaborate, and interact as a young reader, you will have prepared them to perform these new skills in an academic setting.

Your child will head into a school system dominated by standardized tests. These tests are shaped around a new set of Common Core Standards that will be adopted by most schools in the country. The standards can seem daunting at first, especially after emerging from an imaginative, creative, and free home environment. While your teacher will pick the books that they read in school, you can let your child have more freedom at home. At the same time, you can reinforce the comprehension and analysis tools that your child needs for school reading

I shuddered as I explored the materials my daughter would be required to know as she passed through kindergarten and first grade in this new system. But it slowly dawned on me that my focus on interactive reading would actually prepare my daughter for this new world. If you lay the Common Core Standards for English Language Arts side-by-side with the Born Reading Playbook, you will see many happy similarities.

While we shared books with our kids to make them lifelong readers, this gift of reading also prepares them to excel in the Common Core Standards. While most parents (myself included) don't read to our children with the explicit goal of helping them meet certain abstract educational goals, you'll be pleasantly surprised to see how many of these Common Core reading and analysis skills are actually already part of the Born Reading Playbook.

As I wrote earlier, no parent can completely escape this world of standardized tests. Even if you home-school your child through high school, they will probably eventually have to face standardized testing for college entrance exams. The truth is, standardized testing is going to be a part of our children's academic experience.

As a grade-school kid I took a multiple-choice standardized

career test that was supposed to predict what you would be, what kind of career you would be suited for, and what kind of work you would end up doing. I can't even really remember what it told me I would be, but it wasn't a writer. How can you test somebody in grade school to decide what he or she'll grow up to be? Your life is the set of interests, people, and dreams that you end up chasing. It is a wiggly line that you carve through the world, not something that can be charted by blips on a fill-in-the-blanks sheet. I don't trust standardized tests to tell what my daughter is like or where she will go next. But the world is lousy with these tests.

You should balance this rote learning with trips to museums, concerts, art studios, and other places that will inspire your child to follow his or her own interests. Because school will not allow that freedom. Since most parents cannot afford to send their children to private schools where testing might not be a central part of the curriculum, and home-schooling isn't an option for many of us, the job falls to you, the parent, to make sure that your child is creatively inspired at home.

If you have been using the Born Reading Playbook with your child, you will be well prepared to guide your child in his or her future. You can help him or her follow the interest he or she wants to follow, and your habits of interactive reading will actually help your child prepare for this new kind of curriculum.

Even before preschool, you have been preparing your kid to survive in this tough new academic world. By asking your child questions about storybooks, you've taught him or her how to think critically about a story and how to analyze the world around him or her. By relating picture book stories to real life, you showed how to compare different stories—a crucial skill in this new environment. These skills will serve your child well while reading a Dr. Seuss book, a textbook, a Shakespeare play, or even a standardized test.

If you followed the recommended reading throughout this book, then your child has been reading Common Core–recommended books from the age of two. They will be very comfortable tackling all the texts needed during kindergarten and first grade. On a more philosophical level, the Born Reading Playbook also shows parents how to teach their children how to talk about a text and analyze a book the way they will in a Common Core classroom.

By the time our children take these tests, the reading comprehension, analytical, and vocabulary skills required by new school standards will already be a part of their natural thinking process. In fact, the Common Core Standards for first-grade students actually include a number of analytical and comprehension questions that you have been asking for years during interactive reading sessions.

Beyond the kindergarten test we explored last chapter, you can expect what *Fast Company* journalist Anya Kamenetz calls "a grace period" from standardized tests that lasts until third grade in many schools. Then the battery of tests begins from third to eighth grade. She says that there were "particularly key tests in the year of fourth grade (for middle school) and eighth grade (for high school)."

She adds a grim note: "With the Common Core comes a set of new, tougher assessments. They require longer writing, they require the mastery of more complicated concepts, and there's going to be more pre-testing, more practice testing so that the overall burden in terms of time is going to be a lot."

That is the part that worries me the most. I love watching Olive chase her own interests, from Mars to honeybees to quilt-making, but I worry these creative learning experiences will be the first thing cut as teachers struggle to make room for these new tests. Parents will have to do more work outside the classroom to encourage these individual interests.

But on a brighter note, you've already been doing this kind of creative learning with your child for years. Over the next few pages, I will show you how the Born Reading Playbook can work as a powerful tool for entering the Common Core classroom. You can use this advice to help your child read and discuss books at home in order to feel comfortable with the whole process once he or she enters school. I have built the Common Core Standards into the very bones of this book. If you go back through my reading lists at the end of each chapter, you can find all the books listed as "text exemplars" in Common Core materials for teachers.

In the following paragraphs, you can explore the ten English Language Arts "Literacy" tasks outlined in course materials for the Common Core Standards for first graders, augmenting these skills with Born Reading Playbook activities you learned earlier in this book.

You should take this chance to think about your child's strengths and weaknesses as a reader. If they struggle to meet any of these points, you can focus on these activities in your home reading sessions.

1. **Common Core Literacy Skill:** "Ask and answer questions about key details in a text."

This was covered in the Born Reading Playbook when your child was just a baby: "Ask lots and lots of questions." The more questions you ask your child while reading, the more questions they can pose by themselves.

2. **Common Core Literacy Skill:** "Retell stories, including key details, and demonstrate understanding of their central message or lesson."

This is the final point in the Born Reading Playbook, "Encourage your child to retell the story." This is one of the easiest skills to practice with your child. He or she can tell stories while riding in a shopping cart or traveling in the car. It only takes a couple leading questions about a favorite book.

3. **Common Core Literacy Skill:** "Describe characters, settings, and major events in a story, using key details."

This is another key Born Reading Playbook technique: "Share details about the book." Even before a baby can speak, Born Reading parents will highlight colors, shapes, numbers, names, and eye-catching elements of even the simplest board book. Your child should be able to spot these details by him- or herself as he or she is performing a skill you taught him or her from the cradle.

4. **Common Core Literacy Skill:** "Identify words and phrases in stories or poems that suggest feelings or appeal to the senses."

Once again, the Born Reading Playbook has this covered: "Help your child identify with the characters." As Olive grew up, we held long, thoughtful conversations about emotions in her favorite books. From the cozy finger puppets in Sara Gillingham's In My . . . series to Elephant and Piggie's exaggerated emotions in Mo Willems's books, Olive learned how to describe both feelings and sensory details from them. Talk with your child about the characters he loves and the feelings they evoke in him, and have him describe those emotions back to you.

5. **Common Core Literacy Skill:** "Explain major differences between books that tell stories and books that give information, drawing on a wide reading of a range of text types."

Early in this book, we discussed the importance of "Discussing personal opinions about a book." As your child gets older, you can adapt this Born Reading Playbook technique to cover literary genres. Which book did your child like better, Dr. Seuss's *The Lorax* or *A Tree Is a Plant*? Talk about the differences between these books.

6. **Common Core Literacy Skill:** "Identify who is telling the story at various points in a text."

Toward the top of the playbook, parents were encouraged to "Dramatize the story." As your child gets older, you can turn these dramatic readings into learning conversations—helping your child track narrators or shifts inside the story.

7. **Common Core Literacy Skill:** "Use illustrations and details in a story to describe its characters, setting, or events."

Once again, born readers will have learned how to "Share details about the story" from your example, conversing about illustrations from toddlerhood onward.

8. **Common Core Literacy Skill:** "Compare and contrast the adventures and experiences of characters in stories."

Born readers mastered these skills while reading with their parents, following this technique: "Stop and talk about what happened." While talking about what happened in one book, your child will start to compare stories.

9. **Common Core Literacy Skill:** "With prompting and support, read prose and poetry of appropriate complexity."

This is the ultimate goal of the Born Reading Playbook, teaching children to love reading so much that they want to do it themselves.

You can build a reading list for your child using these books, but you can also practice at home and teach how to ask the right questions about the books he or she loves to read.

Common Core Standards for English Language Arts involve three kinds of reading material: stories, poetry, and informational texts. Over the course of this book I've tried to include a text from all three categories. If you visit the Born Reading site, you can actually download free copies of public domain texts that are the backbone of the Common Core list for kindergartners and first graders: it includes read-out-loud books like *The Wizard of Oz* and loads of classic poems. If your child enjoys a particular poem, I recommend you download the complete book online and let your child remix the book on apps like StoryKit, My Story, or Draw and Tell. With these apps your child can add pictures, music, and readings alongside the poems—sharing the homemade digital book with family.

How to Help *Your* Kid Succeed in the Twenty-first Century

You need to write your own parenting handbook now.

My recommended reading material involved private detectives, soccer, and jazz, but your kid might like space, trucks, and magic tricks; or maybe cartoon characters, baking, and dancing.

Your child will gravitate toward his or her own set of unique obsessions, cross-pollinated by all the things you care about in life. Cultivate those themes with books, eBook apps, library visits, and cardboard box crafts.

When you get stuck, make a simple Google search for "best kids' books about _____" or "best books for children about _____." I can guarantee you will discover a whole community of people online who care about that corner of the kids' book world and teaching kids about that particular interest. They will show you where to go next.

Nothing in this book will make your job easier. The digital books and apps and other multimedia resources I showed you will not replace your work as a parent and reader. At the same time, as your child enters school and moves through grade school, the teacher will not replace your role as your child's inspiration. In fact, in our brave new world filled with standardized tests and shared curriculum across the states, it will only make your inspirational job more important.

"My contention is that we're really shortchanging our kids by ignoring what science tells us about emotional intelligence and how motivation, persistence, curiosity, how these things determine people's success," Anya Kamenetz told me.

Gordon Wells began his career by studying how parents read with their children at home, but was appalled by the endless barrage of school testing we inflict on our children. "It will be realized that this is a disaster," Wells told me. "We are really hampering children's interests in the world around them by making them study and learn information to regurgitate on tests about things that don't necessarily interest them. We ignore the excitement of studying things that really do interest them, that would take them deep into history, science, literature, and so on."

We spend our entire educational lives scrambling between quizzes, tests, and mountains of homework. These experiences trained us to believe that this is the best (or perhaps the only) way to learn. During these early years with your child, you will have a chance to watch a young mind develop before worksheets and standardized tests force a very specific way of learning. If you are reading and learning along with your child before he or she starts school, you will yearn for a more interactive academic environment.

"My campaign for the last 25 or more years has been to work with teachers to help them to see that the most effective way of teaching is to be responsive, not to be didactic. And that applies to parents too," Wells concludes.

As I wrote this book, I realized that my daughter will not have the luxury of that hypothetical change that reformers like Wells seek. And neither will your children. This generation of kids will grow up with standardized tests and new educational standards, all while getting unprecedented and unfettered access to mobile devices.

I wrote this book because I cannot wait for a world without a misguided focus on standardized tests, or one in which we understand completely the effects of mobile devices on young brains and bodies. Devices and standardized tests will not make a parent's job any easier. We must compensate for educational and developmental unknowns that no other generation of parents has had to face. So I sought out all the best experts I could find, collected all the data that exists, and archived 15 simple techniques—the Born Reading Playbook—that you can use with your children.

Toontastic creator Andy Russell shared an inspiring thought for parents about how the right kind of digital learning can help children for the rest of their lives. "When kids are out in the real world and they are telling people about their day, use that same framework: what's our set-up? what's our resolution here? Where's the emotional high you are reaching in that arc? Who are the main characters? What are the settings? I'm really hoping that a lot of this stuff transfers over into other mediums, and whether those kids go on to be musicians and they are telling stories through their songs, or whether they go on to be literally writers, writing novels and newspaper articles, or whether they are just building PowerPoint presentations in the business world years from now and giving better pitches because they are going with that classic story arc or a modified version thereof, it's a win for us in any way."

So we can prepare ourselves. Start with this book and the simple tools I have collected. Without spending any money, you can reap the benefits of 30 years' worth of literacy research with your child. These skills I have shown you can apply to digital reading and apps, letting your child flourish in our difficult twenty-first-century soil.

This is the only parenting handbook that won't make your life easier. Obviously, I waited until the end of the book to point this out. If you follow my book, you will add bookshelves of new reading material and countless apps on your devices. You will spend way more time reading than you ever dreamed. But the first time your child tells you a story, it will be worth it.

My mom works as a literacy tutor back home, now that all her born readers have moved out of the house. Someday, I will introduce Olive to the books on my dad's bookshelf. I cruised through his college-level mythology books one summer as a kid, moving on to his elegant hardcover copies of J. R. R. Tolkien's The Lord of the Rings trilogy—feeling like a kid swimming in the deep end of the pool.

Those were magical days.

As I grew up, I always took credit for making myself a reader. But it wasn't until I was a parent that I realized my mom and dad did all the hard work. They spent hours reading to me when I couldn't read to myself. They let us use the record player and cassette deck to play endless audiobooks, and drove us on 30 years' worth of library visits.

Reading is a set of motions, as much as playing basketball or learning the violin. And parents do all the work.

Even though devoted readers like you and me take credit for our bookish lives, it was our parents. And we were so fortunate we ended up with those parents, because they helped us beat some steep statistical odds that we would not be readers.

Someday, your kids will be grateful as well.

Reading List

Books for the First Year

Goodnight Moon by Margaret Wise Brown
F Is for Farm by Roger Priddy
Ten Tiny Tickles by Karen Katz
The Going to Bed Book by Sandra Boynton
Good Night, Gorilla by Peggy Rathmann
Mommy, Carry Me Please! by Jane Cabrera
Lost and Found by Oliver Jeffers
Ten, Nine, Eight by Molly Bang
Baa Baa Black Sheep by Tomie dePaola
Who Said Moo? by Harriet Ziefert and Simms Taback (illustrator)

Recommendations for Library Babies

Curious George Visits the Library by H. A. Rey, Margret Rey, and
    Martha Weston (illustrator)
Library Lion by Michelle Knudsen and Kevin Hawkes (illustrator)

Library Mouse by Daniel Kirk
The Inside Outside Book of Libraries by Julie Cummins and Roxie Munro (illustrator)
Bats at the Library by Brian Lies

Recommendations for One-Year-Olds

Baby Faces series by Roberta Grobel Intrater
Brown Bear, Brown Bear, What Do You See? by Bill Martin and Eric Carle
Baby Happy Baby Sad by Leslie Patricelli
Ten Little Fingers and Ten Little Toes by Mem Fox and Helen Oxenbury (illustrator)
Whose Knees Are These? by Jabari Asim and LeUyen Pham (illustrator)
Bears in the Night by Stan Berenstain and Jan Berenstain
Watch Me Dance by Andrea Davis Pinkney and Brian Pinkney
Hug by Jez Alborough
In My Pond by Sara Gillingham and Lorena Siminovich (illustrator)
Please, Baby, Please by Spike Lee, Tonya Lewis Lee, and Kadir Nelson (illustrator)

Recommendations for Reluctant Readers

In My Jungle by Sara Gillingham and Lorena Siminovich (illustrator)
The Stinky Cheese Man and Other Fairly Stupid Tales by Jon Scieszka and Lane Smith (illustrator)
Fantastic Mr. Fox by Roald Dahl
Squish by Jennifer L. Holm and Matthew Holm
The Adventures of Captain Underpants by Dav Pilkey

Recommendations for Two-Year-Olds

I Want My Hat Back by Jon Klassen
Charlie Parker Played Be Bop by Chris Raschka
Jenny's Birthday Book by Esther Averill
Alice the Fairy by David Shannon
The Cat in the Hat by Dr. Seuss
Where the Wild Things Are by Maurice Sendak
Too Big by Ingri d'Aulaire and Edgar Parin d'Aulaire
Harold and the Purple Crayon by Crockett Johnson
We're Going on a Bear Hunt by Michael Rosen and Helen Oxenbury
Pete the Cat series by Eric Litwin

Recommendations for Three-Year-Olds

Not So Fast Songololo by Niki Daly
Bedtime for Frances by Russell Hoban and Garth Williams (illustrator)
Madlenka Soccer Star by Peter Sís
Poetry Speaks to Children edited by Elise Paschen
Truck by Donald Crews
Cosmo and the Robot by Brian Pinkney
The Big Honey Hunt by Stan Berenstain and Jan Berenstain
Pete the Cat and His Four Groovy Buttons by Eric Litwin and James
     Dean (illustrator)
I Read Signs by Tana Hoban
Ghosts in the House! by Kazuno Kohara

Audiobook Recommendations

Blueberries for Sal by Robert McCloskey
Madeline by Ludwig Bemelmans
Curious George series by Margret Rey and H. A. Rey
Pete the Cat series by Eric Litwin
Charlie Parker Played Be Bop by Chris Raschka

Book Suggestions for Four-Year-Olds

Black Out!: Animals That Live in the Dark by Ginjer L. Clarke
Hip Hop Speaks to Children edited by Nikki Giovanni
This Jazz Man by Karen Ehrhardt
Gorilla by Anthony Browne
The Shark King by R. Kikuo Johnson
Tar Beach by Faith Ringgold
George and Martha by James Marshall
Little Red Riding Hood by Jerry Pinkney
The Munschworks Grand Treasury by Robert Munsch, Michael Kusugak, Michael Martchenko (illustrator), Hélène Desputeaux (illustrator), and Vladyana Krykorka (illustrator)
I Broke My Trunk! by Mo Willems

Informational Reading Recommendations for Five-Year-Olds and Beyond

A Tree Is a Plant by Clyde Robert Bulla
Starfish by Edith Thacher Hurd

Earthworms by Claire Llewellyn

Fire! Fire! by Gail Gibbons

From Seed to Pumpkin by Wendy Pfeffer

How People Learned to Fly by Fran Hodgkins and True Kelley (illustrator)

What Do You Do With a Tail Like This? by Steve Jenkins and Robin Page

A Weed Is a Flower: The Life of George Washington Carver by Aliki

Amazing Whales! by Sarah L. Thomson

Water, Water Everywhere by Cynthia Overbeck Bix

App List

Recommendations for Two-Year-Olds

The Monster at the End of This Book by Sesame Workshop Apps
Fiete by Wolfgang Schmitz
Moo, Baa, La La La! by Sandra Boynton and Loud Crow Interactive
One Fish Two Fish Red Fish Blue Fish by Dr. Seuss and Ocean-house Media
Sago Mini Music Box by Sago Sago
Pango Book by Julien Akita and Studio Pango
StoryKit by International Children's Digital Library
Endless Alphabet by Originator Inc.
ArtKive by The Kive Company
Wheels on the Bus by Duck Duck Moose

Recommendations for Three-Year-Olds

Toontastic Jr. by Launchpad Toys
There's No Place Like Space!: All About Our Solar System by Ocean-house Media

Bizzy Bear on the Farm by Nosy Crow
Sesame Street Family Play by Sesame Street
Draw and Tell by Duck Duck Moose
Felt Board by Software Smoothie
Toca Band by Toca Boca
The Cat in the Hat by Dr. Seuss and Oceanhouse Media
My Story—Book Maker for Kids by HiDef Web Solutions
Roadtrip Bingo by Bright Bunny

Recommendations for Four-Year-Olds

Alien Assignment by Fred Rogers Center
Montessori Numberland HD by Les Trois Elles Interactive
Bedtime Math by Bedtime Math Foundation
Little Red Riding Hood by Nosy Crow
Toontastic by Launchpad Toys
i Learn With Poko: Seasons and Weather! by Tribal Nova
PBS Kids Video by PBS Kids
Sid's Science Fair by PBS Kids
ABC Music by Peapod Labs
Pigeon Presents Mo . . . on the Go! by Mo Willems

Recommendations for Kindergarten and Beyond

Free Books for Children by International Children's Digital
    Library
Rounds: Parker Penguin by Nosy Crow
The Kissing Hand by Audrey Penn and Oceanhouse Media

Storybird by Storybird Inc.
Daniel Tiger's Neighborhood by PBS Kids
Montessori Geometry by Les Trois Elles
CarTOON Makers by TOON Books
Super Why! ABC Adventures: Alphabet by PBS Kids
Toca Builders by Toca Boca
Endless Reader by Originator

Bibliography

American Academy of Pediatrics. "Healthy Children Ages & Stages." http://www.healthychildren.org/english/ages-stages/. Accessed January 2014.

American Academy of Pediatrics. "Policy Statement: Children, Adolescents, and the Media." *Pediatrics* 132 (2013): 958–61. Accessed January 2014.

American Academy of Pediatrics. "Policy Statement: Media Use by Children Younger Than 2 Years." http://pediatrics.aappublications.org/content/early/2011/10/12/peds.2011-1753. Accessed January 2014.

Babble. http://www.babble.com/.

Bentley-Flannery, Paige. "Poetry Paige." http://www.deschuteslibrary.org/kids/poetry/about.aspx.

Campaign for a Commercial-Free Childhood. http://www.commercialfreechildhood.org/.

Campaign for a Commercial-Free Childhood, Alliance for Childhood, and Teachers Resisting Unhealthy Children's Entertainment. "Facing the Screen Dilemma: Young Children, Technology and Early education." Boston, MA: 2012. http://www.commercialfreechildhood .org/screendilemma. Accessed January 2014.

Christakis, Dimitri, and Ari Brown. "Media Use and Early Brain Development." HealthyChildren.org. http://www.healthychildren.org /English/family-life/Media/Pages/Sound-Advice-on-Media-Audio .aspx. Accessed January 2014.

Clark, Lynn Schofield. *The Parent App: Understanding Families in a Digital Age*. New York: Oxford University Press, 2012.

Common Sense Media. http://www.commonsensemedia.org/.

Cordes, Colleen, and Edward Miller, eds. "Fool's Gold: A Critical Look at Computers in Childhood." Alliance for Childhood. http://drupal6 .allianceforchildhood.org/fools_gold. Accessed January 2014.

DeBruin-Parecki, A. "Assessing Adult/Child Storybook Reading Practices." CIERA Report #2-004, 1990. http://www.ciera.org/library /reports/inquiry-2/2-004/2-004.html. Accessed January 2014.

Flood, James E. "Parental Styles in Reading Episodes with Young Children." *Reading Teacher* 30 (1977): 864–67.

Frauenfelder, Mark. "Apps for Kids." http://boingboing.net/tag/appsfor kids.

Fred Rogers Center. http://www.fredrogerscenter.org/.

GalleyCat. "How a Modern Baby Thinks About Reading." http://www .mediabistro.com/galleycat/how-a-one-year-old-thinks-about-read ing_b40042. Accessed January 2014.

Guernsey, Lisa. *Screen Time: How Electronic Media—From Baby Videos to Educational Software—Affects Your Young Child*. New York: Basic Books, 2012.

First Book. http://www.firstbook.org/.

Klesius, Janell P., and Priscilla L. Griffith. "Interactive Storybook Reading for At-Risk Learners." *Reading Teacher* 49 (1996): 552–60.

Kluver, Carisa. Digital Storytime. http://digital-storytime.com/index.php.

Lirenman, Karen. Learning and Sharing with Ms. Lirenman. http://learningandsharingwithmsl.blogspot.com/.

Little eLit. http://littleelit.com/about/.

McCain, Margaret Norrie, J. Fraser Mustard, and Dr. Stuart Shanker. *Early Years Study 2: Putting Science into Action.* Toronto: Council for Early Child Development, 2007.

Miller, Carolyn, Kathryn Zickuhr, Lee Rainie, and Kristen Purcell. "Parents, Children, Libraries, and Reading." Pew Research Center. http://libraries.pewinternet.org/files/legacy-pdf/PIP_Library_Services_Parents_PDF.pdf. Accessed January 2014.

Morrow, L. M. "Assessing Children's Understanding of Story Through Their Construction and Reconstruction of Narrative." In L. M. Morrow and J. K. Smith, eds. *Assessment for Instruction in Early Literacy.* Englewood Cliffs, NJ: Prentice-Hall, 1990. 110–34.

Parent's Choice Foundation. http://www.parents-choice.org/.

Protzko, John, Joshua Aronson, and Clancy Blair. "How to Make a Young Child Smarter: Evidence From the Database of Raising Intelligence." *Perspectives on Psychological Science* 8 (2013): 25–40.

Robb, Michael. "New Ways of Reading: The Impact of an Interactive Book on Young Children's Story Comprehension and Parent-Child Dialogic Reading Behaviors." University of California Riverside, Doctor of Philosophy dissertation, 2010.

Shanker, Stuart. "Dr. Shanker: Self Regulation and Nutrition." http://www.self-regulation.ca/dr-shanker-self-regulation-and-nutrition/. Accessed January 2014.

Shanker, Stuart. "Report of the 2012 Thinker in Residence Self-regulation." http://www.ccyp.wa.gov.au/files/2012%20Thinker%20in%20Residence%20report%20-%20final%20low%20res%20pdf%20for%20web.pdf. Accessed January 2014.

Shifrin, Don. "Setting Limits on Media Use." HealthyChildren.org. http://www.healthychildren.org/English/family-life/Media/Pages/Sound-Advice-on-Media-Audio.aspx. Accessed January 2014.

Society of Children's Book Writers and Illustrators. http://www.scbwi.org/.

Tatar, Maria. *Enchanted Hunters: The Power of Stories in Childhood.* New York: W. W. Norton, 2009.

Teachers with Apps. http://teacherswithapps.com/teachers-with-apps/.

Waldorf Education Frequently Asked Questions. http://www.whywaldorfworks.org/02_W_Education/faq_about.asp. Accessed January 2014.

Wells, Gordon. "Preschool Literacy-Related Activities and Success in School." In D. Olson, N. Torrance, and A. Hildyard, eds. *Literacy, Language and Learning.* Cambridge: Cambridge University Press, 1985.

Wells, Gordon. *The Meaning Makers: Learning to Talk and Talking to Learn.* Bristol: Multilingual Matters, 2009.

Whitehurst, Grover J. "Dialogic Reading: An Effective Way to Read to Preschoolers." Reading Rockets. http://www.readingrockets.org/article/400. Accessed January 2014.

Whitehurst, Grover J., David S. Arnold, Jeffery N. Epstein, Andrea L. Angell, Meagan Smith, and Janet E. Fischel. "A Picture Book Reading Intervention in Day Care and Home for Children from Low-Income Families." *Developmental Psychology* 30 (1994): 679–89.

Whitehurst, Grover J., F. Falco, C. J. Lonigan, J. E. Fischel, B. D. DeBaryshe, M. C. Valdez-Menchaca, and M. Caulfield. "Accelerating Language Development Through Picture-Book Reading." *Developmental Psychology* 24 (1988): 552–58.

Zeviar, Lissa. "The Art of Sign Language: for Babies, Boobs and Bobs." TEDxAmsterdam 2012. http://www.youtube.com/watch?v=S8hiiy3Gksw. Accessed January 2014.

Acknowledgments

I would like to thank the librarians of the Lyons Township District Library in the village of Lyons, Michigan (population 789). This library opened when I was a toddler, and I will never forget the thrill of exploring those seemingly endless shelves. This book (or any book, for that matter) would not have been possible without the librarians, teachers, parents, and other literary angels among us.

I also need to thank all of the authors, app makers, librarians, child-development experts, and parenting experts who helped me during my research. I stumbled into parenthood without a clue, but I found the most amazing people to guide me on my journey. Every single person quoted in these pages generously shared their guidance and support, making me a better father and making this a better book.

I am especially grateful that Betsy Bird, Cen Campbell, Stephen M. Tafoya, Anne Hicks, Betsy Diamant-Cohen, Carissa

Christner, and Genesis Hansen helped me polish my lists of book and app recommendations for children. When it came time to choose the best books and media for my child, two websites were especially valuable: Common Sense Media and Parents' Choice Foundation. Both sites offered hundreds of useful recommendations for parents and they took the time to answer all my questions. I also need to thank Fazia Eltareb for helping me build my research and Sita Patel for connecting us.

This book would never have happened without the inspiration and guidance of my literary agent, David R. Patterson. Michelle Howry and the team at Touchstone believed in my book from our earliest conversations, and I am so grateful that they took a chance with a first-time writer. I'd like to thank Robert Boynton, Brooke Kroeger, and the rest of the NYU Arthur L. Carter Journalism Institute family for their mentorship when I first arrived in New York City. I also need to thank Alan Meckler, Chris Ariens, Rebecca Wright, and Laurel Touby for all their support during my unforgettable years at Mediabistro.

I want to remember Amy D. Hayes, my old writing friend who helped me make it this far. I wish she could read these pages. I owe a debt to my parents, Mike and Joan. They raised me as a born reader and inspired me to follow the same path with my daughter. My siblings Jeff, Mark, Matthew, and Becky were reading alongside me during those weekly library visits—sharing a lifetime of books and stories together. I also want to thank my Los Angeles family: Megan Williams and Michael, Jacob, Carla, and Lulu Shamberg.

Most of all, I must thank Caitlin Shamberg for reading every single draft of this book and helping me find time to write every weekend. And I need to thank Olive for reading and writing with me for the last three years.

Index

About the Author

Jason Boog graduated from the University of Michigan and spent two years in the Peace Corps working with youth groups in Guatemala. He also studied at New York University's Arthur L. Carter Journalism Institute and worked as an investigative reporter at *Judicial Reports*. His work has appeared in *The Believer, Salon, The Los Angeles Review of Books*, and *Peace Corps Writers*, as well as on NPR Books and other outlets. For five years, he served as the publishing editor at Mediabistro, leading the GalleyCat and AppNewser blogs.

He lives in Los Angeles with his wife and daughter.